Fuel Rights Handboo

9th edition 1993/94

Antoinette Hoffland and Nicholas Nicol

CPAG Ltd
1–5 Bath Street London EC1V 9PY

1st Edition (Fuel Debts Handbook)	1977
2nd Edition	1981
3rd Edition	1982
4th Edition (Fuel Rights Handbook)	1985
5th Edition	1986
6th Edition	1988
7th Edition	1989
8th Edition	1992
9th Edition	1993

Antoinette Hoffland has worked in law centres for a number of years. She currently works freelance.

Nicholas Nicol is a barrister at Staple Inn Chambers, specialising in social welfare law. He worked previously at the Southwark Law Project.

© WRUG, 1993
Published by CPAG Ltd, 1-5 Bath Street, London EC1V 9PY

Cover design by Devious Designs, 0742 755634
Typeset by The Bears Communications, 071-272 8760
Printed by Blackmore Press, 0747 53034

ISBN 0 946744 57 2

Contents

Acknowledgements

This is the ninth edition of the Fuel Rights Handbook, and the second since privatisation. As such, it draws on and builds on work from previous editions. The authors would like to extend their thanks to the authors of previous editions and, in particular, to Mary Jane Ashford and Graeme Lyall for their work and support in producing the eighth edition.

Special thanks, once again, to Ian Ford, for his contribution to the Multiple Debt section, which is again largely his work. We would also like to thank our readers for their invaluable criticism and comments: Jim Gray - who checked the manuscript in detail from the point of view of Scottish law and practice – Ian Ford and Lindsey Rhodes. Barbara Montoute also supplied extremely useful comments on the previous edition.

Thanks to Charlotte Evans and the staff at Lambeth Money Advice and to Lewisham Money Advice.

Particular thanks also to Paul Tonkinson, Tony Boorman and Derek Bevan at OFFER HQ, Mr G Evans and Mr Jim Durling of OFFER's meter examiners' service and to the staff of the OFFER Library; Dave Barnes and Denis Long at OFGAS HQ, the staff at the OFGAS Library, and Bob Elbert at the DSS.

Thanks, too, to CPAG staff in getting the book out so swiftly: to Renée Harris for editing and producing it, to Peter Ridpath for promoting it and to Debbie Haynes for overseeing its distribution.

Finally, Antoinette Hoffland would like to give special thanks to Mark Earl for his support throughout the project, and Nicholas Nicol would like to thank Staple Inn Chambers for the use of its facilities.

Foreword

The imposition of VAT on domestic fuel, together with the introduction of a compensation system possibly based on means-tested benefits, signal busy days ahead for fuel rights advisers, especially those working in the colder areas of Britain. Whatever else the Chancellor's Budget proposals achieve, they have already succeeded in raising fuel poverty as an issue to heights not seen since the withdrawal of heating additions in 1988, arousing widespread opposition in the process. A busy time, then, for fuel rights lobbyists and campaigners as well as advisers, for whom this 9th edition of CPAG's authoritative and comprehensive *Fuel Rights Handbook* is particularly welcome.

Fuel rights can, literally, be a matter of life and death. An average of 40,000 people die each winter in Britain because they cannot afford to keep themselves warm and dry in their homes. The rate of 'excess winter deaths' in Britain (ie, the higher number of deaths recorded between October and March compared with April to September) is unparalleled amongst our northern European and American neighbours whose building standards and/or welfare benefits levels are higher. An analysis of Scottish statistics published by the Campaign for Cold Weather Credits in 1992 shows that the risk of excess winter death is higher for low-income groups and especially for older single female pensioners.

Those who survive the British winter still run a high risk of avoidable illness and disease. Dr Brenda Boardman (*Fuel Poverty*, 1991) suggests that the NHS spends around £1 billion each year on treating illnesses, particularly coronary and respiratory problems, which are directly related to life in cold, damp housing. Children and elderly people are particularly at risk. If so many died in motorway pile-ups, the nation would be crying out for something to be done. But because they are barely visible to the majority, these avoidable tragedies only rarely hit the headlines. Other than setting up winter warmth telephone help lines, health ministers have largely ignored the need for effective preventative action in this field.

Awareness of the links between poor housing, poor health and low income is still remarkably limited amongst politicians. None of the major political parties has a co-ordinated strategy for tackling fuel poverty. One government minister claimed that excess winter deaths in Britain result from older British people's unfamiliarity with central heating. "These people", she suggested, "leave their warm homes to catch a bus without dressing warmly enough. Then they come home, start to feel ill and blame it on the house; if only they dressed more warmly there would be no problem." Try telling that to the 7 million households, including a high proportion of elderly people, whose homes cannot be heated, even in one room, to the minimum comfort standard recognised by the World Health Organisation.

This handbook touches on many aspects of law and statutory responsibility which impinge on a person's ability to meet their fuel needs. Until these are extended and integrated into a co-ordinated package of legislation which includes energy rating, enhanced standards in building regulations and adequate benefit levels, low-income households in Britain will never be assured of the basic right to affordable warmth in their homes.

One of the impenetrable mysteries of government for many people is the way in which welfare benefit levels are determined and, consequently, the basis on which ministers can make their claims that these benefits are adequate to meet needs. The amount of money a person needs to heat their home adequately depends on the thermal efficiency of their house, the climatic conditions with which they have to cope and other personal factors – such as disability and age – where additional heating may be necessary. Unemployment also entails more heating in the home where others can depend on minimum levels of heating (secured by government legislation) in the workplace. Despite these obvious differences in fuel requirements, the Government has strongly resisted the idea of individual or even regional variations in benefit levels. When challenged on this, ministers claim that the system of benefits premiums compensates for variations in individual need and that the triggering mechanism of the Cold Weather Payments system makes it responsive to regional variations. Readers of this Guide will recognise the limitations of this argument, as will anyone attempting to secure adequate heating through such inadequate measures.

Scottish organisations obviously have an interest in promoting a regional bias in fuel benefits; identical houses can cost as much as three times more to heat in Northern Scotland compared with the South coast of England. However, the experience of the Campaign for Cold Weather Credits shows that, from the Bristol Channel to Orkney and from East Anglia to Northern Ireland, households in coastal and uplands areas have similar difficulties in keeping warm. The differences lie in the extent and severity of the adverse climatic conditions with which they have to contend. For this reason, where we argue for regional variations in benefit levels, we do so on the basis of 'degree day' measurements which identify the colder areas of Britain. Similar areas should be treated in a similar way.

Ideally, however, we are arguing for a direct relationship between a household's fuel needs and the level of benefits which they should receive. One of the most interesting technical developments in recent years has been the introduction of systems for measuring the energy efficiency of individual homes and the fuel consumption necessary to bring them up to the required standard, of which the best known is the National Home Energy Register (NHER). On the NHER scale of 0 – 10, for example, a new build house constructed according to current building regulations should measure 7.4. By comparison, the houses lived in by people experiencing fuel poverty tend to measure between 0 – 3. The existence of a specific indicator of domestic energy efficiency (accredited by government) transforms the campaign for a right to affordable warmth from a rhetorical aim to a set of practical objectives which forms a 'virtuous circle' of public policy.

What is required is increased capital expenditure in home energy efficiency (which creates jobs and stimulates economic activity). Welfare benefits should be set at levels which would enable households to keep their homes at minimum standard comfort levels. Finally, preventative measures such as the Home Energy Efficiency Scheme should be extended and additional subsidies should be made available to enable the most vulnerable households to tackle the problem of excess winter death and illness. The net effect will include a desirable reduction in CO_2 emissions but not at the expense of the poorest in society. In a society where social justice is perceived to be a desirable objective, a co-ordinated programme for tackling fuel poverty provides a significant opportunity for demonstrating what social justice can mean in practice.

Damian Killeen
Director, Strathclyde Poverty Alliance
Convenor, Right to Warmth and the Campaign for Cold Weather Credits

CHAPTER ONE

Introduction

This book aims to give comprehensive advice to domestic consumers of gas and electricity – for example, how to get a supply, how to find remedies when things go wrong, your position if you are a tenant.

This is a little-known area of the law. It starts with the Gas Act 1986 and the Electricity Act 1989 (as amended by the Competition and Services (Utilities) Act 1992). As well as bringing in the arrangements for privatising the gas and electricity supply industries, these Acts brought in new regulations and regulatory structures. Whatever your views on the concept of privatisation, the new laws are an improvement for the domestic consumer – and for the lawyer, who used to have to wade through perhaps the worst-drafted legislation ever produced to find answers to some questions, particularly on electricity supply!

This chapter covers:

1. Sources for your rights (see below)
2. The structure of the industry (see p2)
3. Using this book (see p3)
4. Developments (see p4)

I. SOURCES FOR YOUR RIGHTS

The sources for your rights in respect of the supply of gas and electricity include:

- Legislation – principally the Gas Act 1986 and the Electricity Act 1989, as amended by the Competition and Services (Utilities) Act 1992;

- Statutory Instruments – regulations made under legislation (eg, the Electricity (Standards of Performance) Regulations SI 1993/1193);

- Law reports/court decisions;

- A gas supplier has to have an Authorisation to Supply from OFGAS and an electricity supplier has to have a Licence from OFFER – British Gas's Authorisation and the electricity companies' Licences are large documents containing a number of conditions which they must comply with or face action from the regulatory bodies, OFGAS and OFFER;

- Codes of Practice – these are devised and published by the suppliers themselves but have to be approved by OFGAS or OFFER. The Codes are not legally binding by themselves, but they do indicate how a supplier should and usually will behave in certain situations. You may be able to get a remedy against a practice or a particular action by a supplier simply because it breaches one of the relevant Codes of Practice. Unfortunately, there is no room in this book to reprint all these Codes and only the main points from them are dealt with. Copies should be available from any local showroom or regional office, free of charge, and no-one who regularly advises in this field should be without the relevant copies for their local area.

Note: if more detail is necessary on a particular problem, the source of any legal assertion will be given in the references at the end of this book, if it is not in the text itself.

2. THE STRUCTURE OF THE INDUSTRY

Gas

Gas is supplied by British Gas plc. It has a monopoly of supply to any customer who wants less than 2,500 therms of gas. (The average household uses about 650 therms.)

Gas suppliers are monitored and regulated by the **Office of Gas Supply (OFGAS)**, headed by the Director General of Gas Supply, and by the Gas Consumers' Council. OFGAS's main functions are the granting of authorisations to supply gas, monitoring the performance of gas suppliers, protecting consumers' interests and resolving individual disputes. OFGAS has wide powers of enforcement (see Chapter 13).

The **Gas Consumers' Council** has 12 regional offices and should deal with anything OFGAS does not. It has wide powers to investigate anything which relates to the use of gas by consumers including service, maintenance and installation of appliances. However, unlike OFGAS, it has no powers of enforcement and only issues reports to be sent to British Gas and OFGAS. Its members are appointed by the Secretary of State for Trade and Industry.

Electricity

Most electricity in Great Britain is supplied by 14 regional companies. They have a monopoly of supply to any customer who wants less than one megawatt of electricity – this will be reduced to 100 kilowatts in 1994 and, after 1998, these guaranteed monopolies go altogether. This means that after 1998, at least in theory, you will be able to choose the company you want to supply you. In fact, this will depend on the technology – particularly for metering – being available.

The companies are monitored by the **Office of Electricity Regulation (OFFER)**, headed by the Director General of Electricity Supply, and by regional Consumers' Committees. OFFER's main functions are the granting of licences to supply electricity, monitoring the performance of electricity suppliers, protecting consumers' interests and resolving individual disputes. Like OFGAS, OFFER has wide enforcement powers (see Chapter 13).

The **Electricity Consumers' Committees** are appointed by OFFER. (Anyone can apply or nominate others to be on these committees – application forms are available from OFFER.) In general, each committee monitors one of the regional electricity companies. They also come together in the National Consumers' Consultative Committee. Like the Gas Consumers' Council, they have no enforcement powers other than the threat of adverse publicity.

3. USING THIS BOOK

In the Gas and Electricity Acts the various supply companies with which this book is concerned are referred to as 'public gas suppliers' and 'public electricity suppliers'. Unless we need to differentiate, all will be referred to as 'suppliers' in this book.

Unless specified, everything in this book applies equally to both gas and electricity. They are substantially similar but there are some differences, partly arising from the different nature of each fuel and partly because of the simple fact that the two industries were privatised at different times, eg, the Electricity Act shows one or two minor modifications, intended as improvements, over the earlier Gas Act.

The Acts apply to England, Wales and Scotland, but not to Northern Ireland. The Scottish legal system is different from that in England and Wales and any points where this produces differences in the applicable law are noted. This book should be equally useful wherever you are in Great Britain.

4. DEVELOPMENTS

VAT

The most controversial and public change for domestic gas and electricity consumers will be the introduction of VAT. Industry and commerce have had to pay VAT on their supplies for some time but it will start for your ordinary bills at home as from 1 April 1994. For the first year, the rate will be a special one of 8%. From 1 April 1995, the full rate (currently 17.5%) will be charged. The rate will be charged on supplies of gas or electricity made within the relevant dates – ie, charging is based on the dates when fuel is used rather than when the bill is sent.

Note: The VAT on your bill is just as much a part of the charges for the supply of gas or electricity as the standing and unit charges. This means you can be disconnected for non-payment of the VAT element alone (see Chapter 7).

Developments Covered in This Edition

Travellers, mobile homes and caravan sites have been included for the first time in new sections in Chapter 2.

Charges for connecting supplies of gas and electricity have been revised and updated in Chapter 2.

New developments affecting security deposits are included in Chapter 2.

Questions of choice of meter and method of payment have been more closely explored and updated with details of the latest decisions by OFFER. See Chapters 3 and 5.

The question of responsibility for the bill has been updated, with details of some county court decisions in respect of gas and new information on OFFER's position.

Recent problems with the Fuel Direct scheme have been addressed in Chapter 3.

New developments in metering technology are explored in Chapter 3, with particular emphasis on the new gas prepayment meter, the 'Quantum' meter.

The difficulties facing customers in arrears and in multiple debt have increased since the last edition. Chapter 6: Arrears has been completely revised and rewritten to reflect this. The problem of suppliers attempting to impose prepayment meters is specifically addressed in section 13 of the same chapter.

The gas industry (OFGAS, British Gas and the Gas Consumers' Council) has completed its review of theft and tampering procedures. The results are covered in the revised Chapter 8.

The latest benefit rates are included in Chapter 10, along with changes due to the implementation of Council Tax and the Child Support Act.

Fuel poverty (the inability to afford a warm home) is a major issue these days. Chapter 11, on energy efficiency, has been improved to reflect the importance of fuel saving, particularly for those living in fuel poverty.

This edition is only the second to cover Scotland as well as England and Wales. In the light of comments on the last edition, the Scottish elements of this book have been revised and improved. Any further comments are always welcome from users to help improve the book for future editions.

Future Developments

The Government is reviewing competition in the gas market in the light of a report from the Monopolies and Mergers Commission. The possibility is that, within the next few years, just as is intended to happen with electricity, you will have a choice of gas suppliers, rather than only British Gas. The likelihood is that, to compensate for the loss of its monopoly, British Gas will be allowed to set higher prices than it is currently allowed.

As from 1 January 1994, OFGAS intends to introduce revised standards of service (see Chapter 13 and Appendix 6).

The Energy Savings Trust (see Chapter 11) is likely to produce a scheme for energy efficiency improvements for low income households soon, called the Affordable Warmth Scheme.

CHAPTER TWO

The Right to a Supply

Electricity and gas will be dealt with separately in parts of this chapter. This chapter covers:

Note: All references to your supply assume that you are legally responsible ('liable') for the supply. You should check Chapter 4 to ensure that you are in fact responsible for the supply.

I. WHO IS ENTITLED TO A SUPPLY?

Electricity and gas suppliers have a general duty to supply you if:

• you are an owner or occupier of premises; *and*

• you request a supply by giving notice in writing.[1]

An occupier is a person who occupies any premises legally, whether paying rent, or other charge, or paying nothing.

There are exceptions to this duty – squatters are not considered to be occupiers and therefore are not entitled to a supply. See below. There are also many other instances when a supplier is entitled to either refuse to connect a supply, or to disconnect a supply which has already been given. See below Electricity – pp8-10, Gas – pp16-17.

2. SQUATTERS AND THE RIGHT TO A SUPPLY

Squatters had no right to a supply of electricity under pre-privatisation legislation. The High Court decided that a squatter was not an occupier for the purpose of the right to a supply of electricity.[2] Although this decision was made under pre-1989 legislation, it is likely that it applies also to current legislation,[3] as this also refers to the right of supply in terms of 'owners' and 'occupiers'. It is also likely to apply to gas legislation for the same reason,[4] and OFGAS has indicated it believes this to be the case.

In practice, in England and Wales the position for squatters is not completely bleak. Both gas and electricity suppliers say that they do supply most squatters and treat them in the same way as other short-term residents. This means they will usually require a security deposit (see p20), or an alternative form of security such as the installation of an electronic prepayment meter as a condition of supply. Electricity suppliers are likely to refuse a supply if you explicitly state that you are a squatter, or if an owner has contacted them to say that a property is empty and not to supply anyone else.

In Scotland there has been a far more hard-line approach to squatters and the practice is still to refuse a supply of electricity and gas. Squatters have no rights in Scottish law, and it is unlikely that they could insist upon an electricity supply.

Both OFFER and OFGAS say that they have not had disputes referred to them from squatters refused a supply. It is important that squatters who are refused a supply seek legal advice as the judgment in the pre-1989 case referred to above was confused, particularly in relation to the definition of a squatter.

3. TRAVELLERS AND THE RIGHT TO A SUPPLY

Local authorities were obliged to set up caravan sites for travellers in England and Wales by the Caravan Sites Act 1968. In Scotland, the position is governed by the Caravan Sites and Control of Development Act 1960. In practice, provision of sites has been scant and patchy.

Local authorities in England and Wales are provided with guidance on practical aspects of site provision and management by the Department of the Environment.[5] The guidance contains the standards for the provision of electricity and water supplies to sites. There are no provisions for the supply of gas. Standards vary according to the type of site provided:

- There are no provisions requiring the supply of electricity to transit or short stay sites or to residential sites which have not yet been developed into permanent sites.

- On permanent sites for long term residential use, every family should have the use of a pitch provided with electricity.

The local authority as landlord will be responsible for the supply and will be entitled to resell electricity. The local authority will be entitled to charge up to the Maximum Re-sale Price for electricity (see p163).

4. MOBILE HOMES AND CARAVAN SITES AND THE RIGHT TO A SUPPLY

Sites for mobile homes are licensed by local authorities. Model standards for the provision of electricity and water to sites are issued by the Department of the Environment to local authorities,[6] who can decide what conditions, if any, to attach to caravan site licences. There are no provisions for gas. Guidance to local authorities is in very broad terms and suggests that sites should be provided with an electricity supply sufficient in all respects to meet all reasonable demands of the caravans situated on them.[7]

You will always need to look at the provisions within the caravan site licence to determine if your site owner is obliged to provide a supply of electricity to your site.

Site owners may resell electricity to you, but cannot charge more than the Maximum Re-sale Price (see p163).

If there is no provision for electricity on your site, there is nothing to stop you from applying for a supply to be connected if you are the owner or occupier of a mobile home or caravan. However, you will need to be mindful of the possibly substantial costs involved. See pp15 -16 for a discussion of connection charges.

5. WHEN CAN YOU BE REFUSED A SUPPLY OF ELECTRICITY?

Electricity suppliers may refuse to supply electricity in a number of circumstances. These may involve refusing to connect a supply to a new premises, disconnecting an existing supply, or refusing to reconnect a supply which has been disconnected. Circumstances in which the supplier is entitled to disconnect are therefore also referred to in outline below. Disconnection for arrears will be dealt with fully in Chapter 7.

You may be refused a supply if:

- **you have not paid your bill** for electricity supplied, for standing charges, meters, and any connection charges within 20 working days of the date of the bill (see p89). You are entitled to two working days' notice of disconnection.[8] Your supply may be disconnected at the premises to which the unpaid bill relates or to any other premises where you receive a supply.[9] You may be protected from disconnection by the provisions of Condition 19 of the Supplier's licence if you cannot pay (see p90);[10]

- **you did not pay your bill for any of the charges above at your previous address.**[11] The supplier may refuse to connect a supply at your new address or may disconnect the supply at your previous address. The supplier is not entitled to payment for your arrears from the next occupier of your previous address.[12] Similarly you cannot be held liable for debts left by previous occupiers of your new address;[13]

- **you have not paid a security deposit** within seven days of being sent a notice requiring you to pay (see p20);[14]

- **you refuse to accept a supply under a 'special agreement' with the supplier.**[15] The supplier is only entitled to insist on supplying you in this way in exceptional circumstances (see p14);

- **your premises are already being supplied by a private electricity supplier** through electrical cables or equipment belonging to the public electricity supplier from whom you have requested a supply;[16]

- **supplying you with electricity would or might be unsafe** – eg, because your wiring is in a dangerous condition;[17]

- **you refuse to take your supply through a meter;**[18]

- **there has been damage to a meter or tampering**[19] (see Chapter 8);

- **the supplier is prevented from supplying you by circumstances outside its control**[20] – eg, if the supplier has been prevented from laying cables because of extreme weather or a civil disturbance;

- **it is not reasonable in all the circumstances.**[21] This is a 'catch all' provision. Most disconnections or refusals to supply will be on one or more of the grounds above, but this provision might be used if those grounds no longer apply – for example, if you were no longer in arrears but the supplier insisted that you could only be supplied through a prepayment meter for future consumption. If you refused to accept a prepayment meter, the supplier would need to be able to demonstrate that disconnection was the only reasonable alternative. The supplier cannot use this catch-all provision unless it first gives you seven days' notice of the intention to disconnect.[22]

Disputes about a refusal to connect a supply or a decision to disconnect your supply could be referred to OFFER (see Chapter 13). Electricity suppliers are not entitled to disconnect where there is a genuine dispute (see p112).

6. GETTING YOUR SUPPLY CONNECTED (ELECTRICITY)

Notice

Most ordinary domestic customers are known as 'tariff customers'.[23] To become a tariff customer and to obtain a supply, you must first give the electricity supplier notice in writing.[24] You can do this by writing a letter or you could fill out a standard application form issued by the supplier. The Electricity Act 1989 says that your notice must include all the following details:[25]

- the premises where you require the supply;
- the date when the supply should commence;
- the maximum power required;
- the minimum period for which the supply is needed.

If you have a preference, you should also specify what type of meter you would like and how you wish to pay for your supply (see Chapter 3).

Many suppliers' application forms do not ask the maximum power required or the minimum period for which you will require a supply. As your rights as a customer are often dependent upon you being a tariff customer, you may wish to ensure that you give notice as required by the Act. It should be sufficient to indicate that you require an ordinary domestic supply, and this may well be implied on the form if it is not explicitly stated. Some suppliers specify on their forms that an application for a supply is for a minimum period of a week. If no minimum period is mentioned on the form, you may wish to specify a similar minimum period.

You are not obliged to give the electricity supplier any information other than the four points listed above, but application forms do frequently request more information about you and about other occupants of your home. If you choose not to give information – for example, about your previous address or creditworthiness – you may be asked for a security deposit. You are not obliged to give information about anyone else occupying your home and you should not be refused a supply if you refuse to give this information. But, be careful – liability for the bill may be decided by who signs the application form or letter. See Chapter 4 for more details.

Some suppliers will connect your supply if you telephone to request a supply. This practice leaves the question of liability for the bill open to dispute. You can safeguard your rights as a tariff customer by making your requests in writing as described above (see p10) or by following up your telephone request in writing.

If the requirements on your application form are acceptable – ie, if the supplier has no objection to your choice of meter, method of payment or other terms and conditions – the electricity supplier will connect your supply. Otherwise, you may be served with a counternotice.

Counternotice

An electricity supplier *must* serve you with a counternotice in response to your notice in any of the following circumstances:[26]

- there has not previously been a supply of electricity to the premises; *or*

- it would be necessary for the supplier to provide electrical lines or plant; *or*

- there are other circumstances which would make it necessary or expedient.

OFFER has ruled that a counternotice should also be served if the supplier wishes to change the terms and conditions of your supply at any time[27] – eg,

- if the supplier wants to insist that you should pay your bills through a prepayment meter rather than through a budget-plan, *or*

- if the supplier wants to change your coin prepayment meter to an electronic prepayment meter.

The counternotice should include details of your right to have a dispute determined by OFFER.[28]

A counternotice must be in writing[29] and must specify the following:[30]

- the extent to which the proposals in your letter or application form are acceptable, and any counter proposals;
- which tariff you will be charged under – ie, the type of meter and method of payment (eg, a credit meter combined with direct debit payments, or an Economy Seven prepayment meter – see p38), or the proposed terms of any special agreement for payment (see p14);
- any outstanding costs of connecting the supply if the original connection occurred less than five years ago (see p15);
- the amount of any security deposit required;
- any restrictions necessary to ensure the supply complies with safety regulations;
- the right for disputes to be determined by the Director General of OFFER.

If you accept the conditions of the counternotice, the electricity supplier will connect your supply. If you disagree with any of the conditions, you could refer the matter to OFFER for an independent decision. See Chapter 13.

How Soon Should your Supply be Connected?

There is no prescribed time limit within which your supply should be connected, though there is a general duty to supply you from the date you specify in your written notice.[31] This duty is watered down in practice by the following:

- if your premises were previously supplied with electricity, you should be given an appointment within a certain number of working days for your supply to be connected and a meter installed under the Standards of Performance set down for all suppliers. The number of days varies from supplier to supplier and is typically between two and six days.[32] (See Appendix 6 for details of the standards which apply to each supplier.) If the appointment is not made within the specified time, you will be entitled to automatic compensation of £20. If the appointment is not kept, you will be entitled to automatic compensation of £40.
- if your premises have never previously had a supply of electricity, and you make a written request for an estimate of the charges of connection, this should be sent within a certain number of working

days if the work is simple, or within a longer specified period if the work is complicated. Time limits are specified under the Standards of Performance set out for all suppliers and range typically from 10 to 20 days for simple work, and from 15 to 30 days for more complicated work. You will be entitled to a compensation payment of £40 if the estimate is not sent within the time limits which apply to your supplier.[33] (See Appendix 6 for details of the Standards which apply to each supplier);

- if an electricity supplier serves you with a 'counternotice'. The supplier must do this as soon as is practical after receiving your written notice.[34] Connection times will then depend on whether or not you choose to accept the supplier's counter-proposals.

If you experience unreasonable delays in getting your supply connected, you could contact OFFER for assistance.

7. CONDITIONS OF SUPPLY

Electricity companies sometimes claim to impose 'Conditions of Supply' or 'Terms of Supply' on their customers. Most often, these simply represent a statement of a customer's rights and duties under the Electricity Act 1989. Some suppliers, however, go further than this by asking customers to sign an agreement to abide by the Conditions of Supply as stated on their application forms. This can represent an unlawful attempt by the electricity supplier to extend its powers.

For example, in a case referred to OFFER as a complaint,[35] a supplier charged a customer for the replacement of a meter and for money which had been inserted into her coin meter following a burglary at her home. The company said that it was entitled to do this because its 'Terms and Conditions of Supply' said that the customer was responsible for the safe-keeping of metering equipment. In this instance, OFFER argued that this was an unreasonable condition which did not comply with the provisions of the Electricity Act. The supplier reversed its decision in this case and altered its procedures.

The legal position is fairly straightforward in cases of this sort. Electricity is supplied under a statutory duty. There is no contract for the supply of fuel outside of the provisions of the legislation. An electricity supplier has no power to impose 'Conditions of Supply' on an ordinary domestic customer over and above anything contained in the legislation, even if the customer has signed an application form agreeing to abide by a condition in the small print.

The only legitimate way that a supplier could side-step some of the provisions imposed by the legislation would be if electricity was supplied under the terms of a 'special agreement' (see below).

8. 'TARIFF CUSTOMERS' AND 'SPECIAL AGREEMENTS'

Most ordinary domestic customers are known as 'tariff customers' under the provisions of the Electricity Act 1989.[36] 'Tariff customers' are owners or occupiers who have requested a supply of electricity in writing and who have been supplied with electricity.[37] Electricity will be supplied and charged for at a particular rate or 'tariff' (see p38 for details of the different tariffs available). There is, however, provision for an alternative status for domestic customers. This is known as a 'special agreement' under section 22 of the Electricity Act.[38] The terms and conditions which bind both you and the supplier would be the terms of the agreement and not certain provisions of the Electricity Act which apply to 'tariff customers'.[39] Note that these 'special agreements' do not represent contracts outside the statutory framework – they are an exceptional provision within the terms of the statute.

There are two sets of circumstances when the question of a special agreement might arise:

- a supplier has the discretion to grant you a special agreement if you ask for one when you give notice requiring a supply;[40] *or*

- you could be required to enter into a 'special agreement' by the supplier if it was 'reasonable in all the circumstances'.[41]

Suppliers usually attempt to impose 'special agreements' only in extreme circumstances and usually only when disconnection is considered to be the only other alternative. In one case referred to OFFER, a supplier attempted to obtain a security deposit in addition to requiring that the customer accept a prepayment meter as a condition of supply. OFFER decided that, even under the terms of a special agreement, this was an unnecessary requirement.[42] A supplier would not be entitled to require both these conditions from an ordinary 'tariff customer'.

If a supplier attempts to impose a special agreement on you against your wishes, you could ask OFFER to intervene. OFFER has a duty to determine disputes about special agreements.[43] But note that in one case, OFFER states that customers entering into special agreements will lose the right to have disputes decided by OFFER.[44] This position is contrary to the provisions of the Electricity Act and clearly wrong. But the existence of the decision means that it is essential that you also seek independent legal advice.

9. CHARGES FOR CONNECTING A SUPPLY (ELECTRICITY)

An electricity supplier may charge for connecting a supply only in the following circumstances:

- **Connection of your premises to the supply network for the first time.** If the supplier has to lay or replace cables or provide equipment to give you a supply, you may have to pay towards the costs incurred by the supplier.[45] This often applies to new housing developments. Suppliers have a general connection fee which covers 90% of new connections. Others, generally those more distant from the supply network or involving more complicated work, are assessed individually and are subject to extra charges. Suppliers publish their policies and these should be available on request. The cost of a new connection could be spread over a period of years. There is plenty of room for argument about what is a reasonable charge. OFFER has issued a statement on Domestic Connection Charges.[46] A number of determinations have now been made on the subject of reasonable charges.[47] In most of these cases, the charges have been reduced.[48] In the event of a dispute, consider asking OFFER to intervene.

- **Connection of premises to supply network occurred less than five years ago.** You may be required to pay extra charges if it has been less than five years since electricity lines or plant were provided to connect a supply to your premises,[49] *and*

  - a charge was paid by the person originally requesting the supply be connected; *and*
  - the supplier's expenses have not yet been recovered in full; *and*
  - the supplier has provided any information you reasonably requested concerning the amount of the expenses, the date the line or plant was provided and how much has been paid by previous consumers.

  You may find yourself subject to such a connection charge, particularly if you require a supply to premises in a rural area where another customer has paid a large connection charge to extend the supply network to the area. If you would benefit from the other customer's expenditure, you can be asked to pay some of the cost.

- Reconnection of your supply following a disconnection (see p120).

10. WHEN CAN YOU BE REFUSED A SUPPLY OF GAS?

A gas supplier may refuse to supply gas in a number of circumstances. These may involve refusing to connect a supply to a new address, disconnecting an existing supply or refusing to connect a supply which has been disconnected. The circumstances in which a supplier is entitled to disconnect are therefore also referred to in outline below. Disconnection for arrears is dealt with fully in Chapter 7.

A supplier may refuse to supply you if:
- **your premises are not close enough to a gas main** – ie, the premises are not within 25 yards of the supplier's gas main or are not connected by a service pipe to a supplier's gas main.[50] The 25 yards must be measured in a straight line on a horizontal plane;[51]
- **you have not paid your bill within 28 days**[52] of being billed and the bill contains charges for gas consumed, standing charges, the supply or fixing of any meter or fittings or VAT.[53] The supplier may disconnect your supply at the premises which relate to the unpaid bill.[54] You are entitled to seven days' notice of the intention to disconnect.[55] You may be protected from disconnection by the Principles adopted under Condition 12A of the Authorisation to British Gas (see p90-91);[56]
- **you have not paid your bill for your previous premises.** The supplier can refuse to connect your supply at any other premises, but is not entitled to payment of your arrears from the next occupier at your previous address.[57] Similarly, you cannot be held liable for debts left by the previous occupiers of your new address;[58]
- **you have not paid a security deposit which has been requested,**[59] unless you are in dispute about the requirement for the security deposit, or you cannot afford the amount being requested. You may be protected from disconnection by the Principles adopted under Condition 12A of the Authorisation to British Gas (see pp90-91);[60]
- **the supplier requires that you have a meter and you refuse.**[61] This might occur in disputes over what type of meter (eg, credit or prepayment) is acceptable (see p51-52);

- you own a faulty meter.[62] Note that in these circumstances the supplier can be asked to supply a meter instead;[63]
- you have not paid a deposit for the loan or hire of a meter;[64]
- it is not safe to connect your supply – eg, because your pipes are in a dangerous condition;[65]
- there has been theft or tampering;[66]
- the supplier is prevented from supplying you by circumstances beyond its control.[67] This might include instances where bad weather or a disaster prevents connection.

Note: there is no power to disconnect for a **consumer credit debt** which is being recovered through a gas prepayment meter. The new generation of gas prepayment meter, the 'Quantum' meter, can be set to recover this type of debt. This could lead to the disconnection of the supply if the customer has insufficient funds for both fuel and the repayment of the consumer credit debt, and may place the supplier in breach of its duty to supply. If a consumer is in difficulties, British Gas could be asked to take the consumer credit debt off the meter. Professional money advice should be sought.

Electricity suppliers are prohibited from this practice.[68]

Disputes about a refusal to connect a supply or a decision to disconnect your supply could be referred to OFGAS as possible enforcement matters or determination matters (see Chapter 13). Gas suppliers are not entitled to disconnect where there is a genuine dispute.[69]

11. GETTING YOUR SUPPLY CONNECTED (GAS)

Notice

If you require a gas supply, the Gas Act 1986 says that you must serve a written notice to an 'appropriate office' of the gas supplier.[70] Gas suppliers must publish the addresses of appropriate offices in their area and bills must carry the addresses of local appropriate offices.[71] The notice must specify:[72]

- the premises where the supply is required;
- the day when the supply should commence.

However, OFGAS' opinion is that the obligation to give written notice applies only to the 'original' connection of the premises because the matters to be specified are only relevant in such a case.[73] For practical purposes, this means that gas suppliers often put little emphasis on application forms or the need for written notice that a supply is required, and will routinely connect premises if you telephone them, or if you call into a showroom in person. They will often leave premises connected if they know you will be leaving, but somebody else will occupy the premises.

The assumption is that it is the premises which are supplied, and not the owner or occupier. However, if you are clear that you want sole responsibility for the bill, make sure you give proper notice in writing. A simple letter will suffice if no application form is available. Otherwise, see Chapter 4 for more about responsibility for the bill.

'Counternotice'

Note that there is no provision for a counternotice as with electricity.

How Soon Should your Supply be Connected?

Your supply should be connected within a reasonable time of service of the notice.[74] 'Reasonable' has not been defined. In practice, gas supplies often remain connected after the previous occupier of a premises moves out, so there is often no interruption to the supply. Situations where a supply has not yet been connected to a particular premises are now also covered by an agreement between British Gas and OFGAS. British Gas has agreed some key standards with OFGAS on aspects of its service delivery and will be developing a compensation scheme similar to that operated by the electricity suppliers. The key standards form part of their commitment to a new condition of the Authorisation to British Gas (see Appendix 6), Condition 13A, which came into force in April 1992. OFGAS is currently re-negotiating the contents of Condition 13A with British Gas.

The provisions of Condition 13A are enforceable by OFGAS (see Chapter 13).

The key standards currently in operation state that when a customer makes contact to request a gas supply:

- If a survey visit is required, contact will be made within two working days to arrange an appointment which will be within three working days, or later if requested by the customer.

- Following such a visit, a quotation for providing a supply will be dispatched within five working days of the visit.

- If no visit is required, a quotation will be dispatched within five working days of receipt of the enquiry.

In the event of an unreasonable delay, you could take the matter up with OFGAS as a possible enforcement matter. You may be able to obtain an injunction (see Chapter 13). In Scotland you may be able to obtain an order of declarator and specific implement (see Chapter 13). You may need to seek legal advice.

12. CHARGES FOR CONNECTING A SUPPLY (GAS)

In most circumstances, there will be no charge for the connection of a gas supply, particularly when you are taking over the supply at premises which are already connected to the gas network.

However, there is likely to be a charge where premises are being connected to the gas network for the first time. You may be charged for all work done on your premises and for any pipe which has to be laid more than 30 feet from any pipe belonging to a gas supplier.[75]

Potential customers in areas which are remote from the British Gas network may face high connection charges. British Gas argues that it cannot subsidise costs in remote areas and currently charges for these new connections on the basis of the incremental cost of laying mains to provide new supplies.[76] This policy led to record levels of complaints to OFGAS in 1992.[77] OFGAS plans to review the present approach as part of a current review of British Gas's gas transportation business.[78]

OFGAS has a duty to resolve disputes concerning connection charges.[79] In the event of a dispute, you may wish to press OFGAS to make an independent decision. See Chapter 13 for more about disputes. Note that OFFER has made a number of decisions relating to electricity connection charges (see p15 for details).

You may also be charged if the gas main through which your premises are supplied is less than five years old at the time that you ask for a gas supply. The extra charge will only apply if all the following conditions are met:[80]

- a charge was paid by the person whose request for the supply led to the main being laid in the first place; *and*
- the amount of the charge is no more than has been made to anyone previously supplied from the main; *and*
- the gas supplier has not yet recovered the full cost of the main; *and*

- the gas supplier has supplied you with any information you reasonably requested concerning the cost of the main, the date it was laid and how much has been paid by previous consumers.

So, if the previous occupiers had a supply put in over the last five years but did not finish paying for it, you may have to pay some of the cost. If you dispute the amount of connection charges, you could refer your dispute to OFGAS for a decision.

13. SECURITY DEPOSITS

Electricity and gas suppliers are entitled to ask for 'reasonable security' as a condition of connecting a supply,[81] or at any time after the supply has been connected.[82] This is generally a request for a cash security deposit, although OFFER has ruled that some methods of payment, such as direct debits, and prepayment meters also represent 'reasonable security'.[83] Some electricity suppliers are now routinely using the principles for requesting a security deposit as a means of imposing electronic prepayment meters on customers in low income groups.

Security deposits are held separately from customers' fuel accounts and are used to offset costs following a disconnection. They should not be regarded as a credit payment towards your next bill.

The supplier may refuse to connect or may disconnect your supply if you have failed to pay within seven days of being billed for the deposit.[84] Your supply may remain disconnected for as long as you refuse to pay the amount requested.[85]

If you are a new customer, you may be routinely asked for a security deposit by electricity suppliers, particularly if:

- you refuse to provide information about previous addresses;

- you cannot demonstrate a satisfactory payment history at a previous address;

- you do not otherwise provide sufficient information about your creditworthiness;

- you are in short-stay accommodation. You should not be treated as being in short-stay accommodation if you are a secure or assured tenant.[86]

- if you are known to be a squatter. This applies only to England and Wales. In Scotland, known squatters are unlikely to be granted a supply.

British Gas has agreed with OFGAS that it will not require any new domestic customer to pay a deposit, except when a bad debt risk is known.[87]

Security deposits may also be required from existing customers:
- when payment plans have broken down.[88] You may be able to have a prepayment meter as an alternative – see p23 below. Remember that the requirement for a security deposit must be reasonable. If the reason your payment plan broke down was that it was unaffordable for you, you may be able to negotiate another payment plan instead of either having to pay a security deposit or having a prepayment meter installed (see Chapter 6).

- if it is not safe and practicable or reasonable for a prepayment meter to be installed,[89] *and*

- in instances when theft, tampering or damage to meters or equipment have occurred.[90]

If a particular group of consumers are always asked for a security deposit – eg, because they happen to live on a particular estate – OFFER should be asked to intervene. OFFER has indicated that discrimination in seeking security deposits is unlawful.[91]

Amount of Deposit

The amount of, or requirement for, a security deposit by an electricity or gas supplier must be reasonable.[92] Electricity and gas suppliers may increase the amount of deposit required if the existing security has become invalid or insufficient. A supplier is only entitled to a security deposit if it serves you with written notice requesting payment of reasonable security within seven days.[93] For electricity only, the notice must inform you of your right to have a dispute decided by OFFER.[94] Non-payment within the seven days will entitle the supplier to disconnect your supply.

The amounts requested vary between suppliers. It can be argued that as the deposit is set against money which may become due, it should never exceed a reasonable estimate of 20 weeks' consumption – ie, the estimated bill for one quarter plus typically the estimated bill for the seven weeks from bill to disconnection.

Electricity:

London Electricity usually asks for £100 as a security deposit, though the amount is negotiable according to the size of premises supplied and the number and means of the occupants. Scottish Power requests around £70 on average, but bases its calculation on the estimated consumption of the two heaviest winter months. NORWEB often asks for much larger sums until challenged on the reasonableness of the amounts. Midlands Electricity Board usually asks for between one and two times the estimated quarterly bill.

The Director General of OFFER has a duty to make a decision in disputes about the amount of or reasonableness of a request for a security deposit,[95] and can prevent disconnection pending the outcome of a dispute.

Gas:

Gas suppliers usually request the highest two quarters' actual or estimated consumption.

If you cannot afford to pay a *reasonable* security deposit for a gas supply straight away, your supply should not be disconnected or refused when financial assistance or counselling is available from the Benefits Agency or another agency, or if a prepayment meter can be installed.[96]

If a gas supplier withholds the supply or threatens to disconnect because you do not pay an *unreasonable* amount, it will be in breach of its duty to supply. You should refer the matter to OFGAS. Your supply should not be disconnected while your dispute is being considered. In the Sheriff Court in Scotland, you will also need the services of OFGAS, though an interdict could be sought to prevent disconnection. If OFGAS failed in its duties, you may need to obtain a declarator with a specific implement to order a connection in the Court of Session as part of an action of judicial review against OFGAS. If British Gas ignored an OFGAS direction, there *might* be a right to start proceedings in the Sheriff Court if the OFGAS Determination is deemed to have the status of a court order. Alternatively, it might be possible to seek a judicial review in the Court of Session. This is not settled law in Scotland and any case will be a test case. Legal advice will be essential.

Return of Security Deposits

There is no legal requirement to return security deposits, though they are often returned after 12 months if payments for the supply have been made promptly.

Interest on Security Deposits

Interest is payable on every sum of 50 pence which is deposited for every three months with an electricity or gas supplier. For electricity, the rate of interest is set by the supplier with the approval of the Director General of OFFER, usually every April. The rate from April 1993 was 10% for London Electricity and 8% for all other suppliers. For gas, interest rates are reviewed every three months on 1 April, 1 July, 1 October and 1 January. Enforcement of interest rates by gas suppliers is one of the roles of OFGAS. The rate at 1st July 1993 was 4%. Interest rates have fallen considerably since last year.

The Costs of Disconnection and Reconnection if a Security Deposit is not Paid

A gas supplier may demand the expenses of reconnection if it has disconnected for failure to pay a deposit.[97] There is no parallel provision allowing disconnection expenses to be charged.

Electricity suppliers may demand the reasonable expenses of both disconnection and reconnection as well as payment of the security deposit prior to reconnecting the supply.[98]

Disputes about Security Deposits

Both OFFER and OFGAS have a duty to resolve disputes over security deposits.[99]

A relevant dispute could include whether it is reasonable for the supplier to provide a prepayment meter or a payment plan as an alternative to a security deposit.

14. ALTERNATIVES TO SECURITY DEPOSITS

Payment Plans and Guarantors

Both electricity and gas suppliers routinely accept direct debit payments and payment plans as acceptable alternatives to security deposits. Guarantors may be accepted as an alternative to a security deposit in some parts of the country only. (London Electricity sometimes accepts guarantors, but they are virtually unheard of in Scotland.)

Potential guarantors should be aware that if the bill is defaulted on, they would be liable for the debt and could be pursued for the debt through the courts. Guarantors of an electricity supply who own or occupy the premises to which the bill relates could have their supply disconnected either at that premises, or at any other premises which they occupy.[100]

OFFER has said in a decision that although such arrangements may be less secure than a cash deposit or prepayment meter, they may in some circumstances be as or more appropriate. They may constitute reasonable security in certain circumstances.[101]

OFFER does not give examples of such circumstances, although, in this case, it decided that a customer who was an habitual late payer should pay his bills by direct debit as an acceptable alternative to a large security deposit.

Prepayment Meters

Electricity

Electricity suppliers are not entitled to a security deposit if you are prepared to have a prepayment meter and it is reasonably practicable for the supplier to provide one.[102] Suppliers are entitled to take into consideration the risk of loss or damage to a meter in deciding if a prepayment meter can be offered as an alternative.

However, in the London region in particular, low-income customers may be asked for a security deposit as an alternative to a prepayment meter, rather than the other way round. This raises the question of choice of method of payment for low-income customers. See p98 for a discussion of this problem.[103]

In extreme situations, an electricity supplier may try to obtain a security deposit as well as the installation of a prepayment meter. This is not normally lawful. It can only do this under a special agreement under Section 22 of the Electricity Act (see pp14-15). This would either require your consent or the supplier would have to be able to show that it was reasonable in all the circumstances for it to insist upon this type of agreement. If a supplier attempts to impose this type of agreement, you should contact OFFER and seek legal advice.

Gas

The position for gas is more restrictive than for electricity. Gas suppliers are not entitled to a security deposit if you accept the installation of a prepayment meter as an alternative to a security deposit. However, you might be refused the option of accepting a prepayment meter as an alternative form of security and instead be required to pay the security deposit, if the supplier thinks that you can afford the deposit, but won't pay.[104]

CHAPTER THREE

Meters and Methods of Payment

This chapter aims to provide information about the choices you may have about types of meters and methods of payment. It is divided into five sections:

1. Types of meters – this section deals with the practicalities of different types of meters, the different ways these meters can charge for fuel, and explores the advantages and disadvantages of the various options (see below).
2. Standing charges and tariffs (see p37).
3. Methods of payment to avoid falling into arrears (see p39).
4. Fuel Direct – this section looks at the Fuel Direct scheme available for claimants of income support (see p42).
5. Can you choose how to pay? – this final section looks at the legal issues about choice of meter and method of payment, and considers some common problems (see p51).

I. TYPES OF METERS

Gas and electricity suppliers offer an often bewildering choice of different types of meters. There are, however, essentially only two different types of meters currently in use:

- credit or quarterly meters when fuel is supplied in advance of payment; *and*

- prepayment meters when fuel is paid for before consumption.

Both credit and prepayment meters charge at the same rate or 'tariff' throughout the day or night. Electricity, however, can also be supplied through an alternative type of meter which may be set to charge different rates or 'tariffs' at different times of day or night. There is usually a cheaper rate for using off-peak electricity. These variable tariff meters are known as 'Economy Seven' or 'Super Tariff' in parts of England and Wales, and as 'White Meters' or 'Comfort Plus' in Scotland (see pp36-37). They are usually an alternative type of credit meter. However, in some areas, Economy Seven prepayment meters are also available (see p33). You will need to check the availability of variable tariff meters with your supplier.

Your choice of method of payment will depend on the type of meter you have. You may wish to change your meter to allow you to use a particular method of payment.

Each gas and electricity supplier publishes a Code of Practice on the payment of bills, outlining the various options available. Many also publish additional detailed information leaflets about the costs of the different options or 'tariffs'.

Credit Meters

Credit or 'quarterly' meters record consumption, are read periodically and a bill is sent at the end of each billing period. Most customers have credit meters.

Advantages

Credit meters often have the advantage of flexibility and convenience: you can pay your bill every quarter or you can spread your payments by using one of a range of different payment methods, including:

- **direct debit**: a system of direct payments from your bank account to be made either quarterly or monthly. You sign to permit the supplier to debit variable amounts, though the supplier must inform you if there is to be a change in the amount debited;

- **standing order**: a system of direct payments from your bank account, usually monthly. You determine the amount debited. You have to sign another form for the bank to change the amount of the payment;

- a range of **flexible payment and budget schemes**: a variety of schemes to allow you to pay weekly, fortnightly, monthly, or whenever you like.

If you pay your bill in full each quarter, you have the option of paying in cash or by cheque or giro at a showroom, by post, or directly into the supplier's account at a bank or post office. If your circumstances change, you will often be able to change to a more suitable method of payment.

The cost of fuel supplied and standing charges is often cheapest if you have a credit meter, though you should always take into consideration the costs of making your payments. Be aware of bank charges if you pay by standing order or direct debit, and of the often substantial costs of being overdrawn.

If you use electric storage heaters or immersion heaters, you should consider the option of a variable tariff meter, such as Economy Seven or a White Meter, to take advantage of their cheaper night-time rates.

Disadvantages

Estimated bills are the largest source of complaint about electricity and gas. A succession of estimates can result in inaccurate billing, with you paying too much or not enough. This often leads to problems with arrears and the threat of disconnection.

To be billed accurately, your meter should be read regularly. Minimum standards exist for the frequency of meter reading, but these only oblige electricity suppliers to read meters once a year for 95% of their customers.[1] Similar standards are being proposed for gas as part of a review of Standards of Service.[2] It is common practice for suppliers to plan to read meters only once every two or three quarters. If a meter reader cannot gain access, or if no reading is planned, your bill will be based on estimated consumption.

If you receive an estimated bill, you can provide your supplier with details of your own reading and request an amended bill. Meter readers sometimes leave a post-paid card for you to complete and return to the supplier with your own reading. You can telephone the supplier at any time to inform them of your reading.

If your bill is an overestimate, you are obliged to pay only for the fuel you have used, together with any standing charges and any other charges. It will be in your interest to provide an accurate reading. If your bill is an underestimate, you are obliged to pay the amount requested in writing on the bill. If you advise the supplier of your actual reading and are re-billed, you will then be required to pay the amount on the revised bill. Remember that underestimated bills only lead to larger 'catch-up' bills in the future.

Reading your meter

Appendix 8 describes how to read your own credit meter.

Elderly or disabled customers should consider taking advantage of the special meter reading registers offered by suppliers. These alert the meter reader to the fact that a customer may not be able to answer the door immediately and enable the meter readers to allow more time for a reading. Quarterly readings can be arranged for those unable to read their own meters. There are also special schemes for repositioning meters free of charge. Consult your supplier's Code of Practice for the Elderly and Disabled for information about services in your area.

If you have problems with arrears as the result of a succession of estimated bills, see Chapter 6: Arrears as a Result of Estimated Bills.

Electronic Prepayment Meters

Major changes have taken place in the technology of prepayment meters in recent years. In most areas, coin meters have largely been replaced by electronic prepayment meters. There are currently three main types of electronic prepayment meters:

- token meters (see below);
- credit key meters (see p29);
- card meters (see p29).

In some areas, Economy Seven prepayment meters are also available. See p36 for information about this type of meter.

Electricity suppliers in each area usually use one of these types of meter. The names of the meters vary from region to region. In Scotland, card meters known as 'Power Card Registers' (PCR) or Power-Card Meters (PCM) are used by electricity suppliers. London Electricity has attempted to improve the image of its key meter by changing its name from 'Budget Meter' to 'Power-Key'.

Token meters

British Gas currently uses a token meter in all regions. This meter system may be known locally by a different name; for example, in the West Midlands it is known as a 'key meter'. British Gas has also just completed trials of a new generation of prepayment meter – the Quantum Meter. See below for more about this new development. Whatever the name ascribed to prepayment meters in your area, you should be able to recognise the type of meter used from the descriptions given below.

All types of prepayment meters can be reset to collect arrears – ie, so they charge for your supply of fuel, standing charges and extra for any arrears you owe.

These meters use plastic tokens which can be bought from showrooms, post offices or from 24-hour vending machines. Availability varies, so check the position in your area. Tokens are generally available in £1 units, but in the Yorkshire Electricity area, £5 is the minimum. Your account is credited only when you buy a token 'officially' from the supplier (and not from neighbours or friends (see p33).

One type of token is electronically coded. When the token is inserted into the meter, the meter records the amount of fuel purchased and automatically cancels the token. You can then either throw the token away, or keep it for your records. The other type comes in the form of a plastic key. When the key is inserted into the meter, the end is snapped off and falls into the meter, providing a record of the number of tokens inserted when the meter is read. If your fuel runs out, you can use an emergency button on the meter to obtain a small amount of credit (typically worth £5 to £6.50). The next token(s) that you insert will be used to pay for the credited amount. No more fuel will be available until this has been paid.

Key meters

These operate in the same way as token meters. The difference is that you are provided with a rechargeable 'key' when the meter is installed. The key can only be used in your meter. It is electronically encoded with the amount of fuel that you buy either at a showroom or from a vending machine outside the showroom. When the key is inserted into the meter, the amount of fuel you have bought is registered and the key is cancelled. You can obtain up to £5 of emergency credit on these meters. Some of these keys are able to read your meter and pass the reading on when you get them charged.

Card meters

This type of meter is used by electricity suppliers throughout Scotland, where it is known as 'Power Card Register' (PCR) or 'Power Card Meter' (PCM).

Card meters are like token meters but are operated by electronically coded, stiff cards. They are cancelled by insertion into your meter and can then be thrown away or kept for your records. Cards are generally available in units of £1 or £5 from showrooms, vending machines and sometimes from local shops or post offices. In Scotland, they are available from showrooms, post offices and selected garages. The emergency credit available with card meters is typically about £5 but, in Scotland, PCRs have a maximum emergency credit facility of £14.

'Quantum' meter: a new development in card metering technology

British Gas is introducing a new card meter – the 'Quantum' meter. This is an electronic card meter. It will be charged by an electronically-coded card, the 'Gascard', which can only be used in your meter. The card is encoded with the customer's reference number and the meter's serial number. It cannot be used to purchase gas for anyone else. The card even reads the meter and passes the reading on to the charging point when you next purchase credit. The card will be available from showrooms or from British Gas Agents. British Gas showrooms should be able to provide you with information about where you will be able to obtain your Gascard locally.

British Gas has produced a clear and easy to read booklet entitled 'How to use your QUANTUM gas meter'.

Unlike the current, crude, mechanical meters, the Quantum meter will have an *emergency credit* facility and a 'Budget' facility. £2 worth of gas will be available as emergency credit at any time when there is less than £1 of credit left on the meter. The *Budget* facility will enable you retain some of your credit for later use. For example, you will be able to purchase £10 worth of gas on your card, but could choose to use only £4 worth of gas. If you want to use the further £6 worth of gas, you will need to reinsert the card.

The meter will be able to recover arrears, but will not operate according to a fixed sum each week. Both the minimum and maximum amounts which will be collected are variable and British Gas will agree the minimum and maximum weekly figures. The amount which is actually collected will depend on how much gas is used. Even if you have been absent from your home for some time, or if you have used up your emergency credit, or both, the meter will always allow you to use gas amounting to a minimum of 30% of the value of the gas purchased on your card. This is an improvement on other types of metering technology and may play a small part in easing problems of self-disconnection.

The meter has a Liquid Crystal Display (LCD) which provides you with information. The display will show a warning to ask that you ensure that all your gas appliances are off before you proceed to turn the supply back on again. This is extremely important for your safety to prevent the leakage of gas into your home and should never be ignored.

These meters would not be suitable for anyone unable to follow the various procedures for obtaining credit from a card or using the emergency credit facility. Similarly, they should not be used by anyone who is at risk of forgetting to turn appliances off before resetting the meter to restore the supply.

The meter is expected to become available in all British Gas areas by the winter of 1993. Orders for 100,000 meters have so far been placed with the manufacturers, with a possible order for a further 40,000 soon to follow. As British Gas currently has only 53,000 of its crude, mechanical, prepayment meters currently in use, this represents a major extension of the use of prepayment meters by British Gas. Advisers will need to watch out for changes to British Gas' current willingness to renegotiate payment plans and its support for the Fuel Direct scheme.

Advantages of electronic prepayment meters

There are three main advantages to electronic prepayment meters:

- They can be useful as a budgeting aid if you are on a low income as they oblige you to restrict your use of fuel according to your means. You are forced to become aware of your fuel consumption. This can be useful if your budget is limited, but you should also consider the risk of self-disconnection. Research suggests that many customers choose to retain their electronic prepayment meter as a budgeting aid even after arrears have been paid off.[3]

- There is no coinbox to attract burglars and the meter does not need to be emptied.

- Meters can be reset to pay off arrears as an alternative to disconnection.

Disadvantages of electronic prepayment meters

There are significant disadvantages to electronic prepayment meters.

- **They can be unsafe for some people to use.** These meters should never be installed for the use of anybody who is at risk of leaving appliances turned on when the supply ends because the money runs out, or who is incapable of operating the meter to obtain credit or emergency credit. They also should not be installed for the use of anyone who cannot obtain the tokens, cards or keys to operate them.

- **They are an expensive way to buy fuel.** Standing charges are usually higher for electricity prepayment meters than for credit meters, though pressure from Electricity Consumer Committees and OFFER has resulted in the charges in some areas being reduced. London Electricity, for example, now charges the same standing charge for its credit and electronic prepayment meters. Coin meters remain more expensive. Standing charges for gas are the same, but the cost of gas per unit is significantly higher than gas supplied through credit meters.

- **There are also hidden costs.** If you cannot afford to buy much fuel at any one time you will need to make frequent journeys to the showroom or other outlet. The extra cost of travel is effectively part of your fuel cost.

- **You cannot spread the cost of large winter bills over the whole year** if you pay for your fuel in advance week by week. A payment plan might be preferable if you could not pay for your heaviest weeks' consumption from your weekly income.

- **Self-disconnection is a major problem** for many low-income house-holds. If you cannot afford to buy tokens, cards or to charge your key, you may face intermittent or extended periods of disconnection. Fuel costs may take up too high a proportion of your income, particularly if you pay for heating costs in winter in hard to heat properties or if your real income is below the level of Income Support.

- **Paying back arrears and emergency credit can result in hardship.** If a meter is reset to pay back arrears, a supply of fuel may not be available until the arrears charge has been paid. With some types of meter, if you are away from your home, or are in hospital, or cannot afford to charge the meter for a week, you will have to insert two weeks' arrears before you will obtain a supply. With all types of electronic prepayment meter, if you have used your emergency credit, you will also have to pay the amount of the emergency credit before obtaining a supply. In some situations – eg, when you come out of hospital – you may be able to persuade the supplier to come out and reset your meter. But check first that this will not involve any extra cost.

- **Your repayment of arrears may be highest when you can least afford it** if you use the crude mechanical prepayment meters currently used by gas suppliers. These operate by overcharging for each unit of gas used, so the more gas you use, the more you pay towards your arrears. This means there is no problem if you are absent from your home for any period of time – you will always get gas for every token you insert.

- **Using the meters can be difficult,** particularly for the elderly, those returned to the community from mental health institutions, people with visual problems or disabilities. Note, however, that meters can often be re-sited free of charge to make them easier for disabled people to use.

- **Obtaining tokens may present problems.** Frequent journeys to buy tokens, cards or keys may present particular difficulties for people who are caring for small children, are disabled, have limited mobility or who are in full-time work.

- **Tokens, cards or keys may be difficult to obtain outside shopping hours.** Vending machines outside showrooms in indoor shopping areas may be inaccessible outside shopping hours. Vending machines have had problems with jamming, vandalism and becoming full up. Consider also the safety aspects of trying to obtain cards out of hours.

- **Cards and tokens may be faulty or become damaged.** Electronically coded cards and tokens may be 'wiped' if brought into contact with other magnetically encoded items, or if they become damp.

- **Cards and tokens can be easily lost or mislaid.** If you lose your token, you could ask the supplier to replace it. Tokens have no intrinsic value, so you cannot benefit from fraudulently claiming that a token has not worked or has been lost. This is because you pay for the fuel when you buy the token. When you insert the token, you will get the fuel, and the meter will record the fuel used. The tokens bought, and the fuel used, should be 'equal'. In the event of a dispute with the supplier, you should seek legal advice.

- 'Token trading' or 'card trading' **can cause endless problems.** If you run out of tokens or cards and buy one from a neighbour, you will have paid £1 or £5 off your neighbour's bill, because the token was bought from the supplier on your neighbour's account. Their account, not yours, will have been credited. Worse still, the supplier will see that you have used more tokens or cards than you have bought (or less if you have sold some to a friend) and may think you have been trying to defraud the company. If you do have to borrow a token or card, pay it back with a token or card bought on your own account. This should avoid problems.

- You may be denied the option of changing to Fuel Direct (see p42) to pay your arrears if you already have a prepayment meter which has been reset to recover arrears.

Economy Seven Prepayment Meters

Economy Seven Prepayment meters are available in some areas only (see pp36-37 for a description of Economy Seven and other variable tariff meters). This type of meter has the advantage of providing customers with cheaper electricity at off-peak times, but the limitations of the technology bring their own problems. NORWEB, for example, frequently routes the lower-rate Economy Seven wiring to bypass the prepayment meter. An estimate of the anticipated lower-rate consumption is then charged as part of the fixed charges on the meter. This means that customers spread their estimated lower-rate charges over the year but pay for higher-rate consumption as it is used.

Advantages
- If the meter runs out of credit, your night-time heating/hot-water is not disconnected.

- The cost of heating is spread over the year, avoiding high winter bills.

Disadvantages

- The estimated lower-rate bill is often inaccurate, so you can still end up owing the supplier money despite having a prepayment meter. Or, you may find that you are paying too much. You will need to look very carefully at the costs involved. It might be preferable to have an ordinary Economy Seven meter and pay on a payment plan (see p36) or through the Fuel Direct scheme if you claim income support (see p42).

Coin Meters

These are prepayment meters that use coins to pay for fuel in advance and have a coin box to collect payment. Each coin pays for a certain amount of fuel, but meters still need to be read. Bills are still provided and any shortfall between the bill and the amount collected by the meter must be paid. There are various types of coin meter. These may be categorised according to who is entitled to empty the coin box: the supplier, the customer or the landlord.

There are now problems with the availability of coin meters as most electricity suppliers are replacing them with electronic prepayment meters, particularly in urban areas. New coin meters are no longer manufactured and suppliers are re-using coin meters from premises where an electronic prepayment meter has been installed instead. Gas suppliers rarely supply new coin meters now. Suppliers are reluctant to install coin meters, but still have an obligation to provide them as an alternative to disconnection if it is not safe and practicable to install a electronic prepayment meter.[4] In practice, though, this will be exceptional.

Supplier-emptied coin meters

Supplier-emptied meters will generally be emptied every quarter and the meter read. Suppliers do not charge for emptying meters each quarter or if the meter is full before it is due to be emptied. Depending on how much fuel you have used, you may be due a refund or you may have to pay extra. This often happens when there has been a price rise, but the meter has not been reset. Suppliers' policies for making refunds vary – some pay immediately in cash, others quarterly in arrears or annually by cheque.

Advantages

Coins are readily available and simple to obtain. There is less likelihood of a time-consuming and costly journey to obtain coins than there is for tokens for a token meter. This makes coin meters particularly suitable for rural areas, and for people on low incomes or whose mobility is limited. British Gas offers a service to elderly and disabled customers, who can have their coin meter fitted with a special handle to make it easier to use.[5]

Disadvantages

There are a number of disadvantages to coin meters:

- Coin meters often attract higher standing charges and costs for fuel than credit meters. Extra costs may also be incurred if you ask for your meter to be emptied before it is full, or if the meter has become full following a scheduled visit when they were unable to gain access. If there are problems with the meter-emptying policy in your area, you could complain to your local Electricity Consumers' Committee or Gas Consumers' Council (see p183).

- You may be deprived of your supply if your meter becomes full before it is due to be emptied. A supplier may be in breach of its duty to supply if it does not empty your meter promptly when it becomes full. You could ask OFGAS/OFFER to intervene in this situation.

- Because of the rising cost of fuel, it is necessary to reset meters at regular intervals, otherwise you may receive a bill in addition to your meter payments. Some suppliers only reset meters at your request.

- The danger of theft is a major disadvantage. (For information about who is liable for money stolen from your meter, see pp126-127.)

- Variable tariffs (such as Economy Seven/White Meter) are not usually available if you have a coin meter.

Customer-emptied coin meters

A supplier may provide you with your own key to empty a meter coin-box yourself. You are then billed periodically and would have to pay any extra standing charges or tariffs resulting from having a coin meter. The meter will need to be reset when prices go up.

Note: NORWEB calls these meters 'budget meters'.

Advantages
- You can empty the meter regularly, diminishing the risk of the theft of large sums of money.

- You can use the meter as a budgeting device if you bank the money collected or pay in instalments towards your bill.

- You do not have the problem of disconnection when the meter is full and do not have to travel to buy tokens.

Disadvantages
- There is no advantage to having this type of meter if you do not use it as an aid to budgeting. If you find yourself recycling the same coin through the meter, consider changing to an ordinary credit meter if you can pay the bill quarterly anyway.

- You may be liable for any cash in the meter if it is stolen. If in doubt, seek legal advice.

Landlord-emptied meters
Your landlord may empty the coinbox to your meter. (See Chapter 12, p164, for more information about this option.)

Variable Tariff Meters (Electricity)

Variable tariff meters are available for electricity only. Suppliers offer different systems, and these may change from time to time. You will need to ask your supplier for information on the type of system it operates. Some typical systems are explained below.

Economy Seven/White Meters
Economy Seven is a scheme allowing you to pay for your electricity at two different rates or 'tariffs' (see p38). You need a special meter, usually an Economy Seven credit meter but in some areas Economy Seven prepayment meters are available as well. 'White Meters' are a similar type of meter which preceded Economy Seven meters. They are still very common in Scotland, but are being phased out elsewhere.

Electricity is charged for at two different rates per unit, with a lower rate at night. The daytime rate is charged at a slightly higher rate than the standard rate for credit meters. The standing charge is often higher than for credit meters. The amount of the charges varies from supplier to supplier.

You should consider changing to Economy Seven/White Meters if you use electricity to heat your home and to heat water overnight.

You may also be able to make savings in your fuel costs if you run electrical appliances (such as washing machines and tumble dryers) overnight, usually by using a timer to ensure the appliances operate within the optimum time-band.

The higher standing charge and higher day-time rate may counter-balance any savings made if your night-time use of electricity is not large enough. Electricity suppliers publish Codes of Practice on the efficient use of electricity and leaflets setting out their tariffs. Both should be available from your supplier. You will need to look carefully at the amount of electricity you use during the day and night, and at the tariff rates, to establish if Economy Seven will save you money. Suppliers should have specialist staff who can advise you if Economy Seven will save you money in your particular circumstances.[6]

'Super Tariff'

Northern Electric offers this three-rate tariff to customers with approved equipment such as electric storage heaters, electric boilers or electric floor warming. Electricity is charged at a low rate for a minimum of seven hours in any 24-hour period for the *specified* appliances. The hours are chosen by the supplier and are usually for five hours overnight and two hours in the afternoon. Electricity used by other appliances is charged at a different rate during the day and at another, different rate during the night.

2. STANDING CHARGES AND TARIFFS

Standing Charges

Standing charges are fixed charges which must be paid regardless of how much fuel you use. Suppliers are entitled to make these charges (see *Tariffs* below) and say that they are to cover costs such as billing, meter-reading, customer services, servicing meters and so on. Standing charges are often higher for Economy Seven and prepayment meters. Standing charges for coin meters may be even higher than those for electronic prepayment meters. Standing charges for gas prepayment meters vary from region to region.

There has been widespread concern that consumers who can least afford fuel are forced to pay the highest standing charges. For example, the Electricity Consumers' Committee for Merseyside and North Wales has voiced its concern for customers forced to use MAN-WEB's Card Meters. It has stated that in view of the level of profits which have been achieved in recent years, the area of card meter rental is one in which the company could show some tenderness to its more vulnerable customers.[7] In the London Region, similar pressure from consumer groups and the Consumers' Committee has contributed to the reduction of the prepayment standing charge to the same level as credit meters.

Tariffs

Electricity and gas are supplied to customers and charged under specific tariffs. Suppliers must publicise their tariffs and the published tariffs must show the methods by which and the principles on which charges are made as well as the prices charged.[8]

Tariffs may include:
- charges for fuel supplied – ie, the rate per unit of electricity or therm of gas;
- standing charges;
- charges in respect of the availability of electricity;
- rental or other costs for meters provided.

Amounts charged under tariffs vary from one electricity supplier to another. The price per unit of gas supplied does not vary from region to region.

What tariffs are available?

Gas and electricity are supplied under a range of tariffs. These may include:
- a standard tariff, with a quarterly or credit meter. The charge per unit does not vary;
- a direct debit tariff. Some suppliers will charge you slightly less for each unit of fuel if you pay by direct debit. This is because the costs of this method of payment are low.
- an electronic prepayment meter tariff. Standing charges under this tariff are often higher than for a credit meter;
- a prepayment coin meter tariff. Standing charges are higher than for the other types of meter.

Electricity only
- Economy Seven – electricity is charged at two different rates: a day-time rate which is higher than for the standard tariff, and a

lower night-time rate. Standing charges are higher than for credit meters.

- White Meter – similar to and preceding Economy Seven with day-time and night-time rates. This is being phased out.
- Comfort Plus – similar to Economy Seven, offered in Scotland.
- Super Tariff – a three-band tariff available to Northern Electricity customers.

3. METHODS OF PAYMENT TO AVOID ARREARS

There are many options available for spreading the cost of fuel bills over the year so that you are not faced with heavy winter bills which you cannot afford to pay.

If you do not have a bank account, look carefully at the hidden costs of making weekly, fortnightly or monthly payments through banks or post offices. Banks now charge large sums (£2 to £3) for paying bills, and post office charges are now 75 pence for each transaction. You may be able to pay your bill for no charge at a branch of the bank used by your supplier. Your supplier should tell you which bank this is. Building societies will provide cheques from savings accounts for no charge, and it will often be cheaper to post these to the supplier rather than making a special journey to your nearest showroom or customer service centre. You could always ask your supplier to provide you with prepaid envelopes to make your payments.

If you have a bank account remember to take into consideration the extra costs of becoming overdrawn if you are considering standing orders, direct debits and payments by cheque.

The following options are available with credit meters (and variable tariff meters such as Economy Seven, White Meters, Comfort Plus or Super Tariff):

- Budget schemes with regular fixed payments
- Flexible payments schemes
- Access or Visa
- Savings stamps
- Budget accounts with banks or building societies
- Other bill-paying services

Budget Schemes with Regular Fixed Payments

An estimate is made of your annual consumption of fuel from the time when you apply to join the scheme, usually on the basis of previous bills. You pay in equal instalments throughout the year. Suppliers usually offer the option of weekly, fortnightly or monthly payment methods within the scheme. Schemes vary around the country.

For example, NORWEB sends a budget statement each quarter showing how much electricity you have used, and what payments have been received. Each year a review is carried out. NORWEB usually recalculates your payments for the next year, adding any arrears to your estimated consumption for the year. You should then clear the arrears over 12 months. Similarly, if you are in credit, repayments will be reduced so that they balance after 12 months. If revised payments cause problems, see Chapter 6.

London Electricity sends a budget statement each quarter, showing how much electricity you have used, what payments have been received, and giving advice on whether you need to increase or decrease your instalments. Each year there is an annual review to work out whether you need to increase or decrease your instalments. If you owe them £50 or two monthly instalments, you will be asked to pay the lower of the two amounts. If you are owed £50 or two monthly instalments, the lower amount will be refunded to you. If you move, you will be asked to pay the final bill for your old address in full.

Payment can be made by one of the following methods:
- **Monthly direct debit** – you sign a form which entitles the supplier to debit variable amounts from your account. In practice, the same amount is usually debited from your bank account each month, with your permission, over the course of the year from the point where you entered the scheme. The supplier should always tell you, in advance, if any balance is due to you or if your monthly instalment is to be changed. The supplier can change the amount debited from your account without you doing anything, so long as it has informed you.

- **Monthly standing order** – 12 equal instalments are paid from your bank account, building society cheque account, or National Giro account. You will need to complete a new standing order application form if you need to change the amount of the instalment. The monthly amount can be changed only by you, not the supplier. You may need to make an additional payment at the annual review.

- **Budget card** – budget card schemes allow you to pay a fixed amount, weekly or monthly, into your account, at showrooms or customer service centres. They are useful if you do not have a bank account. You will need to take into consideration how accessible showrooms are and any extra travelling costs.

- **Payment books** – some suppliers will issue you with payment books which enable you to make payments every week, fortnight or month at the showroom. There have been reports from Manchester of a somewhat bizarre practice for making weekly payments to British Gas. Only fortnightly payment books are issued, but you can pay half the fortnightly payment one week and get a receipt. When you return to pay the following week, your receipt is removed and your book stamped. The authors are interested to hear of any similar or stranger practices from around the country.

Flexible Payments Schemes

These schemes allow you to pay any amount at any time at suppliers' offices, shops or customer service centres, at a bank or by post. The amount paid is credited towards your next bill, which then must be settled each quarter. This is very useful if you have a variable income. *Whatever system you use, the supplier will not refuse money if you give or send it to them.*

Access or Visa

Some electricity suppliers allow payment by direct debit from your Access or Visa account, though you cannot pay by Access or Visa over the counter or by post. This could be a very expensive way of obtaining credit. If you are in financial difficulty it would be worth considering the other budget options available.

Savings Stamps

Both gas and electricity suppliers have saving stamp schemes. You can buy stamps at suppliers' shops and customer service centres and at some post offices. Gas stamps can be used to pay electricity bills and vice versa thanks to common-sense reciprocal agreements. This system of reciprocal agreements does not exist in Scotland.

Budget Accounts with Banks or Building Societies

Some banks and building societies offer special budget accounts which are run independently of the fuel suppliers. These accounts can be used for all regular outgoings. A regular amount is paid into the account each month based on the estimated cost of all household bills for a year. Bills can be paid from the account when they fall due. You are allowed certain credit limits. This approach has the advantage of flexibility and is useful when several bills coincide. If there is a surplus at the end of the year, it can be used for all future bills and not only those for fuel. The bank charges for this credit arrangement, but it can be a cheap way of obtaining credit and retaining flexibility in your financial affairs.

Other Bill-Paying Services

Beware of private firms which offer bill-paying services – this may be an extremely expensive option. Seek advice from your local Citizen's Advice Bureau or Money Advice Service before considering using any private service offered in your area.

4. FUEL DIRECT

'Fuel Direct' is a 'last resort' way of paying for arrears, and for current consumption, of gas, electricity and water directly from income support or from other benefits when they are paid as part of the same giro or order book as income support. The other benefits are:[9]

- unemployment benefit
- sickness benefit
- invalidity benefit
- retirement pension
- severe disablement allowance

Fuel Direct forms part of a scheme for direct deductions from benefit. Not everyone is eligible for Fuel Direct (see p43). Deductions are made from weekly benefit, but are only paid to the supplier once every quarter.

Deductions can be made for arrears only, or for arrears and current charges, or for current charges only after your arrears have been paid off.[10] If you already use a prepayment meter, and this has not been reset to recover arrears, you might want Fuel Direct for the arrears element only.

Fuel Direct is often used as an alternative to disconnection, particularly where a prepayment meter is not an option. The availability of Fuel Direct is often dependent on the attitudes to the scheme of your local gas or electricity supplier and Benefits Agency. This seems to vary according to how aggressive a supplier is about the installation of prepayment meters. Some Benefits Agency offices appear to regard Fuel Direct as a costly and burdensome piece of administration which they are reluctant or unwilling to operate. If the Benefits Agency refuses to allow you to join the Fuel Direct scheme, you can appeal to a Social Security Appeal Tribunal. If the supplier refuses, see p50.

Who is Eligible for Fuel Direct?

The decision to include you in the Fuel Direct scheme is made by an Adjudication Officer in the Benefits Agency.[11] You can ask to be included in the scheme, or the Benefits Agency can include you if it considers that it would be in the best interests of you or your family.[12]

Deductions can be made from your benefit if:[13]
- your arrears are greater than £44 including reconnection charges; *and*
- you will continue to need a fuel supply; *and*
- it is in your interests for direct payments to be made.

The Benefits Agency will refuse to include you in the scheme if:
- the above do not apply; *or*
- you already have a prepayment meter which has been reset to collect arrears (though if you have a prepayment meter for current consumption only, you could still have the arrears paid by Fuel Direct).[14]

How to Arrange Fuel Direct

You will need either to write to the Benefits Agency or to complete their application form for Fuel Direct. If disconnection is being threatened, write to the supplier saying that Fuel Direct is being arranged. Make sure you keep a copy of your letter. Suppliers will delay disconnection of your supply if they know you are trying to arrange Fuel Direct.[15] It is sensible to telephone both the Benefits Agency and the supplier to ensure that they know that your letter/application form is coming and to check that it has been received. If disconnection is imminent, ask the Benefits Agency to telephone the supplier to confirm that Fuel Direct is being arranged and that written confirmation will follow.

Once Fuel Direct has been requested, the Benefits Agency will check that you are eligible, seek a current consumption figure from the supplier, and notify you of your rate of deduction. If the amount of the deduction totals more than 25% of your income support entitlement, the Benefits Agency will ask you to sign a form giving your consent for the deduction to take place. Be sure not to delay returning this to them if you agree that they can deduct the sum stated.

If you are paid by order book, you will not have been properly accepted on to the scheme until your order book has been returned to the Benefits Agency and replaced. The amount paid to you will be reduced by the amount being paid to the supplier. If you are paid by giro, the amount on your giro will change in the same way. You can ask the Benefits Agency to send you a breakdown of your benefit detailing the amount of your deductions.

If you do not hear from the Benefits Agency, make enquiries, as delays could result in disconnection and further costs. Make sure that you are in regular contact with your supplier about the progress of your application for Fuel Direct. If there are any delays, the supplier can be asked to delay disconnection for a longer period. If your application is delayed excessively, or the procedure breaks down at any point, your supply could be disconnected.

Once you are on the scheme, you will continue to be sent *bills for information only*. You should always check these to ensure that the Benefits Agency is paying your deductions across to the supplier and to check that the amounts estimated for current consumption are broadly correct. Remember that deductions from your benefit are only paid across to your supplier about every 13 weeks, so your arrears may appear to increase initially.

Make sure that your meter is read regularly, or provide meter readings yourself to ensure that estimates of your consumption are based on what you actually use. Remember that you will still have to pay for the fuel you use. If your consumption increases (eg, because you are spending more time at home because of illness or the birth of a baby), your deductions will also increase. *Never* assume that the Benefits Agency 'pays for' your fuel. If you leave your heating or appliances on for longer, *you* will be asked to pay more direct from your benefit.

How Much can be Deducted?

Deductions can be made to cover arrears, to cover weekly costs alone after the debt has been cleared, or both.[16]

For arrears:

- £2.20 per week for each type of fuel

- There is a total *maximum deduction* of £4.40 altogether for gas and electricity arrears.[17]

For current consumption:

- In practice, the supplier will advise the Benefits Agency of an estimate of your weekly consumption. The amounts suggested are often high, and it is worth obtaining an explanation of the assumptions used in the calculation.

- The *maximum deduction* which can be made without your consent is 25% of your 'applicable amount' (your income support entitlement before any deductions for income etc., are made). This includes the combined amount of the deductions for arrears and current consumption.[18]

- The final decision on the amounts deducted rests with the adjudication officer at the Benefits Agency, who is not bound to accept the suppliers' estimates of your current consumption.[19] The Joint Statement of Intent on the Direct Payments for Fuel[20] (see p49 below and Appendix 5) states that the Benefits Agency need only take the supplier's estimate into account. OFGAS' position is that the adjudication officer has sole discretion over the calculation of deductions.[21]

- If you disagree with the amounts proposed by the supplier, you could ask the adjudication officer to make a different deduction. You will need to provide information about the assumptions you use in your own calculation. You will need to conduct your negotiations with care to ensure that the Benefits Agency or the supplier do not assume that you are refusing to join the Fuel Direct scheme, as this could ultimately lead either to disconnection or to the imposition of an electronic prepayment meter. If the adjudication officer does not agree to accept your calculations, you could always accept the supplier's calculation to ensure entry to the scheme, and then appeal to a social security appeal tribunal.

Reviews of the Amount of the Deduction

The deduction for arrears is a fixed amount and cannot be varied. Normally, the amount for current consumption is estimated for a period of 26 weeks. You should expect a routine review of this amount every six months, usually as a result of the Benefits Agency being informed of new figures for current consumption by the supplier.

The supplier should normally use a formula in the Joint Statement of Intent for calculating your estimated current consumption.[22] Always make sure that this review is based on an actual reading of your meter. If the supplier bases your estimated future consumption on estimated readings of your meter, the amount of your deductions is unlikely to be correct.

You can ask the Benefits Agency to review the amount of deduction if you can show that the calculation of the deduction is based on a mistake about a material fact.[23] The adjudication officer can ask the supplier to provide details of the basis of the supplier's calculation of estimated current consumption.[24]

You may wish to request a review if you can provide evidence that your actual consumption is likely to be different. You may wish to do this if:

- an actual meter reading shows that the supplier's calculation is based on wrong information;

- your consumption has increased or decreased because of a change in your circumstances such as the birth of a baby, a child leaving home, the need to remain at home more because of illness, a change in a heating system, major repairs or improvements to your home to aid energy efficiency – eg, loft insulation, double glazing, drylining of walls, draughtproofing measures or changes to the way in which you use fuel as a result of energy advice.

You can request a review at any time a relevant change occurs.[25] It is sensible to obtain the supplier's agreement as this will make the decision-making process smoother.

If your consumption is underestimated, or increases for any reason, the Benefits Agency can itself review the amount deducted. The new amount will take effect for the next 26 weeks, unless a further change of circumstances is brought to its attention.

The Joint Statement of Intent on Direct Payments for Fuel makes express provision for regular and irregular reviews (see Appendix 5). If the Benefits Agency refuses to review when there is a change of circumstances, you can appeal to a social security appeal tribunal (see p136).

Other Direct Deductions for Debts

Other debts can also be paid by direct payments from benefit, and payment of these may be in competition with Fuel Direct payments. Regulations provide that certain debts will be paid in the following order of priority:[26]

- mortgage payments;
- other housing costs, eg service charges;
- rent arrears;
- gas and electricity charges;
- water charges;
- council tax and poll tax arrears;
- unpaid fines, costs and compensation orders;
- payments for the maintenance of children.

If you have arrears for both gas and electricity, the adjudication officer decides which debt takes priority.

The following debts can also be paid from benefit, but are not mentioned in the regulation governing priority between debts. You should argue that payments for gas or electricity take a higher priority over these debts:

- Deductions for overpayments of benefit (but check that the Benefits Agency is entitled to recover the overpayment, and seek advice if necessary); *and*
- loans from the social fund.

When Arrears Are Paid Off

Often, Fuel Direct payments continue after arrears have been paid. You can apply to the supplier to have credits refunded. If you wish to stay on Fuel Direct, you should also ask the Benefits Agency to review the amount of the deductions, deducting nothing for arrears and revising the estimated amount for current consumption. If you want to go back to paying your own bills, tell the Benefits Agency and make an arrangement with the supplier to pay.

Advantages and Disadvantages of Fuel Direct

Advantages

- Fuel Direct offers claimants of income support protection from disconnection, particularly when voluntary payment plans have broken down in the past. It is often used as a last resort option, either in preference to, or as an alternative to, a prepayment meter.
- Fuel Direct is an alternative where it is not safe or practicable to fit a prepayment meter, or if you are unable to use a prepayment

meter. It is a useful option if you have difficulty or are unable to budget. It is often the only viable option for people with mental health problems who have had difficulty with coping with other methods of payment.

- the costs of your fuel are spread over a long period.

- the amount of deductions for arrears is fixed. However, this may be a disadvantage, particularly for those with multiple debts or incomes below the ordinary level of income support. See p101 for rates of repayment of arrears.

- the costs of making the deductions and payments is borne by the Benefits Agency.

Disadvantages

- Fuel Direct operates only while you are entitled to income support. If you come off income support, the supplier will be able to threaten to disconnect your supply if you are still in arrears. You will have to make alternative arrangements to pay for your arrears and your continuing supply. The supplier will usually accept you paying at the same rate, at least for a period of time.

- If you go back on to income support, you will have to make all the arrangements for Fuel Direct again.

- The amounts paid for current consumption are estimates of your actual consumption. There are problems with the accuracy of the estimates and obtaining changes may be time-consuming and difficult. On the other hand, you may find the deductions a useful aid to budgeting, or might resent the inability of the scheme to rapidly reflect changes in your patterns of consumption.

- You can still be disconnected and sued for any money owing if the arrangements made with the Benefits Agency break down. You should always check that the money deducted from your benefit is paid over to the supplier at regular intervals. Payments should appear as credits on your electricity or gas bill.

- You will have to deal with both the Benefits Agency and the supplier. There are frequently problems of communication breakdown and misunderstandings when dealing with two large bureaucracies.

Rent Arrears which Include a Fuel Debt

Charges in your rent for heating, lighting, cooking or hot water are not usually covered by housing benefit. If you receive income support, you will be expected to pay these charges out of your weekly benefit. In some circumstances, these payments can be deducted from your benefit and paid directly to your landlord together with a payment for arrears. This will apply if:

- the total arrears are the equivalent of at least four times your weekly rent. Non-dependent deductions are not counted as rent arrears;[27] *or*

- you owe at least eight full weeks' rent and your landlord has asked the Benefits Agency to include you in the scheme;[28] *or*

- you owe less than eight weeks' full rent and the Benefits Agency considers that it is in the overriding interests of your family.[29]

The amount of the deduction will be £2.20 per week for each fuel type towards the arrears plus the current weekly charge. The deduction cannot be made without your consent if it exceeds 25% of your 'applicable amount' excluding housing costs.[30] Payments may continue for current charges only once the arrears are paid off if the Benefits Agency decides it is in the overriding interests of your family. Deductions are subject to rules of priority.

If Your Fuel Direct Arrangement Breaks Down

If your arrangement breaks down because of an error by the Benefits Agency, you could complain to the Ombudsman. If you are sued for nonpayment of the bill, the Benefits Agency could be joined in as a defendant. Or you could sue them yourself. Independent legal advice will be essential.

Regulation of the Scheme

First and foremost, the scheme is part of Social Security provision. It is governed by the Social Security (Claims and Payments) Regulations 1987. There is a Joint Statement of Intent which describes ways in which a claimant of income support, who is in arrears, may be protected from disconnection. It has been drawn up and agreed by the Benefits Agency and the electricity and gas suppliers. The latest Joint Statement of Intent came into effect on 1 November 1991 and is reproduced in Appendix 5.

The Joint Statement of Intent is not a legally binding agreement. It simply represents a policy statement between the parties concerned. If you are in arrears, you will need to consider your rights firstly under Conditions 12A (Gas) and 19 (Electricity) which are enforceable by

OFFER/OFGAS, and then consider the effect of the Codes of Practice and the Joint Statement of Intent.

Can a Supplier Refuse You Fuel Direct?

There have been reports of some suppliers 'refusing' to allow customers Fuel Direct, and insisting that they must have a prepayment meter installed instead.

The Joint Statement of Intent appears to allow the suppliers to refuse to accept direct payments.[31] However, the supplier cannot decide if you should or should not be included in the scheme, since the decision is made by the adjudication officer in the Benefits Agency. The adjudication officer must make a decision based on the regulations governing Fuel Direct only.[32]

The Joint Statement of Intent represents an agreement between the Benefits Agency and the suppliers. It has no force of law and should not affect the decision of the adjudication officer. Any administrative problems which arise are a separate matter.

The supplier will usually assist the Benefits Agency by providing estimates of your current consumption. If the supplier is obstructive and says you 'cannot' join the scheme, you should still contact the Benefits Agency and say that you wish to be considered regardless. If the supplier refuses to provide an estimate of current consumption or otherwise co-operate with the Benefits Agency, you could provide your own estimate of your current consumption based on your previous bills where possible. You will need to satisfy the adjudication officer that it is 'in the best interests of you and your family' that deductions are made from your benefit. The adjudication officer should consider all your reasons for requesting Fuel Direct, including reasons why a prepayment meter is not a suitable option for you.

If the adjudication officer refuses to allow you to join the scheme, you could appeal to a social security appeal tribunal (see p136).

At the same time, you will be in dispute with the supplier over both your arrears and your method of payment. You should complain to OFFER or OFGAS as appropriate. The supplier should not disconnect you as you will be genuinely in dispute (see pp111-112). OFFER or OFGAS could be asked to rule whether or not the supplier is in breach of Condition 19 or 12A by refusing a customer in arrears a method of payment.

In the case of electricity, if the adjudication officer has decided you can have Fuel Direct deductions from your benefit, you could also serve the supplier with a notice specifying Fuel Direct as your method of payment. If the supplier refuses, and you ask OFFER to intervene, the Director General of OFFER will have a duty to determine the dispute. You are strongly advised to involve OFFER.

5. CAN YOU CHOOSE A METHOD OF PAYMENT OR TYPE OF METER?

Important note: all references to 'your supply' in this section assume that you are legally responsible for the supply (see Chapter 4). For more about choice of methods of payment when you are in arrears, see also Chapter 6.

The Legal Position (Gas)

The Gas Act does not contain any obvious provisions which allow customers to exercise choice over the type of meter which is provided, or over the methods of payment which are available.

The Gas Act states only that gas suppliers must provide customers with 'an appropriate meter (whether prepayment or otherwise)'.[33] Gas suppliers and OFGAS consider that this means that the meter should be appropriate for measuring the amount of gas consumed. The argument that it could mean 'appropriate to the customer's preferred method of payment' has not been tested.

Condition 12A of the Authorisation to British Gas and the Principles for the Collection of British Gas Debt regulate the options which are open to customers in debt. Condition 12A provides that customers who cannot pay their bill must be offered a payment plan in the first instance and a prepayment meter as an alternative to disconnection. Prepayment meters must be offered as an alternative to disconnection if a customer cannot pay a security deposit.

The formulation of Condition 12A suggests that customers are entitled to a credit meter in the first instance, and to a prepayment meter as a last resort. It can be argued that Fuel Direct is a payment plan for the purposes of Condition 12A.

There is some obligation for British Gas to consider customers' needs when establishing what method of payment is appropriate. Principle 5[34] provides that where you cannot afford to pay your gas bill, you must be counselled so that British Gas staff can establish the method of payment which would most meet your needs. This does not amount to a right to choose how to pay.

As with electricity, the choices available to customers in debt are restricted by the supplier's ability to require reasonable security. Security deposits and alternatives are discussed in Chapter 2. Choices available to customers in arrears are discussed more fully in Chapter 6.

The Legal Position (Electricity)

The drafting of the Electricity Act 1989 and decisions by OFFER allow customers of electricity suppliers to exercise more choice over the type of meter provided and the methods of payment available. This is in addition to the protection offered to customers in arrears by Condition 19. The comments above relating to Condition 12A (gas) apply equally to Condition 19. See also pp98-99 for a more detailed discussion about the protection offered by Condition 19.

The Electricity Act 1989 is structured in such a way as to provide a mechanism for disputes over types of meters and methods of payment to be resolved by the intervention of OFFER.

Customers can request their choice of meter and/or method of payment by using the procedure for giving notice requiring a supply. This can be done either when moving in or at any other time. This procedure allows customers to specify which 'tariff' is required. As suppliers offer a range of different tariffs, including tariffs for credit meter and prepayment meter use, customers can state which type of meter or method of payment is preferred on an application form or in a letter to the supplier. OFFER considers that any combination of meter and method of payment constitutes a tariff.[35] See p10 for details of how to give notice.

If the supplier does not wish to provide the tariff specified, it must serve a 'counternotice' setting out its objections and alternative proposals.[36] OFFER can be asked to intervene in any resulting dispute and has a duty to make an independent decision which is binding on both parties.[37] In practice, in making such decisions, OFFER will have regard to the provisions of Condition 19 and the supplier's confidential statement of its *methods*.

The effect of this mechanism is not to give the customer an absolute right to choose, but to permit a third party to intervene in the event of a dispute. This may encourage suppliers to be less draconian about limiting customer choice in practice.

You may wish to use this mechanism to:
• specify that you want a particular type of meter or method of payment when you first move into your premises. Note that you do not have to accept a prepayment meter or any other type of meter simply because it is in your premises when you move in.

- formally ask your supplier to change your type of meter or method of payment or both to suit your circumstances, eg:
  - to change your prepayment meter to a credit meter with a payment plan for current consumption once you have paid off all your arrears through the prepayment meter; *or*
  - to change your credit meter to a prepayment meter if you are coming off income support and can no longer pay through Fuel Direct.

Some electricity suppliers – eg, NORWEB – have started to change meters to electronic prepayment meters on some estates on the change of a tenancy. Customers on the estates concerned pay more for their electricity as a result. If there is a policy to target certain estates, it could amount to unlawful 'undue discrimination'.[38] OFFER should always be asked to investigate in similar cases. Anyone in these circumstances could use the procedure above to request their own choice of meter and method of payment.

OFFER has made two decisions which clarify its approach to questions of choice and the legal constraints on suppliers.

The first decision concerned the choices available to a commercial customer who always paid his bills late.[39] The supplier wanted payment of a cash security deposit from the customer concerned. The second related to a domestic customer who also paid bills late. In this case, the supplier wished to impose a prepayment meter.[40]

OFFER's approach in both cases was to consider first the reasonableness of the requirement for a security and, secondly, the form of security appropriate in each case. Payment by direct debit or through a prepayment meter were considered as possible options in each case.

In the case of the commercial customer, OFFER decided that reasonable security was required and that the customer could have the choice of either a monthly or quarterly direct debit option as an alternative to either a security deposit or a prepayment meter. In the case of the domestic customer, OFFER decided that the customer's payment record had been unreasonable, but that the customer had rectified the situation by paying promptly once the threat of the imposition of a prepayment meter had been made. OFFER decided that the customer could continue to pay quarterly on a credit meter.

These cases established the following principles:
- Choice for customers who can demonstrate that they are 'creditworthy' should not be limited. Customers should be able to choose their preferred type of meter or method of payment, provided they have not abused the credit facilities that a particular method of payment may offer (see pp98-99).[41]

- Choice for customers in debt or who are unable to satisfy the supplier that they are creditworthy may be limited by the supplier's power to require reasonable security.[42] 'Reasonable security' can mean a more secure method of payment, such as payment by direct debit or through an electronic prepayment meter, or a cash security deposit (see pp20-24). In practice, OFFER will also have regard to the provisions of Condition 19 and the supplier's confidential statement of its *methods* for dealing with customers in arrears.[43]

- If a supplier wants to change your type of meter or method of payment the supplier must first send you a '*counternotice*' – ie, a written notice containing:

  – the reasons why your existing terms and conditions of supply are unacceptable;
  – the changes to your tariff proposed by the supplier;
  – seven days' notice of the intention to disconnect your supply;
  – your right to have a dispute determined by the Director General of OFFER.[44]

  Note: the supplier does not actually have to disconnect your supply in order to change your meter or method of payment.

- If you do not agree with the change proposed by your supplier you can ask OFFER to intervene and to make an independent decision.[45]

- The supplier should take reasonable steps to inform you of the consequences of an unsatisfactory payment record before seeking to change the terms and conditions of your supply.[46] The supplier should give you an opportunity to rectify the situation.

- If the supplier does not consult you about the proposed change by sending you a counternotice (see above), it may not be entitled to recover any extra charges resulting from a change which it has imposed on you.[47] For example, if a supplier changes your credit meter to an electronic prepayment meter without informing you of its intention to do so and of your right to have a dispute resolved by OFFER, you *may* not have to pay any higher standing charges or consumption costs associated with the imposed prepayment meter.[48] In the event of such a dispute, ask OFFER to intervene.

- Your meter or method of payment cannot be changed without your consent except where the supplier can demonstrate that disconnection would be the only reasonable alternative to the proposed change. This applies to any proposed changes to the terms and conditions of your supply.[49] This means that suppliers would not be entitled to make changes for their own administrative convenience without first consulting you. In many cases they will need your consent to make a change. This will often apply when a supplier wants to change your coin meter to an electronic prepayment meter.

- Late payment of bills in itself is not a reason for a supplier to change the terms and conditions of your supply. However, it may be reasonable for habitual or routine late payers to be denied the option of paying their bills on a quarterly basis and for the supplier to insist instead upon a more secure method of payment, such as payment by monthly or quarterly direct debit. or the installation of a prepayment meter.[50] Normally, the final choice should rest with the customer.[51]

What Happens In Practice

Both electricity and gas suppliers now operate in a commercial environment. Electricity suppliers in particular appear concerned to limit 'credit' to customers, arguing that customers who have quarterly meters have already been given three months' credit when their bill arrives. There appears to be little appreciation that tariff rates already reflect the terms and condition of supply and that customers pay for their 'credit'.

The concern to maintain a healthy and regular cashflow has resulted in suppliers encouraging the use of payment plans which are cheap to administer. Suppliers are particularly keen on the use of direct debit plans and some are offering preferential tariffs to customers who pay this way.

For low-income customers, there has been a marked move by electricity suppliers towards the supply of electronic prepayment meters, particularly in preference to the Fuel Direct scheme for those on income support. Some electricity suppliers routinely deny access to the Fuel Direct scheme to their customers.

British Gas is currently introducing its new high-tech 'Quantum' prepayment meter in all areas. It has ordered large quantities of this meter, suggesting that it is intending substantially to extend the use of this type of meter, presumably for low-income customers. It is to be hoped that it will be more mindful of the needs of its individual customers than some of the more aggressive electricity suppliers. OFGAS is aware of the problems caused by the hard-line attitudes of some electricity suppliers and will be closely monitoring any policy changes within British Gas.

Gas suppliers say that new customers with whom they have had no previous contact are always allowed to choose their method of payment and type of meter. They would seek to limit choice when they have some experience of a customer's payment record.

Electricity suppliers ask for much more detailed information about customers initially to assess creditworthiness and may seek to limit options for new customers. Both gas and electricity suppliers ascribe 'credit ratings' to existing customers, either informally on the basis of individual cases, or systematically by grouping customers according to whether they pay their bills immediately or only after a reminder and so on. With budget payments, they will look at the payment record. Customers with a 'good payment record' will generally be offered the payment method of their choice, while customers with a bad payment record may be asked to accept the choice of the supplier.

CHAPTER FOUR

Responsibility for the Bill

It is always worth checking whether you are in fact legally responsible for a bill, particularly when you are in dispute with a gas or electricity supplier about arrears. Payment of gas and electricity bills is an every-day matter for the majority of consumers. When people move to new premises, one of the first considerations is to establish who will be liable for these bills. You might request a supply yourself in your own name, or together with one or more people. Or your landlord might be liable for the supply. You may have a separate agreement to pay your landlord, spouse, cohabitee, flat-sharer or relative a proportion, or none, of the costs when the bill is in their name.

Deciding who is liable to pay the supplier ought to be a straightfor-ward matter. It can be argued that the legislation[1] provides some clear principles for deciding who is liable for a bill. But, in practice, the suppliers, OFFER, OFGAS and consumers' independent legal advisers have been unable to agree on how the legislation should be inter-preted. The courts as yet have not provided any case law which sets a precedent. In trying to decide whether you are liable to pay all or part of a bill, you will need to consider the differing interpretations of the law.

This chapter covers:

1. A summary of views on liability for the bill (see below)
2. When are you liable for an electricity bill? (see p60)
3. When are you liable for a gas bill? (see p66)
4. Common problems (see p71) – including:

- Does giving notice determine liability? (see p71)
- Your liability when your name is on the bill (see p72)
- Your liability when nobody is named on the bill (see p72)
- Moving in: becoming liable for the supply (see p72)
- Moving out: ending liability for the supply (see p73)
- Who is liable when the person named on the bill has left? (see p74)
- Who is liable for the supply after the person named on the bill has left? (see p75)
- When a consumer dies (see p76)

I. A SUMMARY OF VIEWS ON LIABILITY FOR THE BILL

Introduction

The arguments about who should pay for a gas or electricity bill arise from the nature of the service provided by the suppliers, and their own approaches to securing payment for fuel supplied. Gas and electricity are supplied on credit to the majority of customers. The suppliers' difficulty arises from their duty to supply individuals, who are mobile, at premises which are fixed. If the person supplied moves on without paying the bill and without notifying the supplier about their whereabouts, the supplier may have difficulty in tracing the debtor. The suppliers say this is a particular problem if people share accommodation, or if there is a breakdown of a relationship.

Any other supplier of goods or services would have to pursue their debtor for payment or stand the loss. But gas and electricity suppliers have another sanction: they can withdraw their services by cutting off the supply of an essential commodity.

As a result of this situation, the suppliers adopted interpretations of the legislation which enabled them to use the threat of disconnection as a means of securing payment from people who had not requested a supply, and who were not named on a bill. If the suppliers would not pursue or could not find the missing debtor, this interpretation allowed them to pursue others (eg, a spouse, or joint tenant) for payment. If payment was not forthcoming, they would threaten to cut off the supply.

In particular, electricity suppliers developed an interpretation of the pre-1989 law which became known as the 'beneficial user' argument. The term 'beneficial user' has no status in law. Gas suppliers adopted the same approach in practice, and, in 1988, OFGAS published a similar interpretation of the law on gas.

With the introduction of the Electricity Act 1989, the position for electricity changed so as (in the view of the authors) to render the beneficial user argument obsolete. The arguments all turn on the question of whether giving notice requiring a supply makes an individual liable for the bill, and on who is a 'tariff customer'.

The Electricity Suppliers' View: The 'Beneficial User' Argument

Prior to the Electricity Act 1989, electricity suppliers developed an interpretation of what the then fragmented electricity legislation said on liability. This became known as the 'beneficial user argument'. The precise origin of the term is unknown and it has no legal status in the law of England and Wales or of Scotland. Put simply, this argument asserted that anyone who benefited from the use of electricity could be made to pay for it – regardless of whether they had signed an application form for electricity or were named on the bill. They relied on an English County Court judgment[2] to back up their case, even though County Court judgments do not set precedents in England and Wales or in Scotland. They ignored a precedent setting High Court judgment which did not support their view.[3]

The practice of many electricity suppliers suggests that they do not accept that the Electricity Act 1989 has been drafted in a way which should render the beneficial user argument obsolete. In the absence of any guidance or policy from the industry's regulator, OFFER, many suppliers have continued their pre-privatisation practices. Suppliers will often try to hold individuals liable for a bill which is not in their name, and when they have not signed an application form for the supply. In Scotland, however, electricity suppliers no longer use this argument.

OFFER's View

OFFER has yet to make a comprehensive public statement on its interpretation of the legislation, but has indicated that it does not consider that the question of liability for electricity is clear cut.

OFFER has debated and re-debated the question regularly and in private since it took up its position as regulator of the newly privatised electricity supply industry in April 1990. At the time of writing in September 1993, OFFER had still not made a public statement of its position known. Not surprisingly, there have been no determinations by the Director General of OFFER on the subject of liability.

The Gas Suppliers' View

In practice, gas suppliers operate a version of the electricity suppliers' 'beneficial user' argument. They treat the premises (and not the person requesting a supply) as being supplied, and rarely require notice in writing that a supply is required after gas has been connected to a premises for the first time. New occupants who telephone to request a supply, or to inform the supplier that they have moved in, will have their name put on the bill.

In the event of disputes about the payment of bills, suppliers often regard any occupants as liable for the bill, regardless of whether the bill is in their name. However, the suppliers are expected to comply with the OFGAS interpretation of the law.

OFGAS' View

OFGAS published its own interpretation of the law on liability for gas bills in 1988 as a policy statement.[4] This is reproduced in Appendix 3. The OFGAS interpretation differs from the original 'beneficial user' argument, but has a similar effect. OFGAS concludes that the giving of notice does not determine who should be liable for a bill since, it argues, the details specified within a notice are only appropriate to the original connection of a gas supply to a premises. Who should be considered liable for a bill will depend on the circumstances surrounding occupancy and, in particular, on who has control of the gas supply. OFGAS expects gas suppliers to comply with its interpretation.

2. WHEN ARE YOU LIABLE FOR A BILL? (ELECTRICITY)

The Authors' View

The authors of this book take the view that the legislation for electricity[5] provides some straightforward principles for determining liability in individual cases.

Note: the amounts for which you may be liable may form all or part of the bill. In this section, all references to 'the bill' refer only to 'charges due' for the supply of electricity and do not include other charges such as credit sales charges for appliances. See p111 for more information about 'charges due'.

You *will* be liable to pay the supplier for an electricity bill if:

• you are an owner or occupier of premises; and

• you have given a notice requiring a supply of electricity (see p10 for details of how to give notice); and

• the supplier has a statutory duty to supply you (see p8).

You will be solely liable for the bill if you alone give notice requiring the supply, regardless of whether you live alone or with other adults.

You will be jointly responsible for the bill if you and one or more others also give notice requiring a supply. Your liability for the bill will begin from the date that you require the supply. This will be the date on your notice when you say you want the supply to begin.

Your liability will end:[6]

- Where you give at least two working days' written notice that you intend to leave the premises, on the day that you leave;

- Where you did not give at least two working days' written notice that you were leaving, either

  - two working days after you actually give written notice of leaving; *or*
  - on the next date that the meter is due to be read; *or*
  - when any subsequent occupier gives notice requiring a supply; whichever is the earlier.

You *may* be liable to pay the supplier for the bill if:

- nobody has given notice requiring a supply of electricity; or

- the liability of the person(s) who gave notice has come to an end (see above) and

- you have, in practice, been supplied with electricity.

In this situation, strictly speaking, nobody will have requested a supply of electricity – there will be no 'tariff customer' (see p14 for who is a 'tariff customer'.)

This situation often occurs when people move into new premises where the supply is already connected. There is nothing illegal about continuing to use the supply in another person's name, or where the bill is addressed to 'The Occupier', so long as you intend to pay for it. Anyone who uses fuel without intending to pay for it could be prosecuted for theft. The suppliers could rely on the law relating to 'unjust enrichment' to ensure payment in these circumstances. This applies when someone unjustly obtains benefit at someone else's expense. In England and Wales, the idea of unjust enrichment arises in the law of restitution; in Scotland, the equivalent is found in the law of recompense.

Establishing who should pay the bill will in each case depends on the facts. For example, if you are a **sole occupier** *and*:

- you have taken over responsibility for the supply by requesting this over the telephone; *or*

- you have never filled in an application form because the supply was already connected and you receive bills addressed to 'The Occupier';

– you could be held liable for the bill from the date you moved in simply on the facts.

In situations where there is **more than one occupier,** establishing who is liable will often be more difficult. The criteria for establishing who is liable could depend on any of the following:

- your status as an occupier;

- the extent of control you have over the use of fuel;

- your actual use of fuel;

- the degree of control you have over income within your household;

- the date when you moved in.

You should consider the viewpoint of OFFER and consult the specific problem areas addressed at the end of this chapter. A strict and literal interpretation of the law suggests that there are no provisions for determining when your liability will end if you are not a 'tariff customer' (see p61).[7] It may be advisable to give the supplier notice that you are leaving, to avoid disputes about the end of your period of liability.

You will clearly *not* be liable to pay the supplier for the electricity bill if:

- you are an owner or occupier of a premises; and

- you have not given the supplier notice in writing requiring a supply of electricity; and

- another occupier or owner is liable for the supply by virtue of having given notice requiring a supply and that person's liability for the supply has not come to an end (see p61).

The Legal Basis for the Authors' View

The authors' view is based on a literal interpretation of the construction and contents of the Electricity Act 1989 (see Sections 16-22 and Schedule 6 in Appendix 1). It must be stressed that the authors' view has not been tested by the courts.

Electricity suppliers have a statutory duty to supply electricity to an owner or occupier who has given proper notice that a supply is required at a particular premises[8] (see pp8-10 for exceptions to this rule). The notice must be in writing.[9] Once a supply has been given, any person who gave notice requiring the supply becomes defined under the legislation as a 'tariff customer'[10] and must be charged prices set out in published tariffs.[11] Electricity suppliers may recover charges from tariff customers.[12] The legislation is quite clearly framed in such a way so as to confer rights and obligations on those who have given notice requiring a supply of electricity. For example, when you give notice requiring a supply:

- you may be required to pay a security deposit before a supply is given;

- you have the right to a counternotice from the supplier if the supplier wants to change the terms and conditions of your supply by, for example, wanting you to accept a different type of meter (see p54);

- you have the right to refer certain disputes to OFFER for a decision.

The need to give notice before being entitled to a supply of electricity allows consumers a degree of choice. Where more than one occupier could be liable for the supply, either one or any number could require a supply and be held liable for that supply.

The legislation also prescribes when a tariff customer's liability for the supply ends – ie, when a tariff customer gives notice of leaving a premises, or after prescribed periods of time if no notice is given[13] (see p61, above).

Electricity suppliers are entitled to refuse to supply tariff customers at a new address where the tariff customer has left her/his previous premises without paying the electricity bill.[14] They may pursue the tariff customer for the debt through the courts in the same way as any other creditor.

In addition, the legislation provides that electricity suppliers are not entitled to require payment of the arrears of a tariff customer whose liability for the supply has come to an end from the 'next occupier' of the premises.[15] 'Next occupier' has not been defined, but would definitely include a new occupier whose occupation commenced after the previous tariff customer had left. It is arguable that it might also include someone whose occupation had overlapped with that of the tariff customer, but who was now requesting a supply in their own right.

In view of the effect of all of these provisions within the legislation, the authors are of the opinion that where notice has properly been given in writing, only the person or persons who gave notice can be

held liable for the bill up until the time that their liability is brought
to an end by the circumstances prescribed by the legislation[16] (see
pp60-62). The electricity supplier is not entitled to payment of the bill
from anybody else: not a flat-sharer, partner or anybody else.

A more difficult, grey area is when nobody has given notice and the
liability of the last tariff customer has come to an end as prescribed by
the legislation. In this situation, it is arguable that there is no 'tariff
customer' in so far as there is no-one who has served a notice. In
situations where a supplier does not accept written notice from any of
its customers, there is an argument that these customers could be
regarded as 'tariff customers' on the basis that the supplier has
waived its right to a notice.[17] Deciding who is a 'tariff customer' will
then be a question of fact, not law.

In the event of disputes in these situations, consult the 'common
problems' section of this chapter on pp71-77. You may need to refer
disputes to OFFER. You may also wish to seek independent legal
advice to confirm that OFFER's interpretation of the law is in your
best interests.

The Suppliers' and OFFER's View

In England and Wales, many electricity suppliers continue to approach
the question of who is liable for the bill as though privatisation had
brought no substantial change to the law. They continue to assert that
if electricity has been used, it must be paid for by the people who were
in the premises and may have used it, regardless of whose name is on
the bill and regardless of whether an individual has given notice requiring a supply.

Suppliers vary in their practices. Some suppliers insist that everyone
who wants a supply must complete an application form, while others
simply accept customers' details over the telephone. Some suppliers
attempt to gather as much information as possible about all the
occupants of a premises as a safeguard to enable them to ensure that
someone pays the bill.

The suppliers do, however, acknowledge that they are not entitled
to arrears from the next occupier (see p63 and p75) of the premises,
but usually only in situations where there has been no overlap in
periods of occupancy.[18]

The suppliers' approach to the question of liability relies on the
premise that giving notice requiring a supply of electricity is meaning-
less in terms of deciding liability, except in so far as it provides them
with evidence of who the occupants of a premises might be. The
suppliers' approach assumes that the provisions within the legislation

for determining when an individual's liability comes to an end are of no effect.[19]

But the drafting of the Electricity Act 1989 has clarified and tightened the definition of a tariff customer by clearly setting out that a tariff customer is the person who has given notice requiring a supply of electricity. As the Electricity Act provides that suppliers may charge tariff customers for charges due, it is difficult to see how the suppliers can justify their position in a case where there is somebody in occupation who can properly be defined as a tariff customer.

The only possible exception to this is where no one has given notice, but electricity has been used. In these cases, the supplier will need to consider who can rightly be considered to be the occupier. The supplier will need to rely on the law of restitution ('unjust enrichment') in England and Wales and on the law of 'recompense' in Scotland.

In Scotland, the arguments have been resolved to some extent. Scottish electricity suppliers accept that the person who has signed the application form is the tariff customer. If that person leaves, they will be regarded as liable up to the date that a notice of leaving is received by the supplier.

As yet OFFER has not helped to clarify the position. OFFER has been debating this question internally for years, but has so far failed to make a comprehensive policy statement. As an organisation, it is acutely aware that whatever interpretation it adopts, it will be subject to criticism. As regulator of the industry, OFFER is conscious that it will have to deal with the practical consequences arising from its interpretation of the law.

If OFFER decides that liability for a supply is decided, in the first instance, by reference to the tariff customer being a person who has given notice in writing, it will be faced with the problem that some suppliers have no administrative procedures for accepting written notice. Should it then compel those suppliers to set up costly administrative procedures? Furthermore, OFFER is concerned that if it takes a narrow view as to who is a 'tariff customer', it will effectively be acknowledging that all those customers who have never given notice requesting a supply will have no rights to have their disputes determined by OFFER. OFFER is therefore anxious to find an interpretation which will allow most customers to be classified as 'tariff customers', perhaps by allowing customers who have requested a supply verbally to be classified as 'tariff customers'.

To date, however, OFFER has so far made only limited public statements on the question of liability. In 1992, OFFER's Director of Consumer Affairs gave an indication of a view which might figure in

OFFER's eventual policy statement. In a letter to *The Adviser*,[20] it was stated that:

> generally where people have equal status as occupants (for example, husband and wife) then any one or more of these occupants can be held liable for the bill during their occupancy, regardless of who is named on the account.

This statement does not address the question of liability for the supply when an individual has properly given written notice requiring a supply, as distinct from simply being named on an account. You might be named on an account, but have never given written notice. It is difficult to see how this statement can have any validity in situations where notice has been properly given and where the person giving notice is either still in occupation or has left, but their liability has not come to an end under the terms of the legislation.

Until such time as OFFER makes a public statement on this issue, the vacuum created will continue to permit the suppliers to set their own agendas and policies. Not surprisingly, no determinations on this question have been made by OFFER. While the present situation prevails, it is to be assumed that none is likely to be made, until such time as a consumer insists or compels OFFER to use its duty to determine disputes in an appropriate case.

3. WHEN ARE YOU LIABLE FOR A BILL? (GAS)

The Authors' View

The authors take the view that the legislation for gas[21] provides some straightforward principles for deciding liability in individual cases.

Note: the amounts for which you may be liable may form all or part of the bill. In this section, all references to 'the bill' refer only to 'charges due' for the supply of gas. (See p111 for more information about 'charges due'.)

You *will* be liable to pay the supplier for a gas bill if:

- you are an owner or occupier of premises; *and*

- you have given notice in writing requiring a supply of gas (see p17); *and*

- the supplier has a statutory duty to supply you (see p6 and p16).

You will be solely liable for the bill if you alone give notice in writing requiring the supply, regardless of whether you live alone or with other adults. You will be jointly responsible for the bill if you and one or more others also give notice requiring a supply. Your individual liability for the bill will begin from the date that you require the supply.

Your individual liability for the supply will end:[22]

- where you give at least 24 hours' written notice that you intend to leave the premises, on the day that you leave;

- where you did not give at least 24 hours' written notice that you were leaving, *either*:

  - 28 days after you actually give written notice of leaving; *or*
  - on the next day when the meter should be read; *or*
  - nobody has given notice requiring a supply of gas; *or*
  - on the day when any subsequent occupier of the premises requires a supply,

  whichever is the earlier.

You *may* be liable to pay a gas bill if:

- the liability of the person(s) who gave notice has come to an end (see above); *and*

- you have, in practice, been supplied with gas.

In this situation, establishing who is liable will depend on the facts. This is a common situation for gas consumers, as suppliers very often do not rely on application forms as a means of giving notice. Suppliers routinely put consumers' names on a bill as a result of telephone contact, and many gas bills are addressed to 'The Occupier'. If you are a sole occupier of a premises, you alone will be liable for the bill from the date that you moved in. Establishing your liability might depend on:

- whether you requested a supply of gas in your name;

- your status as an occupier;

- the extent of control you have over the use of fuel;

- the degree of control you have over income within your household;

- the date when you moved in.

You should consider the viewpoint of OFGAS (see p69), and consult the 'common problems' section at the end of this chapter.

You will *not* be liable to pay the supplier for a gas bill if:

- you are an owner or occupier of a premises; *and*

- you have not given the supplier notice in writing requiring a supply of gas; *and*

- another occupier or owner is liable for the supply by virtue of having given notice requiring a supply; *and*

- that person's liability for the supply has not yet come to an end (see p67 above).

The Legal Basis for the Authors' View

The authors' view is based on a literal interpretation of the construction and contents of the Gas Act 1986 (see Sections 10-14 and Schedule 5 in Appendix 1). It must be stressed that the authors' view differs from that of OFGAS. No precedent-setting cases have been decided by the courts, although there have been some county court decisions where district judges decided that women were not responsible for gas debts in the names of their husbands.[23] In one case, the district judge decided that the woman only became liable for the bill when she became the named account holder, and in the other became liable once she had signed a document accepting liability.[24]

Gas suppliers have a duty to supply an owner or occupier at a premises upon being required to do so.[25] Anyone requiring a supply must serve notice on the supplier specifying the premises and the date from which a supply is required.[26] The notice must be in writing.[27] The supply is charged to most domestic customers at a particular 'tariff'[28] (see p37), and these customers are known as 'tariff customers'. Gas suppliers may recover charges from tariff customers, who are defined as 'persons supplied with gas'.[29]

The definition of tariff customer for the purposes of a gas supply is a looser definition than the comparable definition for electricity. A tariff customer for gas is not strictly defined as a person who requests a supply of gas in writing, but as the person who is 'supplied with gas'. It can be argued that where an individual has served notice requiring a supply of gas, that that person has demanded a supply and that the supply is subsequently provided to that customer as a result of that customer's demand. In such a situation, that customer alone will be the 'tariff customer'.[30]

The need to give notice before being entitled to a supply of gas allows occupiers a degree of choice. Where more than one occupier could be liable for the supply, either one or any number could give notice in writing and be held liable for the supply.

The legislation prescribes when a tariff customer's liability for the supply ends – ie, when a tariff customer gives notice of leaving a premises, or after prescribed periods of time if no notice is given (see p67, above).[31]

Gas suppliers are entitled to refuse to supply tariff customers at a new address where the tariff customer has left a previous premises without paying the bill,[32] and may pursue the tariff customer for the debt in the same way as any other creditor.

The legislation also provides that gas suppliers are not entitled to require payment from the 'next occupier' of the premises of the arrears of a tariff customer whose liability for the supply has come to an end.[33] 'Next occupier' has not been defined, but would include a new occupier whose occupation commenced after the previous tariff customer had left. It is arguable that it might also include someone whose occupation overlapped with that of the tariff customer, but who then requested a supply in their own right.

The authors are therefore of the opinion that where notice has properly been given in writing, only the person or persons who gave notice can be held liable for the bill up until the time that their liability is brought to an end by the circumstances prescribed by the legislation. The gas supplier is not entitled to payment of the bill from anybody else: not a flat-sharer, partner or anybody else.

There is a more difficult, grey area where nobody has given notice and the liability of the last tariff customer has come to an end as prescribed by the legislation. As discussed above, who is liable will be a question of fact and evidence. In the event of disputes in these situations, consult the sections on the OFGAS interpretation of the legislation in this chapter and the specific problem areas addressed at the end of this chapter. You may need to refer disputes to OFGAS, but should also seek independent legal advice.

The Suppliers' and OFGAS' View

OFGAS published its interpretation of the question of liability to pay for a gas supply in a position paper as an appendix to its Annual Report 1988. This is reproduced in Appendix 3. The OFGAS position can be summarised as an attempt at a benevolent 'beneficial user' argument (see pp58-60). OFGAS entered into a debate with advisers on the question of liability for gas following the publication of an article on the subject in *The Adviser* in June 1992.[34] While acknowledging the existence of the differing viewpoints expressed, OFGAS decided that it would not be revising its present position.[35]

OFGAS considers that occupiers who are supplied with gas may be liable to pay for it. Who exactly is liable will depend on the circumstances surrounding the occupancy of the premises. Where two or more people are legally entitled to occupy premises, it may be that each of them can be regarded as being supplied with gas. OFGAS asserts that the proper criterion is the amount of control exercised by any person at the premises, and, in particular, their control over the use of gas. On this basis, it asserts that each of two spouses, or each of a group of student sharers could be regarded as being liable for the supply. It would not regard young adults living with their parents as being liable.

The OFGAS position applies regardless of who has given notice originally requiring the supply, except where that person is an owner of the premises and has made it clear that they wish to be supplied as an owner. OFGAS considers that the requirements contained within a notice are only relevant on the original connection of a supply. The obligation to continue to supply gas is based on any 'sufficient indication that a supply is needed'.

By drawing a distinction between the duty to connect a premises initially, and the duty to continue to supply, OFGAS implies that the person giving notice that s/he requires a supply will not always be regarded as the tariff customer. To support this view, OFGAS argues that the requirements contained within a notice (ie, the address of the premises and the date when the supply should commence) do not help to determine who is the tariff customer.

The OFGAS position is dependent on the following assumptions:

- that giving notice requesting a supply requires a supplier only to connect a supply, but not to continue to give a supply;

- that the person giving notice of requiring a supply need not be the same as the person billed as the 'tariff customer' (defined as the 'person supplied with gas').

It would also have the following implications:

- that the legal provisions for determining when liability for a supply will end will apply to any occupant who might be regarded as a tariff customer. Effectively, any such occupier who does not give the supplier notice that they are leaving could be held liable for the bill for up to 28 days after they have left.[36]

- a security deposit could be requested only on the original connection of a premises, since a security deposit can be required only from someone who has given notice requiring a supply.[37]

The authors consider that OFGAS is wrong to assume that giving notice requiring a supply does not also oblige a supplier to continue to supply. The Gas Act 1986[38] specifically words the duty to supply in terms of 'giving' and 'continuing to give' a supply of gas when required to do so, and makes the duty to supply conditional on receiving written notice in a particular form.[39] There is nothing about the terms of the notice to suggest, as OFGAS says, that it only makes sense in relation to the first time a supply is connected. The limited information required (ie, the address of the premises and the date when the supply should commence) would be needed for any customer, not just the first.

It is a pity that the OFGAS interpretation is so convoluted on the question of who is liable for a bill when proper notice has been given. In practice, gas is often supplied in circumstances when nobody has given notice, since most gas suppliers have not set up administrative procedures based on written notice. Most simply accept notice by telephone. In circumstances where no written notice has been given, the OFGAS position paper may be of some use in arguing that individuals should not be held liable for a bill where they had no control over the gas supply.

In assuming that liability should be determined by the extent of control over the gas supply, OFGAS has failed to take into consideration the often unequal control over income in many households. Not surprisingly, a consequence of the OFGAS interpretation has been the experience that suppliers have been holding women deserted by their partners as liable for arrears incurred during their partners' occupancy. This might well have been anticipated, as women often find themselves in the position of using fuel, but of having no means of paying for it independent of their partners' wage or benefits.

4. COMMON PROBLEMS

Notice: Does Notice Determine Liability?

In the view of the authors, the giving of notice requiring a supply will make you liable for a gas or electricity bill until the law says your liability ends[40](see p10 (electricity) and p17 (gas)) for how to give notice).

In the view of OFGAS, giving notice will not in itself make you liable for the supply.

OFFER has not made its view public. In practice, electricity suppliers may try to argue that liability is determined not by the giving of notice, but by occupancy.

Your Liability When Your Name is on the Bill

The person named on a bill will not always be liable to pay. Sometimes only one person is actually named on a bill, disguising the fact that several people actually gave notice requiring a supply, or that nobody gave notice requiring a supply. For example, suppliers often ask outgoing occupants the names of the next occupants. You may find that your name is on a bill without you ever having had any contact with the supplier.

In the authors' opinion, a person who is named on the bill will have sole liability for the bill if they alone gave written notice requiring a supply. Otherwise, the name on the bill will only be evidence of who might be liable.

Your Liability When Nobody is Named on the Bill

When nobody is named on the bill, liability will depend on the facts. See p60 (electricity) and p66 (gas) for the authors' view.

Moving In: Becoming Liable for the Supply

It is in your interest to have some evidence of when your liability begins. When moving to a new address, make a note of the meter reading and preferably agree the reading with the last occupier(s). Arrange to have the meter read by the supplier, and inform them that you require a supply.

If a supplier does not routinely use application forms for giving notice, consider whether you should also give notice in writing (see above). One person can give notice if that person wants to take responsibility. If you are joint occupiers giving notice, ensure that everyone signs the application form or letter. Some suppliers have application forms which suggest that you can apply on behalf of another person who is named on the form as an occupier.[41] This appears to allow the possibility of another person making you liable for the supply without your consent or knowledge. In the authors' opinion, you cannot be made liable for a supply in this way.

If one joint occupant moves out, and you move in to take their place, there is nothing to prevent you from giving notice specifying that you are replacing a joint occupant. The liability of the other occupants will not end until they leave.

It is worth checking your first bill to ensure that it does not include the previous occupiers' charges. Incoming occupiers cannot be held responsible for the previous occupiers' arrears of electricity or gas.[42]

Moving Out: Ending Liability for the Supply

If you are an occupier and you give a supplier proper notice that you are leaving, you will be protected from being held liable for the bill for fuel used after you have left. If you are a tariff customer for either gas or electricity, the law sets out when your liability will end (see p67 – gas; and p61 – electricity). There is no provision for when your liability ends if you are not a tariff customer.

Electricity:

If you have given notice requiring a supply, you will be a 'tariff customer'.[43] You should give at least two working days' notice in writing that you are leaving, or you may be held liable for a substantial bill for a period after you have left (see p61). You could give notice that you are leaving if you are not a tariff customer but are, in practice, responsible for the bill.

Gas:

If you have given notice requiring a supply, in the authors' view you will be a tariff customer. In the view of OFGAS, you may be a tariff customer regardless of whether you have given notice, if you are an occupant who is named on a bill or you have 'equal status' with another occupant – eg, a student-sharer, flat-sharer, joint tenant or spouse. You should give the supplier at least 24 hours' written notice of leaving, or you may be held liable for a substantial bill for a period after you have left[44] (see p67).

When moving, have the meter read by the supplier or agree a meter reading with the incoming occupier. Check your final bill against this reading. You should not be held liable for the next occupiers' consumption if you have given correct notice that you are leaving or once the incoming consumer has accepted liability for bills.

Who is Liable When the Person Named on the Bill Has Left?

Sole liability

If the person named on the bill had sole liability for the supply, their liability will have ended either when they left if they gave notice of leaving, or with the passing of time (see p67 (gas), p61 (electricity)).[45]

In the authors' opinion, a person who is named on the bill will have had sole liability for the bill if they alone gave written notice requiring a supply. As a joint occupier, spouse or cohabitee, you cannot be held liable for their bill if you have not given notice requiring a supply.

In the event of a dispute, involve OFFER or OFGAS and refer to the arguments set out above giving the authors' views and the examination of the views of OFFER/OFGAS. Seek legal advice if you cannot resolve the dispute to your satisfaction – you may wish to resolve the dispute in the county court (in England and Wales) or the Sheriff Court (in Scotland). Note that in England, there have been some cases of liability decided in the county court. See p68 and also Chapter 13: Remedies.

Shared liability

In the authors' opinion, liability will be decided by who gave written notice requiring a supply. If the person who left gave written notice, their liability will end either when they inform the supplier they are leaving or with the passing of time (see p67 (gas), p61 (electricity)).[46] Any remaining occupants who originally gave notice in writing will be liable for the arrears along with the person who has left. In situations where nobody gave notice, who is liable for the arrears will depend on the facts. You could still be held liable for all of the arrears, but may be able to negotiate a compromise.

As a joint occupier or sharer, you could ask for the amount of the arrears to be apportioned between the people responsible for the bill, particularly if the supplier knows the whereabouts of all the parties. Both gas and electricity suppliers are entitled to refuse to supply an occupier who owes arrears,[47] and, in any event, could pursue each debtor separately through the courts. In the event of a dispute, ask OFFER or OFGAS to intervene.

In one case, OFGAS persuaded British Gas to pursue four previous occupants for their share of a bill where arrears had accrued because of a series of estimated bills. British Gas accepted that the fifth (still current) occupant should only pay one-fifth of the total bill.[48]

If the occupant who left was your spouse or cohabitee, and you had little or no control over the income of the household (for example, if

only your partner had a wage or received benefits), you could argue
that you should not be held responsible for any arrears accruing while
your partner was present. You could ask the supplier to pursue your
partner for the arrears. The supplier could refuse to connect a supply
to your partners new premises,[49] providing they are the owner or
occupier.[50]

In other circumstances, it might be appropriate to ask the supplier
to apportion the arrears. In the event of a dispute, ask OFFER or
OFGAS to intervene.

OFGAS has acknowledged that the strict application of its legal
position on liability for a bill[51] has created problems for many customers
with children who are left with large arrears following a desertion.
British Gas agreed with OFGAS to treat these situations sensitively,
taking account of the individual circumstances of each case. They also
agreed to take into consideration the existence of legal agreements
between the parties concerned for responsibility for household expenses including gas.[52] OFFER has indicated that it would regard
husbands and wives as having joint liability for a bill where they have
'equal status as occupants' (see pp64-66).[53]

Disconnection

The supply could be disconnected for arrears which are in another
person's name. This should not happen if:

- there is a genuine dispute about the arrears; *and*

- you have served notice on the supplier requiring a supply in your
  own name (see p10 (electricity) and p17 (gas) for how to do this).
  See Chapter 7 if disconnection is threatened for arrears.

Continuing the Supply After the Person Named has Left

If you give notice requiring a supply in your own name after the
person named on the bill has left, in the authors' opinion you will be
responsible for the ongoing supply from the date your notice says you
want your supply to start. If you do not give notice, who is liable, and
from when, will depend on when the liability of the previous occupant ended and on your current status as an occupant. You will need
to consider the views of the authors, OFGAS and OFFER above to
determine liability.

If a supplier refuses to connect your supply when you give notice
for the ongoing supply, because of arrears accruing from the period of
occupancy of the previous occupier, OFFER/OFGAS could be asked

to intervene. OFFER/OFGAS may order the supplier to connect your supply pending the resolution of your dispute.[54]

When a Consumer Dies

When a consumer dies, the supplier may attempt to secure payment from someone who was living with the customer. In these circumstances, the situation will be as outlined above. Any bills outstanding can be charged to the deceased's estate. This means that outstanding bills must be paid for out of money belonging to the deceased, or out of the proceeds of the sale of any belongings. Electricity and gas debts will compete on an equal footing along with all other debts. They do not take priority (see below). If the consumer left nothing, the bill lapses and the supplier stands the loss. If you have paid the bill of a consumer who has died, in the mistaken belief that you were responsible for doing so, the supplier can usually be persuaded either to credit your own account or refund the money. If the supplier refuses to do so, you should seek legal advice.

Priority between debts

If the consumer dies and leaves some money, but not enough to pay all outstanding debts, then the cost of the funeral and any costs involved in dealing with the estate take priority over all other debts except realised securities (see below). It is normally quite in order to pay funeral expenses and ignore any fuel bills. Other debts are paid in the following order of priority:

- debts of secured creditors – eg, a mortgage – provided the security is realised (ie, the house which is the security for the mortgage is sold);

- specially preferred debts – eg, if the consumer was an officer of a friendly society and held money belonging to the society; one year's income tax and arrears of national insurance contributions; six months' VAT etc;

- ordinary debts – eg, fuel debts. This category includes all other debts except deferred debts, and covers debts to secured creditors where the security is not or cannot be realised;

- deferred debts – eg, a business loan to the consumer's husband/wife.

So, if a consumer dies with an outstanding mortgage and the house is sold to meet this debt, anything left will go first to the funeral and administration costs, and any outstanding fuel bills will get low priority.

Wills

In England and Wales, when someone dies leaving a will, the will usually appoints an executor to sort out the deceased's affairs and pay any gifts left under the will. If no will is left, the deceased's next of kin can apply for letters of administration. This is similar to being an executor. There is no obligation on anyone to become an executor (even if named in a will) or to take out letters of administration. If someone dies leaving nothing, or virtually nothing, it is rarely worth the trouble. In these circumstances, a creditor such as a fuel supplier can take out letters of administration. The supplier should be told that no one intends to take out letters of administration and that it is welcome to do so if it wishes. In Scotland, where there is a will appointing an executor, the executor must apply to the Sheriff Court, submitting an Inventory of Estate to obtain Confirmation as Executor. If there is no will, the next of kin should petition the court to obtain Confirmation as Executor-Dative.

CHAPTER FIVE

High Bills

This chapter looks at ways of checking whether you are paying the right amounts for your gas and electricity. If your bills are correct, you should read Chapters 3, 10 and 11 for help with paying them. Chapter 13 suggests remedies for when a supplier charges you the wrong amount, and looks at the powers of OFGAS and OFFER to determine disputes.

High bills are not always the result of the ordinary cost of fuel or extravagant consumption.

This chapter examines the following issues:

1. The level of the bill (see below)
2. The accuracy of the bill (see p81)
3. The accuracy of the meter (see p82)
4. Circuit and installation faults and faulty appliances (see p86)

1. LEVEL OF THE BILL

Check Consumption

If a fuel bill seems to be too high, you can check whether consumption has actually increased by comparing the units consumed with those used during the same period in previous years. This is done by looking at previous bills.

If you have not kept previous bills, ask the supplier for copies (if it is urgent, you may be able to get the details you need by phone – see below). Some suppliers charge for these. If the charge seems unreasonably high, take the matter up with the Gas Consumers' Council or the relevant electricity consumers' committee (see Chapter 13). If you still cannot pay the charge, try asking the supplier to waive it. If that is refused, you can try one of the following:

- ask the supplier to give the details over the phone (some suppliers keep details of your consumption for the last five or six quarters, including whether it is an estimated or actual reading, and can read them off their computer for you);

- ask the Gas Consumers' Council or the electricity consumers' committee for your area to obtain a record of past consumption;
- exercise your rights under the Data Protection Act (see below);
- ask your MP to request that the supplier produce the information.

Exceptional Reasons for a High Bill

Check whether consumption is higher than usual for an exceptional reason – for example:

- an emergency – eg, a flood;
- a new heating system which you are not used to operating or which might be defective;
- a period of exceptionally cold weather;
- someone in the household being ill, leading to higher heating costs.

(If you think the bill is accurate after taking an exceptional reason into account, read Chapters 3, 10 and 11 for help on how to pay.)

Other Charges in the Bill

Bills may also be high because they contain items other than the cost of fuel and standing charges – eg, instalments on credit sales. The supplier may also include charges for disconnection or reconnection, and for replacing meters. Check to see if these have been lawfully charged by reading Chapter 7 on disconnection for arrears.

Billing Delays

You may find that the supplier has billed you for a longer period of time than normal and, when you finally receive the account, it covers that whole period. Suppliers are not obliged to bill you at any particular interval, but if regular bills have not been sent, or are late, you could point out to the supplier that the high level of debt is partly its own fault by making it difficult for you to monitor or modify consumption. It should be possible to negotiate time to pay.

Also, bills sent after a long time should be examined with care: the tariff or the rate of VAT may have gone up since the last bill. If the tariff has gone up, check to ensure that the supplier has not charged all or too many of the units at the higher rate. If it has, the bill should be reduced appropriately. (Watch out, though, as recently tariffs have just as often been reduced as increased.)

There have been cases of bills being sent out late by months or even years. Unless fraud is involved (see Chapter 8 on Theft and Tampering), charges cannot be recovered –

- in England and Wales if the electricity or gas was used more than six years ago[1] *or*

- in Scotland, if the supplier has not chased you for them and you have not acknowledged the charges for five years.[2]

Otherwise, you must pay for the electricity which was supplied to you (see Chapter 4 on Responsibility for the Bill). With a bill which is very late, much of the bill may be estimated (see below on estimated bills). The longer the billing delay, the better the chances of having part or all of the bill written off, or being given time to pay. OFGAS, the Gas Consumers' Council, OFFER and the electricity consumers' committees could apply pressure on the supplier to settle on a reasonable solution (see Chapter 13 on Remedies).

Obtaining Information under the Data Protection Act

Suppliers can hold a large amount of information about their customers on computer. This may include details of previous bills and consumption, customer credit ratings, and prosecutions. If a supplier refuses to provide information voluntarily, you may still be able to get hold of this information by using your rights under the Data Protection Act.

To exercise your rights, you should write to the supplier. It will send you an application form and a list of categories of information which the supplier has registered on the Data Protection Register (you can look at a copy of the Register itself at your local main public library). You then select the appropriate category from which you want your records, and return the form. You have to pay a fee, of not more than £10, and fill out a separate form for each category. The supplier will then provide the information.

As well as the right to be supplied with copies of information, you have the following rights:

- to have inaccurate information corrected;

- to claim compensation for loss caused by inaccurate information; and

- to complain to the Data Protection Registrar if the supplier fails to provide the information, to correct inaccuracies, or to obtain and process information fairly and lawfully.

Further information is available from the Office of the Data Protection Registrar (see Appendix 10).

2. ACCURACY OF THE BILL

Always check first whether the supplier has got its sums right. If the units consumed are correctly recorded, check that the cost has been correctly calculated. Such an arithmetic error is rare but does happen.

If disconnection is threatened but you think the bill is inaccurate, tell the supplier. A supplier cannot disconnect in respect of that part of a bill which is 'genuinely in dispute'.[3]

Estimates

Check to see whether the bill has been estimated. If it has, there will be an 'E' ('estimated') or an 'A' ('assessed') next to the figure in the 'present meter reading' column. (NB. In some regions 'A' means 'Actual'. Any letter symbols should be explained at the top of your bill and you should check this if in doubt.)

If practicable, you should take your own reading (see Appendix 8). You should take your own reading as soon as possible after receiving the estimated bill and make an allowance for units consumed since the date of the bill so that the comparison is as accurate as possible. You can calculate an average daily rate and deduct that amount for the appropriate number of days.

Alternatively, to decide if an estimate is unreasonable, compare the amount of fuel used over the same period in the previous year with the estimated consumption on the present bill. If a bill covering the same period is not available – eg, if you have only recently moved in – try making a reasonable estimate using any bill you do have, or by calculating how much would be used by the appliances you have and the frequency with which you use them.

If you find the estimate is doubtful, notify the supplier (meter-readers sometimes leave a pre-paid postcard for you to complete and return with your own reading). If your own reading shows that the bill is an overestimate, it must be remedied by a lower bill – a meter reading is presumed to be correct unless proved otherwise.[4]

However, remember that if a bill has been underestimated, a higher bill will result from any complaint. Normally, it will be best to set the record straight as soon as possible because the bill will have to be paid at some time. However, so long as you do not delay simply to put off a difficult problem, consider whether or not it is in your interests to tell the supplier immediately.

Also, beware of cases where a high bill is the result of a low estimate on a past bill followed by an accurate meter reading later. The points made in respect of billing delays above also apply here.

Errors in Reading the Meter

Although actual meter readings are less likely to be inaccurate than estimates, even the supplier's own meter-readers can sometimes make mistakes. You can use the same methods discussed above to detect errors, but the supplier might want to take a second reading to check any reading which you make. If the supplier has made a mistake, the bill should be amended. In houses in multiple occupation, where meters are often grouped together, it is not unknown for readings to be attributed to the wrong meter.

3. ACCURACY OF THE METER

Even if the details on the bill appear to be correct, the meter may be faulty. Meters must be approved and certified by meter examiners.[5] If, as is the normal situation, the meter belongs to the supplier, then it is their responsibility to make sure it is kept in proper working order.[6]

An electricity meter is deemed to be accurate if it does not vary more than +2 to -3½% from the correct reading. For gas meters the limits are +2 to -2%.

Checking Your Meter

You can check your meter by using the following method:

- switch off all appliances, including pilot lights;
- read the meter (see Appendix 8);
- turn on an appliance with a known rate of consumption and note the time (see *Note* below);
- leave the appliance on for a measured period of time, preferably in whole hours;
- switch off the appliance and read the meter again;

- if everything is working properly, the following formulae should work:

Electricity

Difference in readings = rating of appliance (kW) × time on (hours).

For example:
the rating for an average one-bar electric fire is one kilowatt (1KW); if it is switched on for one hour, the figures on each side of the '=' sign should both be 'one'.

Gas

Difference in readings

$$\text{(hundreds of cubic feet)} \times 3.6 = \frac{\text{rating of appliance (kW)} \times \text{time on (hours).}}{\text{(calorific value for region)} \times 2.83}$$

For example:
the rating for an average gas fire is 2.5 kilowatts (kW); if it is switched on for one hour in an area where gas has a calorific value* of 38.2, then the figures on each side of the '=' sign should both be 0.023, ie, the reading should be 2.3 cubic feet.

---

* The 'calorific value' is the amount of heat produced by burning a specific amount of gas.

Note: To find out the rating of an appliance, if it is not marked on the appliance itself, contact the manufacturer, the appliance supplier or the gas supplier. The calorific value for the area may be shown on the gas bill. If not, ask the supplier.

Note also that if gas or electricity appliances are old and/or have not been serviced recently, they may no longer perform in accordance with their rating. If an appliance has a thermostat, turn it to its highest setting so that the appliance works continuously and check it regularly to make sure it is doing so.

Meter Examiners

If you think that a meter is not functioning properly, you should first complain to the supplier who can check it itself. If you are still not satisfied, you can refer the matter to a meter examiner.[7] The supplier can also make such a reference.

If a meter seems to be over-registering, you could pay the supplier for the amount of fuel you think you have definitely consumed, without waiting for the examiner's decision. This would help to avoid disconnection because only the outstanding amount would be in dispute and the dispute would be considered a genuine one (see p81).

The **electricity meter examiners' service** is part of OFFER. An examiner will test the meter and the supply at your premises. The supplier will be invited to send a representative. The meter may then be removed for further tests. Unlike gas, an electricity meter examiner's services are free.[8] You should take a note of the reading on the meter before it is taken away.

If a notice is served by you, the electricity supplier or anyone else interested in the matter, then no one can alter or remove the meter until the dispute is resolved or an electricity meter examiner has finished her/his examination.[9]

The findings of an electricity meter examiner can be produced in court and are presumed to be correct unless proven otherwise.[10]

Gas meter examiners come under the Gas and Oil Measurement Branch of the Department of Trade and Industry. Their examiners do not come to your premises but examine meters which are sent to them by the gas supplier. Again be sure to make a note of the reading on the meter before it is taken away.

If a gas meter examiner finds that the gas meter is working properly, then the person who asked for it to be checked must pay for the removal, examination and re-installation.[11]

On completion of the examination, a gas meter examiner issues a test certificate with details of her/his decision. The decision is final and binding as to whether the meter is working properly or not.[12]

Note: In both cases, if the meter is removed, then a substitute meter should be installed. There should be no charge for this.

Waiting times

Once you ask for an electricity meter examination, the average wait for an examiner's visit is two to three months, although some regions are better than others. No determination should take longer than four months. For gas, the Citizen's Charter specifies one month from the date when the examiners' service receive the meter and they themselves aim to complete examinations in no more than six weeks.

In urgent cases, you should be able to jump the queue for an examination. However, since you should be able to prevent disconnection during most disputes, delay will not normally cause problems.

Results

If your meter is found not to be working properly – ie, outside the limits of variation – then the supplier will have to make a refund or an extra charge to you. The amount of the refund or charge depends on how long and by how much the meter is reckoned to be registering incorrectly. For gas, the meter is deemed to have been registering incorrectly for the whole period since the last actual meter reading.[13] For electricity, the meter examiner has a duty to give his opinion concerning for how long and by how much the meter has been operating outside the prescribed limits.[14]

Older gas meters may run fast – ie, they may over-register the amount of gas consumed. This is because they use a leather diaphragm to measure the amount of gas used and this can dry out. Since 1 April 1981, gas suppliers have installed only meters with synthetic diaphragms, which are more reliable. If you have an older meter and you suspect it is recording inaccurately, you can refer it to a meter examiner. New meters may be distinguished from old ones as they have either a yellow label with a large 'S' on the meter casing or a reference number which begins or ends with an 'S'. British Gas has a programme to replace all the old meters by 1995 and is presently ahead of schedule. However, it is also worth noting that research by OFGAS has shown that just over 1% of the new synthetic diaphragm meters drift slightly into over-reading three to four years after installation.[15]

Note: if a meter is removed by the supplier on an allegation that it has been tampered with (see Chapter 8), it is important that the meter is preserved so that it can be inspected. Each supplier sets out in the relevant Code of Practice how long it will keep a meter in such circumstances before destroying it. Check that the Code of Practice is being kept to.

Prepayment Meters

To check whether a prepayment meter is registering correctly, use the procedure set out on p83 (these formulae will not work if the prepayment meter is set to collect for arrears). It may also be necessary to check whether you are paying the correct amount for each unit of fuel – if so, use the following method:

- allow the money to run out;
- turn off all appliances;
- note the time and put some money in the meter;

- turn on an appliance with a known rate of consumption;
- when the money runs out, note the time again.

If everything is working properly, the following formulae should work so that you can find out the rate of charge:

For electricity meters:

$$\text{cost (pence) per kilowatt hour} = \frac{\text{money spent (in pence)}}{\text{time on (hrs)} \times \text{rating of appliance (kW)}}$$

For example:
an average electric fire has a rating of one kilowatt (1kW); if you put in 15 pence, switch on the fire and the money runs out after two hours, then the cost is 7.5 pence per kWh.

For gas meters:

$$\text{cost (pence) per kilowatt hour} = \frac{\text{money spent (in pence)}}{\text{time on (hrs)} \times \text{rating of appliance (kW)}}$$

For example:
the rating for an average gas fire is 2.5 kilowatts (kW); if you put in 15 pence, switch on the fire and the money runs out after four hours, then the cost is 1.5 pence per kWh.

Compare the result with the local tariff, which is set out in leaflets obtainable at your local showroom or by telephone from the supplier. Any difference between your figure and the tariff should be the amount which is being collected to cover the standing charge (see p37). If there is still a difference, you should challenge the way your meter is set.

4. CIRCUIT AND INSTALLATION FAULTS AND FAULTY APPLIANCES

Faulty Circuits

To check whether a circuit or installation is faulty, turn off all appliances (including pilot lights) and see if the meter is still registering. If an electricity meter is still registering, there may be a short circuit or a leak to earth; if a gas meter is still registering, there may be a gas leak. Quite apart from the effect either of these situations can have on the level of the bill, they are both dangerous and should be dealt with immediately.

Once everything is turned off and the meter has ceased to register, each appliance can be checked to make sure it is registering a reasonable level of consumption by using the formulae given above for checking the meter (see pp83 and 86).

In rented accommodation, landlords are nearly always responsible for gas piping and electrical wiring. If you have told your landlord about defects in installations or in wiring/piping, you can get them to fix the problem and to pay the difference between a high bill and the normal level of the bill, if the difference is down to the defects. Appliances themselves may be damaged by dampness or disrepair in the premises where they are being used and your landlord may be responsible for this (see Chapter 12).

Faulty Appliances – Consumers' Rights

If a fairly new appliance is faulty and uses more fuel than it should, you can claim some of the excessive bill from whoever supplied the appliance by using your rights under the Sale of Goods Act 1979.[16] Under this Act, there are a number of promises by the supplier of the appliance incorporated into the contract between you and it, including the following:

- the supplier has the legal right to sell you the goods;[17] and

- if the supplier sells appliances as its business, the appliance is fit for the purpose for which it would normally be bought.[18]

The Supply of Goods (Implied Terms) Act 1973 puts similar terms into a hire purchase agreement. In England and Wales, if an installation – eg, central heating – is put in defectively, you can use your rights under the Supply of Goods and Services Act 1982 (this Act does not extend to Scotland). This incorporates similar terms to those above, as well as one saying that proper workmanship must be used.

If goods are bought on hire purchase or on credit for £100 or more, and the credit was supplied by a lender associated with the supplier (this includes credit cards), then the lender of the money is liable for faults as well as the supplier, under the Consumer Credit Act 1974.[19] This means you can sue or threaten to sue the credit card company or other lender – this tactic can be used to put pressure on the supplier to settle any dispute or to get redress if the supplier has gone out of business.

If damage is caused by a faulty appliance, you may be able to claim compensation from the producer under the general law of negligence or under the Consumer Protection Act 1987. If the damage includes physical injury to someone, you should take legal advice on the size of compensation you might want to claim.

Damage Caused by Voltage Variations

A problem related to defective circuits and appliances (although not to high bills) is that of damage caused to electrical appliances by variations in the voltage of the electricity supply. Electricity should be supplied at 240 volts, and a variation of 6% is permitted.[20] Voltage in excess of this may cause susceptible appliances, like televisions and videos, to 'burn out'.

You may have a claim against the electricity supplier for such damage, but there are difficulties. In a claim for negligence, it will be difficult to establish that the supplier has actually been negligent, since it will be argued that there is no way that the fault can have been prevented. Alternatively, you can argue that the supplier is in breach of the statutory duty to supply electricity within the voltage limits – this faces the same problem as a claim of negligence and has never been tried before. It may be worth negotiating a settlement as the supplier will want to avoid circumstances which would damage customer relations, such as not being sympathetic to a claim like this.

Under the electricity Standards of Performance (see pp178-179 and Appendix 6), if you complain about a possible variation in the voltage, the supplier must either give an explanation or offer to visit in order to investigate. Failure to do so, or failure to send an explanatory letter or to keep an appointment for a visit, means you are entitled to a payment of £20.[21]

CHAPTER SIX

Arrears

You may find yourself in arrears of electricity or gas for many reasons. You may have spent more time at home because of a change in your circumstances – eg, unemployment, the birth of a child, sickness; you may simply be confronted by a large winter bill which you cannot afford to pay immediately; or you may have a large 'catch up' bill following a meter reading after a number of estimated bills. Whatever the reason for the arrears, it is important to deal with the problem as soon as you can. If you delay or avoid the issue, the arrears may well increase and you could risk disconnection and further costs. Disconnection for arrears is dealt with in Chapter 7.

This chapter covers:

1. WHAT ARE ARREARS?

You will be in arrears of electricity or gas if you are liable to pay a bill, but have not paid your bill on demand. You risk the electricity supplier taking disconnection action if you have not paid within 20 working days of receiving your bill.[1] You risk the gas supplier taking disconnection action if you have not paid within 28 days of the date of your bill.[2] The provisions discussed in this chapter only apply to arrears for 'charges due' for the supply of electricity and gas. See pp111-112 for what this means.

You should be careful to ensure that you are liable for the arrears. If your bill is high, perhaps because of billing delays or incorrect reading of your meter, see also Chapter 5, High Bills.

2. LEGAL PROTECTION WHEN YOU ARE IN ARREARS

The ways in which suppliers deal with customers in arrears are regulated by Conditions within the electricity suppliers' Licence or the Authorisation to British Gas. A supplier must have a licence to be allowed to operate. The licence conditions are laid down by the Directors General of OFFER and OFGAS on behalf of the Secretary of State. OFFER and OFGAS can enforce the licence Conditions using their statutory powers (see Chapter 13). For consumers in arrears, the key conditions are:

Methods for Dealing with Customers in Arrears
Condition 12A (Gas)[3] and Condition 19 (Electricity):[4]

The wording of Conditions 12A and 19 is much the same. Both state that suppliers must adopt *methods* for dealing with customers in arrears. In particular, they provide protection for customers who 'can't pay' as a result of misfortune or inability to cope as opposed to those who 'won't pay'. The methods set out the detailed procedures which the suppliers use to deal with customers in arrears, and incorporate details of their various disconnection procedures and alternatives to disconnection such as the use of payment plans to reduce arrears and the use of prepayment meters.

The detailed 'methods' adopted by British Gas have been approved by OFGAS, but have not been made public. Instead, British Gas has published a summary document entitled 'British Gas: Principles for the collection of domestic gas debt'.[5] This is reproduced at Appendix 2.

OFFER has approved the 'methods' of each of the 14 regional electricity suppliers but has decided that they cannot be required to make their methods public, even in a summary form such as the British Gas 'Principles'. To date, no supplier has published its methods in full. Yorkshire Electricity has made a summary of its 'methods' available to the Yorkshire Electricity Monitoring Group, which includes representatives from local advice centres and Citizens' Advice Bureaux.

The practice of Yorkshire Electricity stands in sharp contrast to that of other suppliers who insist that customers will abuse their procedures to evade payment if they make even a summary of their methods public. In the NORWEB area, advisers have published their observations of NORWEB's practices in the form of a Welfare Rights Briefing.[6] NORWEB has been invited to comment on the briefing and to publish its methods. NORWEB has declined both invitations.

While OFFER can decide if a supplier has breached the methods it has adopted, the secrecy surrounding suppliers' methods means that the full reasons for OFFER's decision might not be open to scrutiny by consumers or their advisers. OFFER states that 'matters of commercial confidentiality would not prevent the making of an Enforcement Order. However, in making public his reasons for making the Order, the Director General would need to consider matters of confidentiality.'

The provisions of Conditions 12A and 19 can be directly enforced in individual cases by OFFER/OFGAS[7] (see Chapter 13).

Condition 12 (Gas) and Condition 18 (Electricity): Codes of Practice

The wording of Conditions 12 and 18 is substantially the same.[8] Both require that the suppliers produce and publish codes of practice setting out their procedures for customers who have difficulty in paying.

The Gas Code of Practice is published in a booklet entitled 'Payment of gas bills – A Guide concerning the payment of gas bills including guidance to domestic customers if they are having difficulty in paying'. This is available from any gas showroom or office. A shortened form of this Code of Practice – entitled 'Please... don't be afraid to ask us about' help if you cannot pay your gas bill' – is now also available.

Electricity suppliers must provide you with a copy of their Code of Practice on request. It is essential to obtain a copy of your own supplier's Code of Practice as the codes differ.

The Codes of Practice provide some detailed information and typically include:

- types of meter and methods of payment available to help you avoid arrears;

- what to do if you cannot afford to pay your bill;

- arranging payment plans to repay arrears;

- when you will be offered a prepayment meter;

- when you will be disconnected;
- when you will not be disconnected.

Remember that the Codes of Practice represent the stated policy of the suppliers. They are not legally enforceable documents. Nonetheless, examples of individual breaches of the Codes of Practice should be reported to OFFER or OFGAS. OFFER/OFGAS should be asked to investigate to ensure that the supplier is not operating a policy which is in breach of Conditions 18/12 or 19/12A.

Many of the electricity suppliers' Codes of Practice make statements which are contrary to the provisions of Condition 19. (For example, some suppliers suggest that you may be obliged to pay a lump-sum towards your arrears if you are to avoid disconnection.) In these situations, Condition 19 will always override whatever is stated in the Code of Practice. In the event of a dispute, ask OFFER to intervene.

3. ARREARS IN ANOTHER PERSON'S NAME

You may not be liable for an electricity or gas bill which is in another person's name if, for example, your partner was previously responsible for the bill and has left home, or if you are a joint tenant or sharer, or if the person responsible for the bill has died. You cannot be held liable for the arrears of the previous occupier of your premises.[9] See Chapter 4 for a detailed discussion of who is liable for a bill, and when.

4. ARREARS AS A RESULT OF ESTIMATED BILLS

OFGAS has indicated that where gas arrears have built up over an extended period because of a succession of estimated bills, repayment of the arrears could be made over an equivalent extended period if you would otherwise be caused hardship. For example, if a meter has not been read for two years, you should be allowed two years to repay the arrears which accrued as a result. Although no comparable statement has been made by OFFER, you could use OFGAS' opinion as a reasonable basis for making repayment arrangements with electricity suppliers.

If you cannot afford the rate of repayment of arrears on this basis, you should be allowed to repay the arrears at a rate you can genuinely afford (see p101).

Estimated bills are a common way for customers to accrue arrears. Suppliers are expected to adhere to minimum standards of meter reading (see p27). It is advisable to take your own readings regularly – at least once every three months – to ensure that a supplier's estimate of your consumption is correct. Suppliers will amend estimated bills if you telephone in with your own reading, or complete and return a card left by a meter reader.

If arrears have arisen because of a supplier's failure to accurately read your meter, you may wish to dispute your liability for the full amount of the arrears. See Chapter 5: High Bills.

5. WAYS OF REPAYING YOUR ARREARS

Once you have established the extent of your liability for arrears, you will need to arrange to pay the arrears. Failure to contact the supplier to make an arrangement to pay will result in the supplier taking action towards disconnecting your supply.

If you cannot afford to pay the full amount at once, you will need to consider paying both for the arrears and for your current use of fuel either:

- in instalments through a payment plan, *or*

- through a prepayment meter, *or*

- through the Fuel Direct scheme if you are on income support.

You should first think carefully about which of the various options would best suit your needs. You will need to consider the costs of the various options to you and the practicalities of using a particular scheme. Your negotiations with your supplier will be more effective if you know which scheme you would prefer and why. Keep in mind that it is in your interests to negotiate a payment method you can keep to – otherwise your options will narrow and you may be forced to accept a prepayment meter against your wishes.

Chapter 3 looks at the advantages and disadvantages of the various methods of payment, including Fuel Direct for some claimants of income support. Consider also the way in which the various options recover arrears.

Payment Plans

Payment plans usually operate with credit meters (or (electricity only) variable tariff meters such as Economy Seven or White Meter). Some suppliers will allow you to have a payment plan in conjunction with a prepayment meter set to pay for current consumption only.

Suppliers calculate an amount which you are required to pay on a weekly, fortnightly or monthly basis. This figure will include an estimated amount for current consumption and an amount for arrears.

Many suppliers will add your arrears to your estimated annual consumption, and then divide by 12 for a monthly figure, or by 52 for a weekly figure. You may be told that this is the figure the computer says you 'have to' repay. This ensures that you will repay the arrears within a year. Often, the use of this formula means that you may be 'required' to repay the arrears at a faster rate than you can afford. This is a clear breach of Condition 19 and you do not have to accept this. If, for example, you can afford to repay £1.50 per week, the supplier should simply add this figure to your estimated weekly consumption.

It is also important to ensure that the amount estimated for current consumption does accurately reflect your use of fuel and that the supplier does not attempt to recover the arrears more quickly than you can afford by overestimating your consumption. You should take particular care to ensure that your meter is read each quarter so that you can accurately track your consumption and, if necessary, ask for a review of the rate of your payments.

Prepayment Meters

Electronic prepayment meters can be reset to pay back arrears over a period of time. For most electronic prepayment meters, resetting means adjusting the meter to reclaim a fixed amount of arrears over each week, irrespective of the amount of fuel used. A timing device in the meter registers the amount due towards the arrears each week. This amount is then deducted from the value of fuel paid for, by inserting tokens, cards or keys, either when the meter is recharged or over the week. This can lead to the problem of self-disconnection (see p32).

Coin meters are rarely available as an option. However, there may be circumstances where you may need to argue that a coin meter really is the only method of payment to suit your needs – eg, if you cannot manage a payment plan, are not eligible for Fuel Direct and cannot use an electronic prepayment meter.

Coin meters can be adjusted so that each coin inserted pays partly for fuel and partly toward the arrears. The effect of this is to spread the repayment of arrears over a longer period if consumption is reduced, and to shorten the repayment period if consumption is increased. This means that your rate of repayment of arrears is highest when you most need to use fuel – possibly when you can least afford it.

If you are likely to spend periods away from home – for example, you are regularly admitted to hospital – a coin meter would avoid the problem of self-disconnection.[10] There may be situations where the installation of a coin meter is 'safe and practicable' for your needs, but an electronic prepayment meter would not be. In these circumstances, you should press for the installation of a coin meter as an alternative to disconnection.

Fuel Direct

Fuel Direct is a system of direct deductions from income support and certain other benefits when these are paid in the same order book or girocheque as income support. Payments are made up of a fixed sum towards arrears and an amount for current consumption of fuel. Fuel Direct is discussed fully in Chapter 3; pp42-51.

Some suppliers dislike Fuel Direct as a method of payment and can make it difficult for customers to choose this option. This particularly applies to suppliers who have invested heavily in electronic prepayment meters. Some Benefits Agency offices also behave as though this scheme does not exist. Do not be discouraged from considering this option – it is sometimes the only sensible way for payments to be made and for disconnection to be prevented.

6. CAN YOU CHOOSE HOW TO REPAY YOUR ARREARS? (GAS)

Condition 12A[11] (see pp51 and 90) allows some choice over method of payment to customers who cannot pay their bills because of hardship. It contains the following provisions:

- If you cannot pay your bill you must be offered a payment arrangement which takes into consideration your ability to pay. This means you must be allowed to repay your arrears at a rate you can afford.

- If you have not been able to manage a payment plan you must be offered a prepayment meter (where safe and practicable) as an alternative to disconnection.

As payment arrangements are associated with credit meters, Condition 12A in effect provides that you are entitled to a credit meter in the first instance, and that a prepayment meter may be installed as a last resort. You are not entitled to a prepayment meter simply because you would prefer one.

If you receive income support, the Benefits Agency may allow you the option of paying your bills through the Fuel Direct scheme (see pp42-51). You would then be able to retain your credit meter.

7. ARRANGING TO PAY YOUR ARREARS (GAS)

Arranging a Payment Plan

You should always be offered a payment plan as your first option when you get into arrears. The Principles for the Collection of Domestic Gas Debt (see Appendix 2) provide that payment arrangements will be the 'preferred option' in all cases.[12] The Code of Practice states that you can make British Gas an offer of a payment arrangement, or they will offer you one. It will help if you have already considered which method of payment will best suit your needs. Consider how convenient it will be for you to make your payments and the costs involved. It is important to choose a method of payment which you can most easily manage to avoid your repayment arrangement breaking down. Where you contact the supplier's debt collection staff, you should be counselled so that the staff can establish the method of payment which would most suit your needs.[13] Gas suppliers currently treat the Fuel Direct scheme as a method of payment for customers on income support and have not attempted to restrict access to this scheme. It is to be hoped that this policy does not change with the introduction of the new 'Quantum' prepayment meter.

Prepayment Meters (Gas)

When will a prepayment meter be offered?

Prepayment meters are considered very much a last resort option at the moment, with British Gas preferring to negotiate or renegotiate payment plans. However, this is all soon set to change with the arrival of the new Quantum Electronic Meter to replace the current crude, mechanical prepayment meters (see p29-30 for more about the Quantum meter). Already, British Gas staff are warning that if a payment plan breaks down, the only alternative will be the installation of a prepayment meter.

However, in some areas it remains difficult to obtain a prepayment meter, with long waiting lists for customers who are not seen as a priority. Until the arrival of the 'Quantum' meter in your area, you will normally be able to obtain a prepayment meter only as an alternative to disconnection, providing[14]

• you cannot manage a gas payment plan; *and*

• it is safe and practical to install.

A coin meter will be offered only if it is not feasible to offer a token meter.[15]

You will not be charged the cost of repositioning a meter to enable a prepayment meter to be fitted, if you demonstrate an inability to handle credit payment alternatives to the satisfaction of British Gas.[16]

When will a prepayment meter be refused?

The shortage of mechanical prepayment meters and the development of the Quantum prepayment meter as the 'next generation' of high-tech meter led to a policy of prepayment meters not being installed in situations where often electricity suppliers would be only too keen to impose a prepayment meter. This may change once the new meters become widely available. Because of the nature of the fuel, there are also additional safety considerations which may prevent the installation of a gas prepayment meter. If you cannot have a prepayment meter installed, you will need to negotiate a payment plan instead.

The Principles for the Collection of Domestic Gas Debt (see Appendix 2) provide that a prepayment meter will not be installed if:[17]

• there are any secondary (subsidiary) meters supplied with gas through that meter; or

• the position of the meter physically prevents installation – eg, a prepayment meter cannot physically be fitted into a semi-concealed meter box. However, the possibility of relocating the meter will be considered in this situation;

• the location of the meter prevents safe operation of the token mechanism by the customer, taking account of the customer's circumstances – eg, in the case of a disabled person who could not cope with a meter located above a door, relocation of the meter would be considered;

• there has been no contact with the customer, including non-return of the 'Helpline' card.

Note: The Helpline card is a card delivered to all British Gas customers who are threatened with disconnection. It asks customers to get in touch with British Gas if they wish to prevent disconnection. It advises customers that payment plans may be available and that a prepayment meter can be installed as an alternative to disconnection.

Returning the Helpline card to British Gas will delay and possibly prevent disconnection.

- the customer has refused a prepayment meter.

8. CAN YOU CHOOSE HOW TO REPAY YOUR ARREARS? (ELECTRICITY)

Condition 19 of the supplier's licence allows some choice over method of payment to customers who cannot pay their bills because of hardship. It contains the following provisions:

- If you cannot pay your bill you must be offered a payment arrangement which takes into consideration your ability to pay.

- If you have not been able to manage a payment plan you must be offered a prepayment meter (if safe and practicable) as an alternative to disconnection.

As payment plans are associated with credit meters, Condition 19 in effect provides that you are entitled to a credit meter in the first instance and to a prepayment meter as a last resort.

If you receive income support, the Benefits Agency may allow you the option of paying your bills through the Fuel Direct scheme. Although Fuel Direct is often considered a 'last resort' option by suppliers, it is arguable that it is a payment plan for the purposes of Condition 19 and therefore should be considered as an option before a supplier attempts to impose a prepayment meter. This argument is supported by the fact that the supplier's Codes of Practice typically allow for the disconnection procedure to be suspended for between 14 and 21 days to allow customers to contact the Benefits Agency for help. If no help is forthcoming, only then are the suppliers entitled to offer a prepayment meter as the last option before disconnection. See pp42-51 for more details about the Fuel Direct scheme.

Some electricity suppliers are so keen to impose prepayment meters upon any customer in arrears that this may be presented as the only available option. Such a policy breaches Conditions 18 and 19. OFFER should be actively working towards eliminating such practices. It will help if you (and advisers in particular) always refer details of such disputes to your local electricity consumers committee, who may have a working party or subcommittee working on debt issues, and to OFFER.

OFFER can intervene in disputes about the choice of a meter or method of payment.[18] While this does not necessarily result in more choice for individual customers, it may assist to curb some of the more draconian policies of the suppliers. OFFER's independent decision would be binding on both parties.

In one case, OFFER decided that a supplier was not entitled to impose a prepayment meter on a customer with a history of late payment without first having served a counternotice on the customer. The counternotice should have informed the customer about the proposed change to their terms and conditions of supply and of the right to have a dispute decided by OFFER.[19]

OFFER further decided that the customer ought to have been offered a choice between paying through a direct debit plan or accepting a prepayment meter. Either of these options would have given the supplier reasonable security for the future payment of bills. The final choice should have rested with the customer. As the supplier had failed to use the proper procedures to inform the customer of the proposed changes to the terms and conditions of the supply, the supplier was not entitled to the extra charges for the installation of the prepayment meter. See Chapter 3 for more about choice of meters and methods of payment.

The amount of say you have finally on your choice of a way to pay for your arrears will often depend on your payment arrangements in the past. You may be less likely to obtain your choice of method of payment if you have had a succession of broken agreements.

9. ARRANGING TO PAY YOUR ARREARS (ELECTRICITY)

Payment Plans (Electricity)

You should always be offered a payment plan as your first option for the repayment of arrears.[20] Do not be persuaded that this is not the case by suppliers who see prepayment meters as your only possible option when you are in arrears.

Look carefully at the terms of a payment plan offered by the supplier. Many suppliers will calculate your first year's payments under a payment plan by adding the amount of the outstanding bill to an estimate of a year's consumption. They will then divide by either 12 or 52 to produce a monthly or weekly repayment figure. This system ensures that the arrears are repaid over a year. You will effectively be paying for five quarters over four quarters. In practice, it is often worse than this. If there is a delay in arranging your payment plan, for example, by two months into the next quarter, suppliers will often add your estimated consumption for this period to the arrears and demand payment of the total sum over the following ten months. In this situation, you will effectively be asked to pay for 15 months' consumption over ten months.

You do not have to accept such demands from a supplier – you are entitled to repay your arrears at a rate which is genuinely affordable for you. See p101 for more about rates of repayment.

Many electricity suppliers (eg, Eastern Electricity) state in their Codes of Practice that they will recover arrears within a reasonable period. If a supplier attempts to rely on such provisions in its Code of Practice, it should be pointed out that this is totally contrary to the provisions of Condition 19. Condition 19 makes it quite clear that it is the amount you pay which must be reasonable, not the length of time it takes the supplier to recover the money. If the supplier is obstructive in negotiations, you could ask OFFER to assist.

If a payment plan is your preferred option for repaying your arrears, make sure that you negotiate an arrangement you can keep to. Otherwise your payment plan may be set up to fail. When your payment plan breaks down, suppliers will often attempt to use this as a justification for imposing a prepayment meter. Many suppliers' Codes of Practice say that they will do this if your first payment plan breaks down. You can challenge this, but it will always be more satisfactory if you can make a lasting long-term arrangement in the first instance. (See p49 for when your repayment arrangement breaks down.)

Prepayment Meters (Electricity)

When will a prepayment meter be offered?

Obtaining a prepayment meter when you want one is rarely a problem. You can request one at any time. See Chapter 3 for how to do this.

The Codes of Practice state that prepayment meters will be installed if your payment plan breaks down or if you cannot pay a security deposit. In practice, some suppliers will attempt to install prepayment meters on any customer who is in arrears, or whom it feels might get into arrears. Suppliers may rely on their powers to request a security deposit and to install a prepayment meter as an alternative to a security deposit as a means of imposing prepayment meters on new customers. See p104, Resisting the Imposition of a Prepayment Meter.

When will a prepayment meter be refused?

It is rare for a supplier to refuse to install a prepayment meter. If a prepayment meter is refused against your wishes, you could ask

OFFER to intervene. (See p51 on Choice of Meter and Method of Payment.)

The suppliers say only that a prepayment meter will be fitted where it is safe and practical. The suppliers assume that these requirements refer only to the question as to whether it is physically safe or practical for the meters to be fitted into a premises, and not whether it is safe or practical for a customer to use them. However, if a supplier insisted on imposing a prepayment meter upon a customer who was clearly unable to operate it, it would be in breach of its duty to supply.

10. RATE OF REPAYMENT OF ARREARS

Both gas and electricity suppliers are required to make arrangements for the recovery of debts which take into account your ability to pay.[21] This applies whether you are offered a payment plan or a prepayment meter.[22]

The rate of Fuel Direct deductions is often used as a yardstick to determine the period over which a debt should be repaid within a payment plan or through a prepayment meter. A single fuel debt of £114.40 would be repaid over a year on basic Fuel Direct payments. (This figure is based on repayment rates of £2.20 per week.)

If you receive income support, you may wish to consider the Fuel Direct scheme, but note that this would result in fixed deductions for your arrears. This may not be appropriate if your arrears should be recovered at a lower rate.

Repayments Below Fuel Direct Rates

If your income is low or roughly equivalent to basic income support levels (for example, you receive family credit, housing benefit, or community charge benefit), you should argue that you should not repay your debt at a higher rate than the Fuel Direct rates.

There are many situations where a supplier should accept less than this level of repayment, particularly if your income is less than basic income support levels (for example, you may not be entitled to benefit because you work, but have to pay childcare or mortgage expenses which are not taken into consideration, or your benefit is reduced because of a trade dispute or you are an asylum seeker and therefore receive less income support than other claimants), or if you have multiple debts.

British Gas now says that it is primarily concerned with ensuring that customers pay for their current consumption as the first priority, and that it will accept payments of arrears over extended periods of time at rates which customers can afford to sustain. For customers with multiple debts, British Gas has accepted that gas debts should be treated in the same way as other debts, accepting payments for gas arrears on a pro rata basis alongside other debts to banks, catalogues and so on.[23] Although electricity suppliers have not made an explicit statement to this effect, it is implicit in their licence agreement that they must do the same. If your arrears have built up as a result of successive estimated bills, see also p92.

In practice, electricity suppliers usually seek to recover debts within a year and at rates not below £2.20 per week (the Fuel Direct deduction level), adjusting the period of debt recovery accordingly. If you cannot afford this rate of repayment, you could ask to pay at a lower rate, providing information about your income, necessary outgoings and other debts. If the supplier refuses to accept lower payments, you could ask OFFER to intervene, as a potential breach of Condition 19 of the supplier's licence is an enforcement matter (see p100, above).

Paying For Your Current Consumption

Whatever your rate of debt repayment within a payment plan, you will also have to pay for your estimated current consumption over the year. It is important that this estimate is as accurate as possible, otherwise you may end up paying more than you can afford. Where possible, the estimate should be based on your use of fuel as determined by actual meter readings.

You can check the estimate provided by the supplier either using your own bills or by asking for details of the actual readings of your meter over a past period. Suppliers often have computer records for up to eight quarters. Try to make sure that the readings cover at least a year so that you make allowances for seasonal variations in your consumption. You will need to calculate the number of units of fuel you have used over the period covered by meter readings and then divide by the number of weeks in that period to calculate the number of units you use on average each week. Multiply that figure by the cost of the units of fuel. Then add on the amount of the standing charge for each week.

If you have not been in your property for long, the suppliers' energy efficiency advisers should be able to advise you on the likely size of your bills if you provide them with details of the size of your home, family and the appliances you use.

Once you have joined a payment plan, be careful to ensure that your meter is read every quarter, either by the supplier or by you so that you can check the accuracy of your estimated current consumption.

11. LUMP-SUM REPAYMENTS TOWARDS ARREARS

The Electricity Act 1989 should have brought to an end demands for large sums of money as part-payment towards arrears as a requirement of allowing a customer to pay arrears in instalments. Condition 19 of the supplier's licence specifically provides that suppliers must allow customers in debt who 'can't pay' to pay arrears in instalments, taking into account their ability to pay.

However, for example, London Electricity's Code of Practice contains a clause stating that where it agrees a payment arrangement or to install a prepayment meter, it might require a part-payment towards the debt first.[24] This is clearly contrary to the provisions of Condition 19. A dispute arising from such a request could be referred to OFFER for a decision as a potential enforcement matter.

Similarly, gas suppliers should not demand lump sums from customers in arrears through hardship, though in recent years gas suppliers appear to have abandoned this practice.

12. WHEN YOUR PAYMENT ARRANGEMENT BREAKS DOWN

Gas and electricity suppliers differ in their approaches to the breakdown of repayment arrangements. British Gas states that payment plans are its preferred option for debt repayment.[25] In practice, this means that gas suppliers will often try to negotiate another payment arrangement. However, this practice may change once the 'Quantum' prepayment meter becomes widely available.

Electricity suppliers are not as likely to renegotiate payment arrangements once they have broken down. They have moved much more quickly into the provision of electronic prepayment meters and, particularly in urban areas, may insist on a prepayment meter as the only alternative to disconnection.

Eastern Electricity and London Electricity are among suppliers whose Codes of Practice state that if you do not enter into, or keep to a payment arrangement, the only alternative to disconnection will normally be the installation of a prepayment meter.

If a change of circumstances has occurred which has affected your ability to pay, you could ask the supplier to consider a revised payment arrangement. Both gas and electricity suppliers would be obliged to consider this under the terms of Conditions 12A and 19 respectively. This would apply regardless of what is said in their Codes of Practice. (The provisions within Conditions can be enforced by OFGAS or OFFER in individual cases, in contrast to the provisions within the Codes of Practice.)

If your circumstances have not changed, it may well have been that the level of repayment was too high in the first place. If this is so, you could argue that the original agreement was in breach of Condition 19/12A. You could ask for a revised payment arrangement based on a more detailed picture of your financial circumstances. Otherwise, you may be obliged to accept a prepayment meter as an alternative to disconnection.

In the event of a dispute, ask OFFER/OFGAS to intervene.

13. RESISTING THE IMPOSITION OF A PREPAYMENT METER

The emphasis some electricity suppliers place on attempting to impose prepayment meters on their low-income customers has been a theme discussed in many of the sections above. Some suppliers will often attempt to impose a prepayment meter on new or existing customers in the following circumstances:

- if the supplier decides that a security deposit is required from you because you are a new customer with no previous payment record, or because as an existing customer you have consistently paid your bills late;

- if you claim income support or otherwise have a low income;

- if you have arrears, by refusing to consider you for a payment plan or refusing access to the Fuel Direct scheme or otherwise presenting the prepayment meter as your only option;

- if you have previously had an arrangement to pay arrears in instalments, but you have missed a payment.

Some suppliers have made it extremely difficult for their customers to pay by any other method. Money Advice workers in some areas have reported that suppliers will not consider a payment plan for some customers unless the customer can produce medical evidence that a prepayment meter is unsuitable.

In all of the above situations, OFFER can intervene as regulator of the industry. OFFER can use its powers of enforcement to take action against a supplier who breaches Condition 19 of its licence condition. A supplier will be in breach of Condition 19 if it does not offer customers in arrears access to a payment plan or to the Fuel Direct scheme if the customer claims income support, if a customer has difficulty in paying or has arrears.

OFFER can also take enforcement action against suppliers who systematically ignore the provisions of their own Codes of Practice. In individual cases, OFFER has a duty to make decisions about the reasonableness of the request for security, including the request for a cash security deposit or the imposition of a prepayment meter as an alternative.

In individual cases, it is important to begin by reminding the supplier of its obligations under Conditions 18 and 19 and negotiate for an affordable payment plan in the first instance. Ensuring that a payment plan is affordable will reduce the chance of it failing and avoid more difficult negotiations to reinstate a revised payment plan. Where a supplier is citing the requirement for a security deposit, you may need to make efforts to show that you will be able to manage a payment plan, perhaps by referring to other bills you have successfully managed to pay in instalments, eg, catalogue debts or consumer purchases. If negotiations fail, you should always involve OFFER. If there is sufficient pressure for a change in the supplier's bad practices, OFFER may be forced into action.

If a supplier attempts to impose a prepayment meter on someone who will not be able to operate it, it will be in breach of its duty to supply. Action could be taken against the supplier either by complaining to OFFER or by considering court action. See Chapter 13.

14. MULTIPLE DEBT

Dealing With Multiple Debt

For many people, gas and electricity arrears are just parts of a bigger problem of unpaid bills. It is beyond the scope of this book to give detailed advice about debts other than those for fuel. Often, the best thing to do is to seek advice if you can. This section tells you where you may be able to get advice and outlines what you need to do if you cannot get the advice you need.

It is important to deal with your debt problem as a whole. Do not file your bills in a carrier bag or bury them in a drawer – they won't go away. You may instead risk losing your home, or having your gas and/or electricity cut off, or the bailiffs (in Scotland, Sheriff's Officers) may call to take away your possessions. If you are seeking advice about your fuel debts, you must tell the adviser about your other debts as well or you may not get the best advice.

Where to go for advice

Some places have specialist money advice centres or debt counselling services – sometimes independent, sometimes run by your local council – often by the social services, welfare rights or consumer advice departments. Your local Citizens' Advice Bureau will tell you what is available locally. Some CABx have specialist money advisers themselves.

There is now a national telephone helpline for England and Wales: 'National Debtline': Telephone 021-359 8501 (Birmingham). Advisers will counsel you on the phone, but cannot attend court with you. They produce two 'Do-it-yourself' guides for dealing with multiple debt. One is for people who pay rent, the other for people with mortgages. Both include a very useful sheet to help you work out your own financial statement. You should be careful about running up large phone bills if you are making a long-distance call.

If you are offered advice from anywhere that is not suggested above, make sure that it is free and genuinely independent of your creditors.

You may wish to consult the following publications:

- *The Debt Advice Handbook* – a guide to debt in England and Wales – has been published by the Child Poverty Action Group (CPAG).[26]

- *A Guide to Money Advice in Scotland* has been published by Drumchapel Community Organisations Council in association with CPAG.[27]

Helping yourself

Whether you choose to seek advice or to help yourself, you should gather together the following information and take the following steps:

Stage 1: Work out your income and essential expenditure
Before you can decide what to do with your debts, you need to look at your income and your essential expenditure.

- First, add up all the money you have coming in from wages, benefits, maintenance and any other income every week or month, depending how you get paid. Check that you are receiving all the benefits you should, and that you are not paying too much tax. A local advice agency, Citizens' Advice Bureau or welfare rights service can help you to do this.

- Second, work out what you spend each month on essentials. Ignore any *payments for arrears* at this stage. Include your normal payments for the following items:

  - rent;
  - mortgage and any other loans secured on your home;
  - gas (your average weekly or monthly bill over the last year);
  - electricity (again, your average bill);
  - transport to work;
  - council tax;
  - water (in England);
  - childminding;
  - food;
  - clothing;
  - other housekeeping expenses – eg, newspapers, cigarettes, cleaning materials etc.

Be realistic. Work out what you need to live on over a long period and not over a week. Remember that clothes and other items wear out and need to be replaced.

Do not include even current payments on loans, credit agreements, catalogues.

- When you have done this, take away the total of your expenses from your total income. The difference is what you have available to deal with your debts. If this is nothing, or your expenses are more than your income, seek advice (see p106).

Stage 2: Work out your debts
- Make a list of everything you owe to everyone. Include:

  - arrears of rent/mortgage;
  - arrears of gas/electricity/water/telephone;
  - the total amount owing (not just the arrears) on loans, credit cards, catalogues, credit agreements etc.

- Some debts must take priority because there are serious consequences if you cannot pay them. For most people these are:

- rent, mortgage or secured loan;
- council tax.

If you are in arrears with any of these, contact the people you owe and try to arrange repayments. If you explain your position fully, they will usually allow you a period to pay off your arrears. This will often be one or two years. Sometimes it may be longer – particularly if you are on income support, or your income is very low. If you cannot reach agreements, or if you think you have agreed to something you cannot afford, *seek advice* (see p106).

- Take away the total of what you have to pay on these priority debts from the amount you had available to pay all the debts. If there is nothing left, *seek advice* (see p106).

- Now you have to share out what is left fairly between all the other people you owe money to.

Stage 3: Work out how much to pay your creditors
You now have to share this money between your creditors. The basic rule is, the more money you owe to one creditor, the bigger share they get.

- Add up all your debts (except the priority ones you dealt with at stage one above).

- Next, work out what percentage of your total debt is made up by each individual debt. For example, if your total debt is £2,400 and you owe British Gas £120, the percentage of the total debt owed to British Gas is

$$\frac{£120 \times 100}{£2,400} = 5\%$$

- Now simply take that percentage of the weekly or monthly amount you have available to pay your debts.

In the example above, if you have £15 per month money for debts, you should pay British Gas 5% of that or:

$$£15.00 \times 5\% = £0.75 \text{ a month.}$$

Once you have worked out all these details, you will need to contact all your creditors. They will all need to see your financial statement if they are to understand why you will only be making a small payment to each of them.

Electricity or gas suppliers ought to agree to accept whatever you can afford to pay using this calculation. They may try to argue that they should be priority creditors, but they must accept what you can reasonably afford to pay.[28]

Seek advice in any of the following circumstances:

- you have any difficulty with any of your creditors;

- you have difficulty preparing a financial statement;

- you want to know what legal powers your creditors have – or the ways in which the law protects you.

Administration Orders

Some people with multiple debts can apply to their local county court in England and Wales for an administration order as a way of getting the county court to take over the administration of their debts.[29] This is a little-used, but extremely useful, provision whereby the court will decide how much you can afford to pay to each of your creditors. You make one monthly payment to the court, who will then pay your creditors on your behalf.

In terms of fuel debt, the making of an administration order by a court must be the definitive statement of a tariff customer's ability to pay under Conditions 12A (Gas) or 19 (Electricity). Suppliers who sought to recover arrears outside the terms of the administration order could find themselves in contempt of court.

Suppliers, however, are not used to people putting their debts on to administration orders. You should always contact your supplier in advance to explain your proposed course of action. You will also need to make arrangements to pay for your current supply. The supplier will almost certainly insist that you pay using a method of payment which offers the supplier greater security such as a prepayment meter, Fuel Direct or through a payment plan using direct debit. The supplier will not be permitted to recover *arrears* through any of these methods of payment, since the court will take over the payment of arrears.

Note also that the law on administration orders is changing. A change to the law has been passed, but has not yet taken effect.[30] Applications will in future be open to more people and the details of the effects of the order will be more clearly defined, particularly in relation to fuel suppliers who will be prevented from disconnecting a supply without the permission of the court.

To be able to obtain an administration order under the current rules:

- you must have a county court judgment against you;
- the total of your debts must be less than £5,000 (excluding your mortgage if you have one.

To apply for an administration order, you need to obtain form N92 from your local county court. When you have completed the form, you need to take it back to the court, where you have to swear that the contents of the form are correct. The court will then contact all the creditors on the list and either make the agreement or arrange a private hearing with a district judge to consider your application.

Advantages of an administration order:

- The order usually runs for a period of three years. (This may vary in some courts.) Provided you have paid your monthly payments, the rest of the debt is written off at the end of this period.
- Interest is frozen on accounts.
- Your creditors cannot chase you or take other court action against you while the order runs.
- You have to make only one payment each month. The court divides it up and pays it to your creditors.

Disadvantages:

- Your name will appear on a register of court orders and you will find it hard to obtain credit. Although it is not illegal to take on more credit while you have an administration order, the court will expect you to sort out your existing mess before you start another one.

If you think you could be helped by an administration order, seek advice from one of the places suggested in the section above or ask your local county court staff for help.

CHAPTER SEVEN

Disconnection for Arrears

This chapter covers:

I. WHEN CAN YOU BE DISCONNECTED FOR ARREARS?

Electricity

An electricity supplier may disconnect your supply if you have not paid all 'charges due' (see below) in respect of your electricity supply[1] within 20 working days after the date of the bill or other written request to pay.[2] You must be given at least a further two working days' written notice of the intention to disconnect,[3] and cannot be disconnected for any amount which is *'genuinely in dispute'*.[4] Charges due includes any amounts for the electricity supply, standing charges, meter provision or the provision of electrical line or plant.[5] It does not include:

- other charges such as those for credit sale agreements;

- charges for altering the position of a meter or replacing a meter with a specially adapted meter when either of these changes was made by the supplier to meet the needs of a person with disabilities.[6]

Note: 'charges due' can only be properly established on the basis of a meter reading. Estimates cannot be used, and you should not be disconnected on the basis of an estimated bill. However, you must ensure you pay the amount actually due, otherwise disconnection may take place. The supply can be cut off at the premises to which the bill relates or to any other premises which you occupy.[7] Failure to give the required notice of disconnection is an enforcement matter and OFFER should be asked to intervene.

Gas

Gas suppliers may disconnect if you have not paid any 'charges due' (see below) for gas within 28 days of the date of the bill or other written demand for payment.[8] You are entitled to a further seven days' notice in writing of the intention to disconnect.[9] This will usually be given in the final demand. A gas supplier is not entitled to disconnect your supply for any amount which is *'genuinely in dispute'*.[10]

Charges due are any charges in respect of the supply of gas, or the supply and fixing of any meter or fittings. Disconnection must be at the premises to which the supply relates.[11] If you leave arrears at a previous address, the gas supplier may refuse to connect your supply at your new address until the arrears have been paid.[12] Failure to give the required notice of disconnection is an enforcement matter and OFGAS should be asked to intervene.

2. DISCONNECTION WHEN YOU PAY IN INSTALMENTS

Electricity

If you have an arrangement to pay in instalments, either for your current supply only or for your current supply plus an amount for arrears, the electricity supplier is not entitled to disconnect for arrears while you keep to the terms of your agreement, since you are paying the amounts requested in writing.[13] If you miss a payment, the supplier will be entitled to disconnect for arrears 20 working days after the date of your missed payment, but only if there are still charges due (see above), and subject to having given you two working days' notice of the intention to disconnect. If your account is in credit, based on a reading of your meter and allowing for any standing and other charges, the supplier is not entitled to disconnect.

Gas

As with electricity, a gas supplier is not entitled to disconnect if you keep to an agreement for paying your current fuel costs and/or arrears in instalments. If you break the agreement, the supplier is entitled to disconnect after 28 days, providing you have been given seven days' notice of the intention to disconnect.

Electricity and gas

If the breakdown of your arrangement to pay in instalments has occurred because you cannot afford to pay, you may be able to arrange another payment plan and, in any event, the supplier must offer you a prepayment meter as an alternative to disconnection, providing this is safe and practical (see p114, below).[14]

3. PROTECTION FROM DISCONNECTION

The following provisions may prevent disconnection in certain circumstances:

- If you are having difficulty paying your electricity bill, Condition 19 of the Licence and the Codes of Practice may offer some protection.
- If you are having difficulty paying your gas bill, Condition 12A of the British Gas Authorisation, the Principles for the Collection of Domestic Gas Debt and the Code of Practice may offer some protection.
- If you claim income support, you should also look at the Joint Statement of Intent on the Direct Payment of Fuel (see Appendix 5).
- If you dispute that the supplier is entitled to disconnect, see p121 below.
- Note that local councils can help with paying tenants' bills (see pp165-167).

4. CONDITION 12A AND CONDITION 19

If you are threatened with disconnection because you cannot pay your bill, Condition 12A of the Authorisation to British Gas and Condition 19 of the electricity supplier's Licence give you the following rights:

- You are entitled to a payment arrangement to repay your arrears at a rate you can afford.

- If you have not been able to manage a payment arrangement, you must be offered a prepayment meter (if safe and practicable) as an alternative to disconnection. The meter must be set to recover arrears at a rate which you can afford.

The suppliers are obliged to develop 'methods' for dealing with customers in arrears under the terms of these conditions. The 'methods' set out the procedures which should be followed by each supplier. They provide the practical mechanism for the protection of the rights set out above. Any departure from the 'methods' may constitute a breach of Condition 12A and Condition 19 and could be referred to OFFER/OFGAS for investigation as a potential enforcement matter.

5. CODES OF PRACTICE

Suppliers are obliged to publish Codes of Practice which set out their policy on dealing with customers in arrears and situations where they will or will not disconnect. These codes cannot be directly enforced in individual cases. Sometimes they contain provisions which are contrary to your rights under Condition 12A (gas) or Condition 19 (electricity). In these situations, the Codes of Practice cannot override your rights. Otherwise, the Codes of Practice are a useful guide to what actually happens when disconnection is threatened. All suppliers offer a limited moratorium on disconnection for certain groups of people, often for particular times of year only. Codes of Practice will also advise you of when disconnection can be delayed by you taking action to help yourself. For example, all the Codes of Practice say that if you contact the Benefits Agency or social services for help with dealing with the problem, the supplier will delay disconnection, typically for 14 or 21 days. You must tell the supplier what you are doing.

Examples of some provisions within the Codes of Practice which offer some protection if you are threatened with disconnection are given below. You should obtain a copy of your own supplier's Code of Practice as they do vary.

Codes of Practice (Gas)

The gas Code of Practice states that a gas supply will not be cut off if:

- you agree and keep to a payment arrangement for your gas and pay off the debt by instalments at a rate which you can manage;

- it is safe and practical to install a prepayment meter. This will be set to collect the debt at a rate which takes into account what you tell the gas supplier about your circumstances and ability to pay;

- they know that all the people in the house who have incomes are over retirement age, in which case the supply will not be cut off between 1 October and 31 March. This will not apply if you can pay but have not paid. In these cases the supply may not be reconnected for the following winter.

- the supply is in the name of a past customer. You must have made proper arrangements to take over the supply.

- there is no adult at home, unless you have been given a warning that you will be disconnected on or after a particular date. The supplier will obtain an entry warrant if they need to enter your home. (Note that this does not mean you will not be disconnected if you have young children);

- the debt is only for credit sale or hire purchase. The supply can only be cut off if you are in debt for gas.

Codes of Practice (Electricity)

Midland Electricity

Midland Electricity's Code of Practice is just one example of the electricity suppliers' codes. It is essential that you obtain a copy of your local supplier's code as they do vary. Midland Electricity states that your electricity supply will not be cut off if:

- you have a prepayment meter fitted (although they might ask you to pay part of the debt first);

- you agree to and keep to a payment arrangement to pay off the debt by instalments over a reasonable time;

- they know that all the people in your home get a state pension or are severely sick, in which case they will not cut off your supply between 1 October and 31 March. They will cut off your supply after 31 March if they have not been able to agree a payment arrangement with you;

- the debt you owe is not for electricity – eg, it is for an appliance bought from their shops. Any money you pay towards a bill which is only partly for an electricity bill will be first set against the electricity bill. They may take you to court to collect debts that are not for electricity;

• the debt belongs to the person who lived in your home before you.

Note: Condition 19 gives you more rights than this Code of Practice implies. You are not obliged to make part-payments towards arrears if you cannot afford to pay your bill. (See p103 for more information about lump-sum payments.) You must be offered a payment plan as a first option before being asked to accept a prepayment meter. Payment plans cannot impose an upper time limit on when the arrears should be paid back: they can only recover arrears at a rate that you can afford.

London Electricity

London Electricity's Code of Practice says that your supply will not be cut off if:

• you agree to a payment arrangement to clear the debt by instalments within a reasonable period at a rate which you can manage, while also covering the cost of your ongoing use of electricity;

• you have a prepayment meter installed (where this is safe and practicable). The meter will normally be an electronic prepayment meter and will be set to collect your debt at a rate which takes account of your circumstances and ability to pay;

• they know that all the people in the house are of pensionable age or severely sick, in which case your supply will not be cut off between 1 October and 31 March. This will not apply if you could pay, but have not paid;

• your debt is not owed for the supply of electricity (eg, it is for an appliance bought from their shop);

• the person (or persons) to whom the electricity bills are addressed is no longer responsible for the supply and someone else has properly accepted responsibility for it.

6. PREVENTING DISCONNECTION

There are overwhelming reasons why you should always try to prevent disconnection from occurring:

• You cannot solve a debt problem by being disconnected. The supplier will still want the money you owe and will take court action to get it. You will also be charged the costs of disconnecting the supply.

- If you later want your supply reconnected, you will have to pay any arrears still owing, plus the costs of reconnecting the supply.

- If the supplier has had to get a magistrate's warrant (or JP's or Sheriff's warrant in Scotland) to disconnect your supply, you will also have to pay the costs of obtaining the warrant.

- You may have to pay a security deposit as a condition of being supplied following the disconnection.

It is always preferable to deal with your problems sooner rather than later. You are more likely to be able to obtain a solution which genuinely meets your needs if you have time to think about your own proposals to the supplier, or what the supplier is prepared to offer you. If you delay resolving the problem to the point of disconnection, you will be negotiating under far more stressful conditions and may find yourself agreeing to something inappropriate or undesirable. For example, electricity suppliers in particular are very keen to impose electronic prepayment meters, often without offering a payment plan first.

You will normally be able to prevent disconnection if:
- you contact the supplier;

- you arrange to pay your arrears at a rate you can afford;

- you ask the Benefits Agency to include you in the Fuel Direct scheme (a system of direct payments from your income support – see pp42-51);

- as a last resort, you agree to accept a prepayment meter set to collect the arrears at a rate you can afford.

See Chapter 6 for how to negotiate a payment plan you can genuinely afford, if you feel you are being pushed into agreeing to a payment plan which is unaffordable for you or if you want to resist the imposition of a prepayment meter.

All suppliers say that disconnection is seen as a last resort. Some suppliers will routinely install a prepayment meter rather than completely disconnect a supply. In practice, disconnection most often occurs where there has been no contact between the customer and the supplier. Once you contact the supplier, the supplier is obliged to consider your situation and to look for a suitable way for your supply to continue and for you to repay your arrears at a rate you can afford. The Codes of Practice usually make some provision for disconnection to be delayed if you tell the supplier that you are going to ask the

Benefits Agency or social services (social work in Scotland) for help with the bill.

Disconnection is usually delayed for a certain number of days to enable the Benefits Agency or social services to consider whether they can help you. The time allowed varies between suppliers, so you will need to consult your suppliers' Code of Practice.

However, here are some examples:

- MANWEB's Code of Practice tells you to let MANWEB know if you are going to contact social services or the Benefits Agency. MANWEB will also contact them on your behalf. It says it will not cut off your electricity for at least 15 working days after your case has been referred to the Benefits Agency or social services. This period may be longer if MANWEB is still investigating your case.

- Northern Electricity and Seeboard allow you 10 working days.

- British Gas allows 21 days.

7. AT THE POINT OF DISCONNECTION

The Supplier's Right to Enter Your Premises

Suppliers may, with your consent, enter your premises to disconnect your supply providing they have served you with the correct notice of disconnection (see p111 and Chapter 9). If you do not consent, the supplier must obtain a warrant from the magistrate's court (or Sheriff Court in Scotland).[15] The costs of the warrant will be added to your bill. In some cases, the supplier will disconnect your supply from outside – which makes reconnection extremely expensive. The premises must be left no less secure than they were before entry. Any damage caused by legally gaining entry must be made good or compensation paid. If the supplier failed to secure your premises and your possessions were stolen as a result, you will be able to sue the supplier. Suppliers sometimes change locks and leave a note telling you to pick up a key from the showroom. There has been at least one case of compensation for overnight expenses resulting from this.

Disconnecting External Meters

A warrant is not required for the disconnection of an external meter. Disconnection will be lawful providing that the correct notices have been given (see p111 for details of notice required).

Last-Minute Negotiations

If the supplier agrees not to disconnect at the last minute, but an official turns up to carry out the disconnection, the disconnection should not be agreed to and the disconnector should be asked to telephone the supplier's office. The difficulty here is that suppliers cannot usually contact their vans during the day. Many suppliers will accept payment on the doorstep, but some will make an extra charge to cover their expenses. Some routinely carry prepayment meters with them and will offer you one as an alternative, even at this late stage. If you accept the meter, you will need to check that it has been set to collect arrears at a rate you can afford. If it has not, you should ask the supplier to change the setting. Do not be put off by such folklore as 'it can't be changed' or 'it is set at the factory'. This is not the case. If in doubt, seek legal advice and contact OFFER/OFGAS.

If you refuse to allow entry, the supplier will have to obtain a warrant or may disconnect from the road. This will involve you in more cost, unless you are able to negotiate keeping your supply and paying off the arrears at a rate you can afford in the meantime (see Chapter 6).

8. GETTING YOUR SUPPLY RECONNECTED

Your Rights

Electricity suppliers must reconnect the electricity supply within two working days of you paying the expenses of disconnection and reconnection and any security deposit.[16]

This also applies if you have been able to reach an agreement with the supplier to pay off the arrears in instalments as a condition of being reconnected.

In the event of unnecessary delays, either you or OFFER may force an electricity supplier to reconnect your supply within the time limit, for example, by obtaining an injunction or interdict in civil proceedings.[17] Any individual affected by the failure to restore a supply would also be entitled to bring civil proceedings for damages against the electricity supplier. The supplier will have a defence if it can prove that it took all reasonable steps and exercised all due diligence to avoid failing to reconnect within the time limit.

Gas suppliers must reconnect your supply once you have paid the expenses of reconnection.[18] A gas supplier is also entitled to recover from you the expenses of disconnection.[19] In practice, your gas supply will not be reconnected unless the costs of both disconnection and reconnection are paid. Your supply should be reconnected within a 'reasonable time'. This also applies if you can reach an agreement with the supplier to pay the arrears in instalments.

Failure to reconnect your gas supply within a 'reasonable period' can be dealt with by OFGAS (see p18 for your right to a supply, and Chapter 13 for legal remedies).

In practice, if you agree to accept an electronic prepayment meter reset to collect the arrears, the supplier will reconnect your supply. You may have to pay the expenses of reconnection separately but usually they will be added to your arrears.

If You Do Not Want Your Supply Reconnected

The supplier will continue to submit bills regardless of whether or not you want your supply reconnected. If you do not pay, it will usually seek recovery of the debt through the small claims court.

Assuming you are liable for the bill, you should try to negotiate payment in instalments prior to any court action. Otherwise, if the supplier has a summons issued, you should respond to the summons – providing a statement of your financial circumstances – and ask to pay in instalments. In these circumstances, the court will usually order payment in instalments. If the court has made an order for payment of the whole debt at once, you could apply to the court to have the order varied to payments in instalments. You do not have to pay any costs for applying to have the order changed. The court will not order you to pay an amount you cannot afford – even if you can only afford £1 or £2 a month. You would not be liable for the supplier's legal costs if you lost in the small claims court.

In Scotland, you can apply for a 'Time to Pay' Direction before a decree (court order). If you break this arrangement by allowing three instalments to pass unpaid, you will lose the right to pay by instalments. If you allow a decree to pass without defending or seeking time to pay, then you will have to wait until the supplier seeks to enforce the decree before you can ask for a 'Time to Pay' order. You will be liable for up to a maximum of £75 of the supplier's legal costs if you lose your case, but only if the debt is over £200.

The Costs of Disconnection and Reconnection

Charges for disconnection and reconnection must be 'reasonable' and must reflect the actual costs involved.[20] Charges vary between suppliers. For example:

Midlands Electricity charges   £
  disconnection with customer's consent – fixed charge   25.25
  warrant obtained, but customer allows
  disconnection   60.00
  warrant issued and executed   91.00
  call out charge where customer pays on the
  doorstep   8.25
  where warrant has been issued, but customer pays
  on the doorstep   24.25
  service disconnection, ie, digging up the road   *from* 276.50

East Midland Electricity charges
  'voluntary' disconnection – eg, if a customer
  requests disconnection of an empty house   15.00
  disconnection with customer's consent   30.30
  disconnection where a warrant has been issued   67.00
  service disconnection – fixed charge   161.00

These charges all include the cost of reconnection. In practice, there are no separate charges for reconnection.

9. DISPUTES: UNLAWFUL DISCONNECTION

If you dispute that the gas or electricity supplier is entitled to disconnect, you could ask OFFER/OFGAS to intervene. They can order the supplier to connect or continue your supply pending a decision on your dispute.

Unlawful disconnection of either a gas or electricity supply is an enforcement matter. Suppliers may be forced to comply with the law by an order from OFFER or OFGAS respectively. If the supplier ignores the order, either you or OFFER/OFGAS can apply for a court order to enforce the order (see Appendix 7).

Clearly, if disconnection was unlawful, you cannot be required to pay the costs of disconnection or reconnection.

Theft and Tampering

This chapter covers:

I. INTRODUCTION

Unlike other goods, gas and electricity are delivered to you without the supplier being present. Suppliers cannot see what you are doing with their meter or with the fuel they have supplied. This makes suppliers vulnerable to theft. And, perhaps because of this vulnerability, suppliers sometimes make allegations of theft on quite flimsy evidence. The consequences of such allegations against you can be severe, as a supplier has the power to 'punish' you by disconnecting the supply without having to go to court to prove the allegations first.

Theft from or tampering with a meter are both criminal offences and can result in both criminal prosecution and civil proceedings. However, it is important to realise that not in every case of tampering will you necessarily have to pay for damage or alleged stolen fuel.

If a consumer is legally liable for the theft or tampering, a supplier may be entitled to disconnect the supply, although this right does not follow automatically from liability (see p116).

British Gas has a detailed policy on procedures to deal with theft and tampering. It has produced a summary of this for advice agencies which is reproduced in Appendix 4. For detailed examination of the legal issues, OFGAS has produced two very helpful papers entitled 'Disconnection of supply on grounds of injury to or interference with gas meters' and 'Liability of tariff customers for money stolen from prepayment meters'.[1] OFFER's view is set out in its Determination s23/c/001(B). (Determinations are explained on p183.)

2. TAMPERING WITH A METER

Evidence of Tampering

Since a supply of gas or electricity is charged for on the basis of metered consumption, the most obvious unlawful method of reducing a potential fuel bill is to interfere with a meter to prevent it registering or to reduce the amount it has registered. There is a variety of possible techniques, including fixing wires or pipes to bypass a meter, using a wire to inhibit the rotation of the disc or making the meter run backwards so that recorded consumption apparently diminishes. There arc tell-tale signs on a meter that has been tampered with – eg, the seals are cut or missing, the casing is cracked or badly scratched or a small hole has been drilled in the side. These descriptions are included not as a guide to people who might want to try it, but for advisers who may have no idea what tampering involves or how to tell if a meter has been interfered with.

However, never simply assume that an allegation of tampering is correct, whatever technical evidence is quoted by the supplier. The evidence is not always clear cut and the supplier's experts do not always get it right. You can get your own expert (listed under 'Electrical Engineers' and 'Gas Engineers' in the *Yellow Pages*) to examine the meter for an objective assessment. Where appropriate, legal aid can be used to cover the cost.

Meter tampering will not always be seen when the meter is read in the normal way. The meter reader may not be trained for detection and is only there for a short time. Holes or cracks may be on the far side of the meter in a dark cupboard and so difficult for anyone to spot.

Theft due to tampering can be detected by unusual patterns of consumption – eg, if the bills suddenly go down or if they go up after the installation of a new meter. A meter examiner employed by the supplier will then come to look at the meter. Sometimes, they will be accompanied by the police; they would normally come with a colleague to assist them. If they detect signs of tampering, the meter will be removed and the supply disconnected as a result. If they cannot detect any evidence there and then, the meter will normally be taken away for further examination, but a replacement will be left so that the supply is not disconnected straight away.

Examining the Evidence

If a supplier alleges that a meter has been tampered with, there are two key areas to consider:

- You must establish what method of tampering is being alleged. In some cases it will be obvious that the only explanation for damage to a meter is tampering (eg, a hole drilled in the meter casing with a wire inserted). In other cases there may be alternative explanations (eg, if meter seals are missing, it may be that these are company seals which were never put on, or were removed by the supplier but not replaced, or have been removed by electricians rewiring a house).

  Note: Electricity meters have two sorts of seals: Prescribed Copper Seals (PCS seals) and company seals. PCS seals are put on a meter by or on behalf of OFFER at the time when the meter is originally certified – some meters still have ESMA seals (Electricity Supply (Meters) Act seals) but PCS seals have been used for all new meters in the last ten years. Company seals are put on the meter by the supplier. Although, in theory, electricity meters should have no seals missing, suppliers carrying out wiring work or installing meters commonly leave off a number of company seals. So, if company seals are the only ones missing, that in itself is weak evidence of tampering.

- You must investigate whether the supplier has evidence that it was you, and not someone else, who tampered with the meter. Usually, the supplier will not know who did the tampering. If that is the case, the action they can take is considerably more limited than if they have direct evidence against the consumer. It will help if you can explain why it has been tampered with – for example, you know that the meter was taken over from a previous occupier who had tampered with it, or that it was damaged by builders.

Examining the Law

As well as looking at the evidence, if a supplier alleges that the consumer is liable for theft or tampering, it is important to find out which legal provision they are relying on. This is because different considerations apply when dealing with different parts of the law. Normally the supplier will point to particular provisions in the Gas Act or Electricity Act, as appropriate, but liability can also arise under general common law principles.

General legal principles

In England and Wales, when you receive or take on a meter, you become 'bailee' of it. A bailee is under a duty to take 'reasonable care' of bailed property (in this case, a meter). For example, if you leave your home unlocked and a thief breaks open a coin meter, damaging it and removing its contents, you may well be liable to pay compensation for failing to take reasonable care.[2] There is no definition of 'reasonable'.

In Scotland, 'bailment' does not apply, but the concept of 'restitution' may be used – ie, if you are in possession of goods which do not belong to you, you are under an obligation to look after them until the owner returns for them.

Of course, if you intentionally damaged a meter, you would be liable to pay compensation to the supplier. The supplier can sue you, or you may be prosecuted for criminal damage which is an imprisonable offence. On conviction, the court can order the offender to pay compensation to the supplier.

Responsibility for meters under the Gas Act and Electricity Act

If a consumer requires it, a supplier must provide a meter. The supplier can sell it, lend it or hire it out.[3] If you own the meter you must keep it in proper order for correctly registering the quantity of gas or electricity supplied. This must be done at your own expense and failure can lead to disconnection.[4] However, in most cases the meter has been hired or loaned and, under these circumstances, the meter is the supplier's responsibility.[5]

If you hire the meter then you may have to enter into a hire agreement with the supplier. Suppliers have no powers to impose conditions concerning the care of the meter in such an agreement other than what is allowed under the Acts.

There are three specific meter offences under the Acts, each punishable by a fine of up to £1,000 on present court scales:

- damaging or allowing damage to any meter, gas fitting or electrical plant or line;[6]
- altering the meter index or register by which consumption is measured;[7]
- preventing the meter from registering properly.[8]

In each case, the offence can only have been committed if the act was done 'intentionally or by culpable negligence' – ie, if it was the alleged offender's fault.

If you are prosecuted for either of the latter two offences, possession of artificial means for altering the way the meter is registering will be taken as *prima facie* evidence that the alteration was caused by you.[9] If such artificial means are not found, a conviction would be difficult to obtain, especially if the case concerns a house in multiple occupation or where there has been a burglary.

Note: Always check any claim by a supplier against the actual law rather than its own documents. Most documents issued by the suppliers to explain these provisions to the consumer paraphrase them, sometimes in a way which comes close to rewriting them in the supplier's favour. Some suppliers still try to impose an additional condition in their standard 'Terms and Conditions of Supply' which attempts to make consumers responsible for meter damage however it arose and whoever's fault it was – this will not be binding by itself unless it is a proper part of a 'special agreement' (see p14).[10]

3. THEFT OF CONTENTS OF A COIN METER

Prepayment coin meters are on their way out as new technology provides alternatives which the suppliers prefer and which are often better for consumers. However, there are still many around. They have some advantages over other meters but are also obvious targets for burglars.

If your coin meter is broken into, you have two problems:

- convincing the supplier that you were not responsible for the theft;

- the supplier may try to get you to pay for damage to the meter, and for the contents of the meter.

Consumer Liability

There are a few points you should note concerning possible liability for theft of coins from a meter:

- Once a coin has been placed in a prepayment meter, payment has been made to the supplier.[11]

- Unless there has been negligence or deliberate damage by the consumer, the risk of storing the coins in the meter is borne by the supplier (or the landlord if it is a landlord's meter).

- The consumer is the 'bailee' of the coins, with a duty to take reasonable care of them; or, in Scotland, may have a duty to take reasonable care of them under the principle of 'restitution'.

- If there is a burglary and you had taken reasonable care (eg, by locking all the doors and windows), the supplier bears any loss.[12]

As with tampering, if money is demanded by the supplier following a break-in to a coin meter, you should:

- find out what argument the supplier is using to claim liability;

- eliminate allegations that the consumer stole the contents by asking the supplier what evidence there is of the consumer's involvement, and also by reporting the theft to the police.

As well as specific offences related to tampering (see p125), anyone who breaks into a coin meter will be guilty of criminal damage[13] and theft.[14] On conviction, the court can order compensation to be paid to the supplier. Prosecutions are unusual because it has to be proved beyond reasonable doubt that the particular individual charged committed the offence, and it is normally easier for the supplier to try to rely on its other powers to recover money. Also, British Gas states in its policy on theft and tampering that it regards prosecutions as a matter for other authorities such as the police and it is only concerned with the security and safety of the gas supply (see Appendix 4).

Suppliers' Policies

Regardless of the legal position, suppliers may have policies, including those set out in their Codes of Practice, or staff guidelines which are more generous than the minimum provisions of the law. Some of these are not published in order that they cannot be taken advantage of dishonestly, but it is always worth checking the policies of your local electricity supplier or gas region. Also, see Appendix 4 for British Gas' policy on meter tampering.

Insurance

Some household insurance policies cover against theft from prepayment meters, though many insurance companies are reluctant to offer such policies. Age Concern offers an insurance policy for people aged 60 or over which includes cover for such theft. Contact Age Concern Insurance Services for details (see Appendix 10).

4. THEFT OF FUEL

Theft of gas and dishonest use or 'abstraction' of electricity are criminal offences.[15] Penalties include fines or imprisonment. You can be convicted of theft even if there is no damage or evidence of interference with a meter.[16] However, as with tampering, suppliers are more likely to recover the value of the stolen fuel by other means – ie, by threatening disconnection.

Accuracy of Meter and Estimates of Stolen Fuel

In cases of alleged tampering or theft of fuel, suppliers will try to recover the cost of fuel stolen by estimating the consumption during the period of tampering or theft. This often leads to a dispute about whether a meter has recorded consumption accurately or not. If you disagree with the supplier about whether a meter is recording consumption properly, either of you can refer the matter for consideration by a meter examiner (see p83).

If the consumption of fuel has been under-recorded, whether because of tampering or otherwise, extra charges will be due. Suppliers will claim that, since the meter has been tampered with, consumption must be estimated – and they often come up with extremely high estimates. If you dispute an estimate and want to challenge it, you should ask the supplier how the estimate was made and on what assumptions. *Just because a meter has been tampered with does not necessarily mean that fuel was successfully stolen – it is still up to the supplier to prove that it was.*

There are various ways in which suppliers estimate consumption. One measure is to compare your consumption during the period of tampering with your normal rate of consumption, either before the meter was tampered with or after its replacement. The comparison should be over a period of at least a year, as consumption tends to increase in winter.

This method may not be appropriate for you – because, for example, your pattern of consumption has changed, or you have recently moved home, or because the supplier claims tampering began after the meter was last read or inspected. There is another method based on the number and type of appliances which you use. Suppliers make assumptions about the running costs of appliances and how often you use them and then calculate the level of consumption in accordance with those assumptions. You should look at these assumptions critically to see if they bear any relationship to actual usage. Suppliers sometimes assume the existence of appliances which you do not actually have or assume that you use the appliances you do have for maximum periods of time and at maximum settings.

If a meter examiner has been called in, she/he will decide the amount of extra fuel charge. You can get your own electrical expert (listed under 'Electrical Engineers' and 'Gas Engineers' in the *Yellow Pages*) to make an independent assessment for you – if appropriate, legal aid can be used to cover the cost. See Chapter 13 for other methods of solving disputes on charges.

Inspection of Meters

In cases of alleged tampering or theft of fuel, suppliers often remove meters quickly. Each supplier must state in its relevant Code of Practice the minimum length of time it will keep a damaged meter. In the event of legal action, you will need to be able to have your own expert to inspect the meter, so check that the meter is being retained correctly and, if necessary, quote the supplier's own Code of Practice (see Chapters 1 and 13 on Codes of Practice).

5. DISCONTINUING THE SUPPLY BECAUSE OF METER DAMAGE

If a supplier alleges theft or tampering, as well as holding you liable for damage to the meter or any financial loss, it will also want to disconnect the supply until you make arrangements to pay for that loss. See Appendix 4 for British Gas' policy in these circumstances.

However, disconnection powers arise under a number of different provisions and it is useful to find out which power it is relying on; each power has its own limitations and it is important to make sure they are not exceeded. In particular, the powers to disconnect for damage to or tampering with a meter are different from the power to disconnect for arrears. For instance, notice must be given before disconnection takes place (see Chapter 7) but not in tampering cases on the basis that the tamperer could be forewarned to get rid of the evidence. See Chapter 9 for the supplier's rights to enter your home in order to carry out the disconnection.

Note: A supplier may claim to be able to disconnect on the basis that money is owed for the damage to the meter, and that this constitutes arrears for which the general power to disconnect can be used, in the same way as if an ordinary quarterly bill was unpaid. This argument is wrong. Firstly, this power can only be used in respect of the actual supply of gas or electricity; and secondly, you only have to pay for damage to a meter if it is specifically your responsibility under the legal provisions discussed on p125.

Specific Powers of Disconnection

There are three specific meter offences under the Electricity and Gas Acts which are discussed above on p125. If any of the offences are committed in respect of a gas meter or fitting, then the supplier can only disconnect the supply of the particular person who has committed the offence.[17] This is also the case with the first listed offence of damaging an electricity meter or electrical line or plant.[18]

However, if anyone tampers with an electricity meter so as to commit one of the latter two listed offences, then the supplier can disconnect the supply from the premises regardless of whether the person who committed the offence is the tariff customer and whether or not other users of electricity live there.[19]

The suppliers' rights to enter your home in order to disconnect the supply are dealt with in Chapter 9. However, it is worth pointing out here that gas suppliers do not have the right to enter to disconnect for theft or tampering unless they have given 24 hours' notice or have a warrant from a magistrate or, in Scotland, also a Sheriff or justice of the peace.[20]

To get a criminal conviction, it must be proved beyond all reasonable doubt that an offence has been committed. However, to exercise the power to discontinue the supply, the supplier need only be able to prove it on the balance of probabilities (ie, more likely than not). There does not have to be an actual conviction of anyone before the power to disconnect can be used.[21]

The supplier can only discontinue the supply until the matter has been remedied.[22] In the case of tampering with a meter, this includes paying for the cost of any damage to the meter and for any stolen fuel, but the two should be treated separately. Obviously tampering is normally done in order to reduce the fuel bill, which amounts to theft. However, if a meter has been damaged, that does not necessarily mean any fuel has successfully been stolen and proof of damage is no proof that any money is owing to the supplier in respect of fuel. (It has been known for tampering to go wrong so that the meter actually registered a *higher* consumption.) Therefore, unless the supplier can show that, on the balance of probabilities, the damage in question caused financial loss other than the cost of replacing the meter, then the matter will be remedied once that cost has been met.

Often the supplier will assess an amount of fuel which it reckons has been stolen, and will also demand payment for that before it reconnects. It can only do this if it can prove that there was a theft, and that it was caused by the particular damage in question[23] – see pp81 and 128.

If the supplier can prove that fuel has been stolen, and can justify its assessment of its value, then it can disconnect for non-payment.[24] However, suppliers cannot use this power if the amount charged is 'genuinely in dispute' (see p81 and Chapter 7).[25]

Disconnections for Safety Reasons

Both gas and electricity suppliers have powers to disconnect your supply for safety reasons. A tampered meter can be in an unsafe condition (although not always, as with a meter which is simply missing its seals).

Electricity suppliers can disconnect your supply if they are not satisfied that your meter and wiring are set up and used so as to prevent danger and not to interfere with the supplier's system or anybody else's electricity supply.[26]

Gas suppliers have similar powers for 'averting danger to life or property'.[27]

Suppliers do not have to give notice for disconnection in emergencies. Electricity suppliers must send you a written notice as soon as they can, telling you the reason for the disconnection.[28] If you think the disconnection should not have been carried out, you can apply to OFFER for a decision on the dispute (see Chapter 13).

Gas suppliers must send you a written notice within five days of the disconnection, telling you the nature of the defect, the danger involved and what action has been taken.[29] If you want to object, you have 21 days to appeal to the Secretary of State for Trade and Industry against the disconnection.[30] The meter stays disconnected until the fault is remedied or the appeal is successful.[31] Reconnection without the consent of the appropriate authorities is otherwise a criminal offence.[32]

When the supply is disconnected for safety reasons, a supplier may provide alternative appliances – eg, electric heaters and cookers – although this is unlikely if they think tampering is involved.

Up to once a year, British Gas will provide a free gas safety check for installations and appliances for some customers. The check includes a basic examination and minor work. If any additional work is necessary there may be a charge. To qualify, you must request the free safety check yourself, and you must:

- be over 60, registered disabled, or in receipt of invalidity benefit, severe disablement allowance, mobility allowance, disability living allowance, disablement benefit or income support with a disability premium; *and*

- live alone or with a person who also qualifies.

6. REMOVAL OF METERS

Suppliers have powers to remove, inspect and re-install meters.[33] These powers may be exercised when tampering is suspected, as well as the powers discussed in this chapter. Suppliers must install a replacement meter of the same type and so leave the supply connected on the same terms as before unless they are exercising powers to disconnect the supply itself.

However, if gas or electricity is unpaid for, the supplier can disconnect supply by whatever means it thinks fit. This includes removing the meter without replacing it. But seven days' notice must be given by a gas supplier,[34] and two days' notice by an electricity supplier.[35] This notice is usually given in the 'final demand'.

CHAPTER NINE

Rights of Entry

This chapter covers:

1. Entering your home (see below)
2. Right of entry with a warrant (see p134)

The Gas Act 1986 and the Electricity Act 1989 give suppliers certain rights to enter your home. These rights can only be exercised if:[1]

- you consent; *or*
- the supplier obtains a warrant from a magistrates' court (in Scotland the Sheriff Court, a justice of the peace or a magistrate); *or*
- there is an emergency.

1. ENTERING YOUR HOME

Suppliers have the right to enter your home:

- to inspect fittings or to read the meter[2] – no advance notice has to be given;
- to remove, inspect or re-install a meter[3] – electricity suppliers must give two working days' notice;[4]
- to discontinue supply or remove a meter under their powers in connection with theft and tampering (see Chapter 8)[5] – gas suppliers must give 24 hours' notice;[6]
- to discontinue supply or remove a meter where they are no longer wanted[7] – electricity suppliers must give one working day's notice and gas suppliers 24 hours' notice;
- to replace, repair or alter pipes, lines or plant[8] – electricity suppliers must give five working days' notice (unless it is an emergency, in which case notice must be given as soon as possible afterwards[9]) and gas suppliers seven days' notice.

Any notice which has to be given should be in writing and can be served by sending it by post, sticking it through the letter-box or attaching it to any obvious part of the premises.[10] Once any required notice has been given, suppliers may use these rights at any reasonable time. There is no definition of 'reasonable' but it probably means at reasonable times of the day – ie, not late at night.

Suppliers do not have the power to inspect or read the meter if you have written to them asking for the supply to be disconnected and this has not been done within a reasonable time.[11]

Gas suppliers also have the right to enter your premises to do any necessary work or to cut off your supply, if they have reasonable cause to suspect that gas is, or might be, escaping or that escaped gas has entered your premises, and there is a danger to life or property.[12]

Officials representing the supplier must produce official identification when using any of the above powers.[13]

If you intentionally obstruct an official exercising any of the above powers, you can be punished by a fine of up to £1,000 on present scales,[14] although you cannot be punished if the official does not have a warrant.[15] On the other hand, suppliers must leave the premises no less secure than they found them, and must pay compensation for any damage caused.[16]

2. RIGHT OF ENTRY WITH A WARRANT

If you do not consent to the supplier entering your premises in accordance with any of the above rights, the supplier must get a magistrate's warrant (or the Scottish equivalent).[17] When there is an emergency, a supplier does not need to get a warrant to exercise the right of entry, but can still go and get one if entry is obstructed despite the emergency.

To get the warrant, the supplier must apply to the magistrates' court or, in Scotland, to a justice of the peace, a magistrate or a Sheriff. The warrant will be granted if the court is satisfied that:

- entry to the premises is reasonably required by the supplier;

- the supplier has a right of entry under the powers discussed above, but that right is subject to getting consent to enter;

- any conditions the supplier is supposed to meet in order to exercise the right of entry – eg, to give notice – have been met.

As well as the above, the court must be satisfied of at least one of the following:

- if the right of entry does not itself have a requirement for notice, 24 hours' notice has been given after which entry was refused; *or*

- there is an emergency and entry has been refused; *or*
- the purpose of entering would be defeated by asking for consent – eg, if tampering is suspected.

There is no general requirement that the supplier or the court should inform you that an entry warrant is being applied for, or has been issued. You have no right to be notified or to be present at the hearing.

The court should not grant the warrant unless it is satisfied that the legal requirements have been met, but, in practice, courts tend to rubber-stamp suppliers' applications for warrants. If you suspect that a supplier will be applying for a warrant, you should write to the supplier setting out the reasons why a warrant should not be granted, and send a copy to the court asking that it be shown to the magistrate (or other Scottish court officer) who will deal with the application.

CHAPTER TEN

Fuel and Benefits

Note: This chapter does not cover benefits for people subject to the immigration rules. It is essential to seek specialist legal advice before claiming benefits, as your immigration status may be jeopardised if you have recourse to 'public funds' by claiming certain benefits (see CPAG's *National Welfare Benefits Handbook* for detailed information).

This chapter deals with the limited payments and loans available within the social security system for fuel and related costs. It is not intended to be a comprehensive guide to the benefits system, but should help you to establish if you may be able to obtain direct help with a fuel-related cost. It covers:

1. Income support (see p137)
2. Cold weather payments (see p137)
3. Housing benefit (see p138)
4. Charitable payments and benefits (see p141)
5. The social fund (see p142)

If you cannot afford to pay for fuel or related expenditure, you should obtain specialist benefits advice to ensure that you are receiving your full entitlement to benefits. You should not delay in this, as there are time limits for claiming all benefits and restricted opportunities for back payments. Do not be put off from seeking advice and do not assume that you are not entitled to any help or to more help than you are getting at present. Many benefits are unclaimed or underclaimed. This applies particularly to benefits for the sick and disabled, and to low-income families with one or more working parent. Whatever your circumstances, your local citizens' advice bureau, neighbourhood advice centre or welfare rights service should be able to provide you with a benefits check free of charge.

If you are refused a benefit and need to appeal, for example, to a Social Security Appeal Tribunal, consult CPAG's *National Welfare Benefits Handbook* for detailed information or seek advice. If you are not entitled to any benefit, see Chapter 11 which deals with other limited sources of financial and other help. See also p145 for details of social fund payments which are available in certain limited circumstances whether or not you are entitled to income support.

I. INCOME SUPPORT

Income support is the national 'safety net' means-tested benefit. It is administered by the Benefits Agency on behalf of the DSS. It is a key benefit if you need direct help with fuel-related costs. You will not qualify for social fund community care grants, budgeting loans or cold weather payments unless you are on income support. (Note that you do not have to be on income support to qualify for a crisis loan.) If you are on income support, you may be able to avoid disconnection by paying for your fuel and any arrears by using the Fuel Direct scheme (see pp42-51).

You may be entitled to income support if:

• you do not work, or work less than 16 hours per week; *and*

• you have savings of less than £8,000.

You will not be entitled to income support if:

• you have a partner who works 16 hours or more per week, *or*

• if your income exceeds the income support assessment of your financial needs.

Full details about rules of entitlement and how to calculate income support can be found in CPAG's *National Welfare Benefits Handbook*.

Income support does *not* recognise fuel costs as a separate and variable need arising independently of age, health and disability. There is, therefore, no provision, for example, for an extra weekly payment because housing is difficult to heat or because a heating system is expensive to run.

2. COLD WEATHER PAYMENTS

These are occasional extra payments from the regulated social fund to some claimants of income support only. They are intended to assist with the extra costs of heating during exceptionally cold weather, but only when the weather has been exceptionally severe for seven consecutive days. £6 is paid for each week of exceptionally severe weather.[1] Payments should be made automatically by girocheque to those who qualify.[2] If you think you should have received a payment, but have not, contact your local Benefits Agency Office.

Who Qualifies?

You will qualify if you receive income support (see above) *and*:

- your normal home is in an area where an official 'period of cold weather' has been forecast or recorded;[3] *and*
- you have been awarded income support for at least one day during the period of cold weather; *and*
- *either* your income support includes at least one of the following premiums:
  - pensioner premium,
  - higher pensioner premium,
  - disability premium,
  - severe disability premium,
  - disabled child premium;
- *or* you have a child under five years of age.[4]

You will still qualify even if you have not spent any extra money on heating or have been away from home during the period of cold weather. The amount of capital you have does not affect entitlement.

What is a 'Period of Cold Weather'?

Temperatures recorded at government weather stations are used to calculate when a period of cold weather has occurred. The weather stations record the minimum and maximum temperatures each day. The average of these two figures produces the 'mean daily temperature'. A 'cold weather period' occurs when the average of the mean daily temperature over seven consecutive days is equal to or below 0 degrees Celsius.[5] Regulations determine which weather station covers each area.[6]

3. HOUSING BENEFIT

When Does Housing Benefit Assist With Fuel Costs?

Housing benefit does not assist with most fuel costs paid with your rent. You are expected to find the money for these charges from any other income you may have, such as benefits or earnings. However, the following charges can be included as part of your housing costs which may be met by housing benefit:

- Service charges for communal areas, but only if the charge is separately identified from any other charge for fuel used within your accommodation.[7] Communal areas include access areas – eg, halls and passageways.[8] In sheltered accommodation only, rooms in common use – eg a TV room – would also be included;[9]

- Charges for the provision of a heating system – eg, for boiler maintenance, will be eligible if separately identified from any other fuel charge.[10]

How Fuel Charges Are Calculated

Housing benefit will not be paid for fuel charges which are included in your rent – eg, heating, hot water, lighting, cooking.[11] If the amount of your fuel charge can be identified (eg, in your rent agreement, rent book, or letter from your landlord), the amount specified will be deducted from the amount of your total rent. The remaining amount will be eligible for housing benefit.[12] For example, if your rent is £20 per week and your rent agreement states that this includes £5 for heating, £15 would be counted as rent in assessing your entitlement to housing benefit.

A flat-rate deduction will be made if no fuel charges are specified as part of your rent.[13]

If the local authority considers that the amount your landlord says you have to pay for fuel is unrealistically low compared to the cost of the fuel provided, or if this charge contains an unknown amount for communal areas, it may instead apply the flat-rate deductions below.[14] This would lead to a lower assessment of housing benefit. This does not apply to council tenants as the regulations assume that fuel charges for council tenants will always be specified.[15]

Flat-rate Deductions from Housing Benefit

If you pay for fuel charges in with the rent, the amount of rent which is eligible for housing benefit will be calculated by making flat-rate deductions if your fuel charge:[16]

- is not readily identifiable; *or*

- is considered to be unrealistically low; *or*

- contains an unknown amount for communal areas.

The following amounts will be deducted:
If you and your family occupy more than one room
for

heating	£ 8.60
lighting	£ 0.70
hot water	£ 1.05
cooking	£ 1.05
Total	£11.40

If you and your family occupy one room only:
for

heating alone	£ 5.18
with lighting and/or hot water	£ 5.18
cooking	£ 1.05

If fuel is supplied for more than one purpose, the appropriate charges will be added together. If you are a joint tenant, the deductions will be apportioned according to your share of the rent.[17]

The local authority must notify you if it has used flat-rate deductions in calculating your entitlement to benefit. It must also explain that these can be varied if you can produce evidence of the actual approximate amount of the fuel charge.[18]

The *Housing Benefit Guidance Manual* says that the lower rate applies if you occupy one room, even though you may share a kitchen or bathroom.[19] You should argue for the lower-rate deduction if you are forced to occupy one room due to disrepair, damp or mould growth in your home.

Maximum Deductions from Housing Benefit if You are on Income Support

This transitional protection for claimants of the old supplementary benefit ended in April 1993. Extra payments of housing benefit were paid to some tenants who paid high fixed fuel charges in with the rent. Full details can be found in the 8th Edition of the *Fuel Rights Handbook*.[20]

4. CHARITABLE PAYMENTS AND BENEFITS

As social security and housing benefit help with fuel costs is so limited, charities are increasingly stepping in to help with fuel or reconnection costs, particularly when 'vulnerable people' have been disconnected. Many citizens' advice bureaux and advice agencies will be able to help with applications for charitable payments. This section deals with the effect of charitable payments for fuel on income support, housing benefit and family credit. Unless specified, the provisions below apply to all three benefits.

Irregular Charitable Payments

Charitable payments which are made irregularly and are intended to be made irregularly are regarded as capital.[21] Payments from the Independent Living Fund and the MacFarlane Trust are disregarded in full.[22] You will be treated as having an income from any capital above £3,000. For every £250, or part of £250, above this figure, you will be treated as having a tariff income of £1 per week. You will not be entitled to benefit if a charitable payment takes your total capital above £8,000 (for income support and family credit) or £16,000 (for housing benefit). For income support, the charitable payment will be treated as income if you are involved in a trade dispute, and for the first 15 days following your return to work.[23]

Regular Payments

Regular charitable payments for fuel are taken into account as income,[24] but the first £10 per week will be disregarded.[25] For income support, the payment will be counted in full if you are involved in a trade dispute. Voluntary payments to maintain a former partner or children will be treated as maintenance.

Payments in Kind

Any payments in kind by a charity are ignored completely.[26] Coal donated by a charity would therefore be ignored, as would fuel stamps.

5. THE SOCIAL FUND

This section is not intended to be a comprehensive guide to the workings of the social fund. You are advised to use this section simply as a tool to help you determine where financial help may be available for different aspects of fuel and related costs. You should consult the CPAG's *National Welfare Benefits Handbook* for detailed information about the operation of the social fund, and for advice on tactics and methods of making a claim. This section is arranged in three parts:

- a general introduction which should be sufficient to provide you with some terms of reference;

- an outline of types of social fund payments, specifying any excluded items and items which might receive a high priority within the social fund budget;

- options available for different fuel-related costs – eg, fuel costs, disconnection charges, the cost of heaters.

Introduction

The social fund is a discretionary, cash-limited system of social security provision. It is intended to provide grants or loans for a variety of needs. It is not subject to clear rules or regulations which determine entitlement. Instead, each application for help is decided on the basis of its priority within the social fund budget of a local area.

There are some broad rules. An Act of Parliament allows the Secretary of State to issue directions which are binding on the social fund officers who administer the scheme. The directions are in broad terms and set out the circumstances in which a social fund officer can make a payment.

The Secretary of State's interpretation of the directions is published in the form of guidance in the Social Fund Manual. The guidance is not legally binding, but social fund officers should take account of it. Social fund officers also set local guidance. Where social fund guidance is mentioned in this section, the reference is to national guidance. You may wish to refer to local guidance in your area where this assists your case.

To be successful in obtaining a grant or a loan from the social fund, it helps if you can argue that the items you need fit into your local office's list of high priority items. (Certain items and certain circumstances are allocated a 'high' priority in local and national guidance.)

Social fund officers must look at your individual circumstances in reaching a decision.

Social fund payments are made in the form of community care grants and loans (budgeting loans and crisis loans). Obviously the loans are repayable where grants are not. Most often, the loans are recovered through reductions in benefits.

Social fund officers' decisions can be challenged firstly by way of an internal review procedure. There is then a limited right of 'appeal' to the Social Fund Inspectorate. The Social Fund Inspectorate is not independent of the Benefits Agency and is bound by the same budgetary constraints as the local office, but it does sometimes change decisions. If you are refused a grant and offered a loan instead and you desperately need the item, you could consider taking the loan. When you have the money, you could apply for a review of the decision to try to get it turned into a grant. But be sure to seek independent legal advice first. See p106 for where to seek advice.

Community Care Grants

You may get a community care grant if you are on income support and[27]

- you are coming out of institutional or residential care; *or*

- you or a member of your family need help to avoid going into care; *or*

- you and your family need help to ease 'exceptional pressure' on yourselves.

You may also get a community care grant if you are coming out of residential care within six weeks and are likely to be claiming income support.[28] You are excluded from claiming a community care grant for most purposes if you have been disqualified from unemployment benefit because of a trade dispute.[29]

Excluded items

You cannot get a grant for:[30]

- consumption costs and standing charges for gas and electricity;

- service charges for fuel.

High priority items

The following items are given high priority for a grant:

- cookers;

- heaters;
- connection and reconnection charges;
- bedding;
- washing and drying facilities for heavy laundry needs.

High priority situations

Certain groups of claimants are given high priority in the guidance:

- elderly people;
- mentally ill people;
- mentally handicapped people;
- people with disabilities or chronic or terminal illnesses;
- people who are dependent on drugs or alcohol;
- ex-offenders;
- families under stress;
- young people leaving local authority care.

Budgeting Loans

You may get a budgeting loan if you have been on income support for the past 26 weeks (one gap of up to 14 days is ignored).[31] You are excluded if you are unable to claim unemployment benefit because of a trade dispute.[32]

Excluded items

You cannot get a budgeting loan for:[33]

- consumption costs and standing charges for gas and electricity;
- service charges for fuel.

High priority items

The following items have high priority for a budgeting loan:

- meter installations;
- reconnection charges;
- cost of non-mains fuel – eg oil, bottled gas, paraffin, coal;
- any item where a refusal could cause hardship or damage or risk the health or safety of anyone in your family.

Crisis Loans

You do not have to be entitled to income support to claim a crisis loan. Loans are available to people aged over 16 if the loan is the only means of preventing serious damage or serious risk to the health and safety of yourself or your family.[34]

You will not be entitled to a payment if you are:[35]

- in residential care or hospital, unless you are to be discharged within two weeks;

- a prisoner or otherwise lawfully detained;

- a fully maintained member of a religious order;

- in full-time non-advanced education and not entitled to income support;

- a full-time student, unless you are on income support, or it is your long vacation, or you are suffering a disaster;

- you are a person from abroad and are not entitled to income support unless there is a disaster.

Excluded items

The only fuel-related item which is excluded is service charges for fuel.[36] Fuel consumption and standing charges are not excluded.

High priority items

High priority is given to items requested by income support claimants during the first 26 weeks of their claim.

Options for Different Fuel-related Costs

Fuel bills

You cannot in any circumstances get a community care grant or a budgeting loan to pay for bills for the consumption of gas or electricity or any standing charges. You may, in very limited circumstances, be able to get a crisis loan for these costs if:

- you do not qualify for Fuel Direct; *and*

- the installation of a prepayment meter is not safe or practicable; *and*

- there is a serious risk to your health if the supply is not reconnected/continued.

Crisis loans are most likely to be paid to help people who are very young, elderly or seriously ill.

Connection and meter installation charges

You may be able to obtain a community care grant for the reasonable costs of fuel connection alongside any costs for furniture, furnishings, bedding, household equipment as part of a general start-up grant.

You should also apply for a community care grant for connection costs alone if this is your sole need. Relevant connection costs might include security deposits for the supply or for meters, or the costs of providing wiring or cables to connect your supply.

The guidance suggests that a community care grant may be made for the installation of prepayment meters, including the cost of any piping or wiring if you have difficulty in budgeting for quarterly bills. The guidance suggests that this would only be done for families with a child under 5 or a disabled child.[37]

According to the guidance, meter installation costs would usually be high priority for budgeting loans.

Reconnection charges

Community care grant guidance suggests that a grant may be made if your supply has been disconnected and you are going onto Fuel Direct. If the debt leading to disconnection was caused by a breakdown in the Fuel Direct system, you should ask the Benefits Agency for an ex-gratia payment.

Reconnection charges would usually be a high priority for budgeting loans, though it would obviously be better to obtain a community care grant in preference. If you are going onto Fuel Direct and cannot get a community care grant, try to have the costs of reconnection added to your debt rather than taking out a budgeting loan for this – otherwise you may have to repay an unnecessary extra charge from your weekly benefit.

Re-siting a meter

There should be no charge when an electricity meter is re-sited to meet the needs of a disabled customer (see p149). The guidance suggests that a community care grant may be available for re-siting meters if a disabled person needs easier access.

Cost of replacing a damaged meter

Meter installations are not excluded items for community care grants or crisis loans. They are high priority items for budget loans.

Money stolen from meters

Help when money is stolen from meters is not excluded by the guidance for community care grants or budgeting loans. It is arguable that the money lost is not a fuel charge, since the fuel has already been paid for. However, in practice, it will be very difficult to obtain a grant or loan for this.

Draughtproofing/insulation

Consider applying for a Home Energy Efficiency Scheme (HEES) grant for these items (see p150).

Heaters

The guidance suggests that community care grants may be made for the provision or repair of a heater to allow you to continue living in your home.

Non-mains fuels costs

This would include oil or bottled gas. Coal is not mentioned in the guidance, but is a non-mains fuel cost. Non-mains fuel costs would normally be high priority items for budgeting loans.

CHAPTER ELEVEN

Other Sources of Help

This chapter covers:

1. Help from social services (see below)
2. Energy efficiency (see p149)
3. Help from charities (see p151)

1. HELP FROM SOCIAL SERVICES

In England and Wales, local authorities have duties under the Children Act 1989 section 17 to provide services to safeguard and promote the welfare of children in need and promote the upbringing of such children by their families. This would include negotiating with a supplier on your behalf when necessary.

In exceptional circumstances this can also include providing assistance in cash.[1] Under the equivalent provisions of the Child Care Act 1980 (now repealed), many local authority social services departments were extremely reluctant to provide help in this way. However, a policy not to provide such assistance in any circumstances at all would almost certainly be unlawful. If such payments are available, you can argue that they can be used to meet all or part of a fuel bill, to buy alternative means of cooking or heating, or to provide other aids for keeping warm, such as blankets.

In Scotland, there are powers under section 12 of the Social Work (Scotland) Act 1968 to promote social welfare by 'making available advice, guidance and assistance' to persons in need due to infirmity, youth, age, illness or mental disorder. These powers can be used to make cash payments if this will diminish the need to take a child into care or to refer them to the Children's Panel, or if the local authority would later have to go to greater expense providing some other form of assistance. Therefore, a local authority social services department in Scotland may also help negotiate with a supplier, or even contribute to fuel bills or the purchase of alternative means of cooking or heating.

If you are seeking help from social services in an emergency – because, for example, the supplier is threatening disconnection – then you should tell the supplier. Suppliers' Codes of Practice allow for a delay in disconnection, normally for about two weeks, while a local authority investigates whether it can help, but this delay will only happen if the supplier knows of the local authority's involvement.

Social workers may also have good links with and/or be prepared to make referrals to charities for you (see below).

See also p165 on local councils' powers in England and Wales to protect occupiers and tenants when an owner or landlord fails to pay fuel or water bills.

People with Disabilities

Local authorities also have powers to assist adults with severe disabilities.[2] They must decide whether or not to use these powers if asked to do so by the disabled person or their carer or authorised representative,[3] and must allow that person or their authorised representative an opportunity to present their case. See the *Disability Rights Handbook*, available from CPAG.[4]

Note: Each supplier has a Code of Practice on services for the elderly and disabled (see Chapters 1 and 13).

2. ENERGY EFFICIENCY

Fuel poverty (ie, where people cannot afford to heat their homes to appropriate levels) is often caused by properties which are badly insulated or in a poor state of repair or where people use expensive or inefficient appliances (see Chapter 12 on how tenants can exercise their rights against low-standard property). You can get help, both financially and with advice, on how to make your home more energy-efficient.

Home Improvement Grants

Local authorities have powers to make grants for repairing or improving people's homes in order to bring them up to a standard fit for human habitation.[5] These grants are means-tested on a basis similar to the housing benefits means test. Grants are available to owners and landlords, but to tenants only if they have repairing obligations.

More relevantly, local authorities in England and Wales can also assist with *minor works*, including thermal insulation.[6] You must be wholly or mainly resident at the relevant property; an owner or a tenant of it; and in receipt of income support, family credit, housing benefit or council tax benefit. The grant will be 100% of the cost of the works, up to a maximum of £1,080 per application and £3,240 in each period of three years.

Works covered by these grants can help you to put your home in such a state that you need to use less fuel. Apply to your local authority (usually the housing, environmental health or technical services department) for details.

HEES

Grants are also available for improving the energy efficiency of your home under the Home Energy Efficiency Scheme (HEES).[7] You qualify for a grant if you are a resident householder, tenant or homeowner and you or your spouse are receiving income support, family credit, housing benefit, council tax benefit or disability working allowance. Grants of up to £289 can pay for roof insulation, draughtproofing and insulation of your hot water tank and for energy advice, subject to a small contribution of up to £16 and an upper limit. Both the contribution and the upper limit depend on what items of work are being done. You can also get grants for works to communal areas.

HEES is administered by the Energy Action Grants Agency (see Appendix 10 for how to contact them).

Energy Savings Trust

The Energy Savings Trust (EST) is a partnership between the Government, British Gas and the 14 electricity companies to promote efficient energy use in the UK, funded mostly from a levy on gas and electricity bills. At the moment, it has four programmes which are of interest.

The **Condensing Boiler Rebate Scheme:** if you install a condensing gas boiler in place of any existing boiler (whatever fuel it uses) or as part of a new central heating system, you can claim a rebate of £200 from the EST. A condensing boiler, although more expensive than ordinary boilers, is much more efficient, producing savings of up to 30% on current gas bills. The scheme is being administered by the Heating and Ventilating Contractors' Association (details of HCVA and EST in Appendix 10).

Combined Heat and Power: this is a scheme for more efficient (and so cheaper) production of heat and power. Previously, it has only been used in large-scale situations, but the EST wants to promote its use for homes. However, it is still only relevant for places like blocks of flats and old people's homes, rather than individual dwellings. Details can be obtained from the EST or the Combined Heat and Power Association (see Appendix 10).

Affordable Warmth: this is a programme which EST is still working on. When it is ready, the idea is to fund energy efficiency improvements for homes of people on lower incomes, but on a larger scale than HEES.

Energy Advice Centres: EST is looking to establish 30 local independent advice centres. They will provide energy advice but mostly aimed at middle and higher income customers.

Advice

Each supplier has to produce a Code of Practice on using fuel efficiently. A copy of each Code should be available at your local showroom or by telephoning the supplier. The Codes say that suppliers will provide certain levels of advice on energy efficiency, including which appliances are best for using your supplies of fuel most efficiently. However, a survey by *Which?* magazine suggests that, although there are some exceptions, suppliers cannot generally be trusted to give you the best advice, particularly if they might lose money as a result.[8]

Most DIY stores, where you would expect to buy the materials with which to make your home more energy efficient, seem not to have enough expertise to give good advice.

However, there are some useful sources of independent energy advice. Energy advice is provided most thoroughly by having a full energy survey done of your home. There are two energy survey schemes: the *National Home Energy Rating Scheme* (cost £50-100, depending on the size of the property) and the *Starpoint Home Energy Label Scheme* (cost £49.95) – see Appendix 10 for how to contact them. A survey is carried out by an inspector who comes to your home and looks at things such as the size and age of the property. The details are fed into a computer which produces a 'score' that measures how energy efficient your home is. You will then be advised on improvements you can make to cut your heating bills.

There are also some specialist energy advice agencies around the country which aim to help people on lower incomes.

3. HELP FROM CHARITIES

Some charities, particularly charities for ex-service personnel, offer help to meet fuel bills. It is helpful if an advice agency or social worker can write to the charity to explain your circumstances. The

Charities Digest (available in reference libraries) lists relevant charities. Another very useful book is *A Guide to Grants for Individuals in
Need*. Your local reference library may be able to help locate useful
local charities.

However, the introduction of the social fund has resulted in considerably less help from the state for those with fuel debts, leading to an
increase in demand for charitable payments. It is likely that many
charities will refuse to help with fuel debts if Fuel Direct or some
other budgeting scheme is available. If you are on income support,
housing benefit or family credit, you will need to check that a charitable payment does not affect your benefit.

CHAPTER TWELVE

You, Your Landlord and Fuel

This chapter covers:

1. Introduction (see below)
2. Can your landlord increase rent for fuel or fuel-related services? (see p154)
3. Resale of fuel by landlord to tenant (see p163)
4. Defective housing and heating systems: tenants' rights (see p169)

I. INTRODUCTION

Most arrangements for payment of gas or electricity are made direct with the supplier. However, many tenants pay for fuel or fuel-related services (eg, heating, cooking, lighting or hot water) indirectly through their landlord – ie, the supplier supplies the fuel to the land-lord who re-sells it to the tenant. Frequently a landlord will:

- provide gas or electricity, pay the bill and recover charges from tenants by sharing out costs on a fixed or variable basis;
- pay the bill and recover charges from tenants by using a slot meter;
- provide heating from a central boiler and recover charges on a fixed or variable basis.

It can be more economical if your landlord provides fuel-related services – eg, a common boiler in a block of flats may be relatively cheap. However, the involvement of your landlord can lead to disputes over sums charged for fuel or heat, or over your position if your landlord fails to pay the bills.

A *note of caution*: Before exercising your rights, you should always consider the strength of your position. For a tenant, this means considering how secure the tenancy is. This depends on the type of tenancy you have (protected, statutory, assured, assured shorthold/short assured, secure or none of these). A full discussion of security of tenure is outside the scope of this book but it is important because, for example, if you have no security and start a dispute with your landlord, you could end up losing your home.

2. CAN YOUR LANDLORD INCREASE RENT FOR FUEL OR FUEL-RELATED SERVICES?

The circumstances in which your landlord can increase the rent because of increases in charges for fuel or fuel-related services will depend partly on the type of tenancy you have – ie, council or non-council. If you are a non-council tenant, your rights will also vary according to whether you took up the tenancy before or after 15 January 1989 (2 January 1989 in Scotland) – see p160.

A landlord's power to increase charges for fuel or fuel-related services can be limited in one of three ways:

- payments for fuel or fuel-related services are 'service charges', so legislation which affects service charges may be relevant;

- the courts have held that fuel charges are normally part of the rent,[1] so where legislation controls the rent, fuel charges are included;

- a tenancy agreement is a type of contract and may include limits on your landlord's power to increase charges.

Council Tenancies

You have a council tenancy if your landlord is a local authority, unless you have used your right to buy or if, in England and Wales, your tenancy has a fixed term of more than 21 years. Most council tenancies are called 'secure tenancies'.

In England and Wales, there is no law dealing with service charges or rent control for council tenants. There is a power for the Secretary of State for the Environment to make regulations covering heating charges, but this has not yet been used.[2]

In Scotland, local authorities are limited to making service charges which they think are 'reasonable in all the circumstances'.[3] There is no definition of 'reasonable' (see p160), but if you think the charges are unreasonable, you can apply for judicial review (see Chapter 13).

Otherwise, the only protection for council tenants is contractual. If fuel or fuel-related services are provided as part of your tenancy, a failure to provide these will be a breach of contract. If there is such a breach, you can go to court to claim damages (ie, money in compensation) and a court order requiring the local authority to obey the terms of the tenancy agreement.

The terms of your tenancy may be contained in a written statement, in which case any terms relating to fuel or fuel-related services will be clear. However, in most cases not everything will be in writing – sometimes there is no written agreement at all. You will then have to work out whether your fuel problem is covered by terms implied into your tenancy. An 'implied term' is one which, although not written down, is considered by the courts to be included automatically in any tenancy.

Every tenancy agreement in England and Wales has an implied term that the landlord will allow a tenant to have 'quiet enjoyment' – ie, that the landlord will not interfere with or interrupt a tenant's ordinary use of the premises they occupy. In this case, that would mean not interfering in any way with your use of fuel or fuel-related services. The Scottish equivalent is the tenant's right to full possession of their premises, which has the same effect.

In England and Wales, terms will also be implied by the Supply of Goods and Services Act 1982 which says that services must be provided with reasonable care and skill, within a reasonable time and at a reasonable charge.[4] Problems with fuel supply or fuel-related services can often come within these terms.

Local council heating systems

All local councils have the power to produce and sell heat.[5] There is no specific protection in relation to heating charges, but the local authority must:

- keep a separate account of them;[6] *and*

- when fixing the charges, act in good faith, not for ulterior or unlawful purposes, and within the reasonable limits of a reasonable local council;[7] *and*

- comply with the law on maximum resale of fuel (see p163).

London boroughs have additional powers in respect of the provision of heating by hot water or steam.[8]

They may prescribe scales of heating charges which apply unless there is a specific agreement setting different charges.[9] The charges must be shown separately on rent books, demand notes or receipts, and be differentiated from rent generally.

London boroughs must balance their books in respect of heating[10] – ie, they are not allowed to subsidise heating. In providing heat or fixing charges, they must not show 'undue preference' or exercise 'undue discrimination'.[11] Some preference or discrimination is inevitable, as not all tenants paying the same charges will be provided with identical heat. To decide if the preference or discrimination is undue you should consider:

- the cost of providing the heat to you compared with the cost of providing it to other tenants;
- the level and consistency of heat;
- restrictions or terms governing the heat provided (eg, in winter only).

If you can show undue preference or discrimination, you can recover the amount you have been overcharged by taking legal action (see Chapter 13).

London boroughs have a choice of using either the general power which all local authorities have, or the power which is specific to them. They have more freedom to do what they want if they exercise the more general power. It is not clear how the two powers relate. If a borough has resolved to apply the general power (which came into force on 14 February 1977), then the position will be clear for tenancies starting after that date. If a tenancy started before that date and has simply continued, then a court may decide that the more detailed powers apply.

Challenging the way heating is provided

If you challenge the legality of the way a heating system is being run or charges for heat, complex legal issues arise. As well as the matters mentioned in relation to undue preference or discrimination by London boroughs (see above), a court can consider matters such as where the local council:

- charges tenants for assumed heat delivery instead of actual heat delivered, if there is a significant difference;
- charges for heating costs which are significantly higher than those of other heating systems;
- charges amounts unrelated to heat delivered or assumed to be delivered.

When some heat is provided but it is inadequate, it is difficult to prove breach of the tenancy agreement, unless there is a specific agreement stating how much heat is to be provided and at what times of the year. If nothing is specifically agreed or set out in the tenancy agreement, it is probably an implied term that 'reasonable heat' should be provided – but this is extremely vague. If there is to be a dispute, you should keep a detailed diary of when the heat was sufficient, when it was inadequate or off altogether, and even when there was too much.

Tenants' group pressure

Because of the difficulties with such legal proceedings, it may be easier and more effective for tenants' associations to put pressure on a local council to change the way it manages the heating system or the charges for it. In challenging high heating charges and looking for an explanation, these are some of the matters your tenants' association can look at:

- copies of council committee reports on heating systems and charging policies;

- a comparison of income from, and expenditure on, individual estate systems and across a local council area;

- expenditure charged to the heating account: does it include all fuel expenditure, maintenance, insurance, caretakers' wages, interest on the cost of the system? Is this consistent with other public landlords?

- district heating systems: the number of dwellings supplied, the costs and type of fuel used;

- level of service: heating and hot water, hours per day, winter and summer, temperature standards assumed and achieved;

- method of calculation of charges: pooling of costs, property by property, flat charge, charge related to size and numbers of bedrooms;

- energy efficiency of dwellings: insulation quality, double glazing;

- a temperature survey could be organised to find out what heat is being delivered. Temperatures in all rooms at different times of the day can be measured simultaneously in a number of dwellings. A useful booklet to help you is *Taking Action on Cold Homes* (see Appendix 9).

Heating standards used by local councils

A local authority may provide heating to a set standard. These are examples of such standards in use today:[12]

- 'Parker Morris': from 1969 to 1980, local authorities were required to meet the standard recommended in the Parker Morris Report of 1961 which is to supply 18°C (65°F) in living rooms and 13°C (55°F) elsewhere;

- Chartered Institute of Building Surveyors: used from the mid-1970s to recommend 21°C (70°F) in living rooms, 18°C (65°F) in the kitchen and 16°C (60°F) in hall and bedrooms;

- British Standards Institution (Code of Practice BS 5449): to supply 21°C (70°F) in living room and dining room, 22°C (72°F) in bathrooms, 18°C (65°F) in bedrooms, kitchen and toilet, 16°C (60°F) in hall.

Some landlords will use their own standards. You should ask your local authority or other landlord what standards they use as these will probably be used in setting the charges.

Note: An alternative to relying on a landlord who supplies heat to a block of flats or apartments is for the residents to get together and buy gas or electricity jointly. In the case of gas, if the total power purchased is over 2,500 therms, then an ordinary contract can be negotiated with British Gas (or any other supplier if one exists). In either case, negotiating bulk purchases could produce better terms.

Non-Council Tenancies

This applies to you if your landlord is not a local authority. There is legislation on variable service charges and also on rent control. The legislation on variable service charges does not apply in Scotland but there are some court cases which give rights to tenants in this area. The provisions for rent control are different for all tenancies granted before 15 January 1989 compared to most of those granted after 15 January 1989 – the corresponding date in Scotland is 2 January 1989.

Variable service charges in England and Wales

Variable service charges are covered by the Landlord and Tenant Act 1985 sections 18-30. If your landlord used to be a council but it sold the property to a private landlord, then you have similar rights under the Housing Act 1985 sections 47-51. A variable service charge is defined as:

> an amount payable by a tenant as part of or in addition to rent... directly or indirectly for services... the whole or part of which varies according to the landlord's [costs or estimated costs].[13]

This is a wide definition and includes payments for electricity or gas, whether made direct to the landlord or indirectly through a landlord's meter. As long as the rent varies according to the landlord's costs, it does not matter whether a charge is simply a share of a bill (with little or no regard to your actual consumption) or an accurate assessment of your consumption. These provisions apply to all tenants unless you are:

- a tenant of a council or any other public authority (eg, a housing action trust), unless your lease is for over 21 years or was granted under the right to buy legislation;[14] *or*

- a tenant whose rent has been registered with a service charge stated to be a fixed sum.[15]

Note: tenancies with variable service charges may be treated as fixed sum charges if the mechanism of variation is unreasonable.

Your landlord can recover the costs of the services she/he provides – such as heat, light or cooking facilities – only if the service is of a 'reasonable' standard and the costs are 'reasonably' incurred.[16] If the charges are based on an estimate in advance, the estimate must be reasonable and, after the costs have actually been incurred, the charges must be adjusted by repayment, reduction of future charges or additional charges, whichever is appropriate. If they are paid in arrears, most charges cannot relate to periods of more than 18 months before.[17]

If you think costs were unreasonably incurred or estimated, or a service was of an unreasonable standard, you can apply to the county court for a declaration to that effect.[18] There is no definition of 'unreasonable' but it probably means something which is obviously excessive.

Access to Information

The right to challenge unreasonable charges would be almost useless without access to supporting information about how the charges are made up. You have the right to require your landlord to provide information. Your request must be in writing. Your landlord must provide a written summary of costs incurred over 12-month periods. Your landlord must comply within six months of your request.[19]

If the service charges are payable by tenants of more than four dwellings together, the summary of costs must be provided by a qualified accountant.[20] This is aimed mostly at tenants such as those in mansion blocks, but also applies if you live in a house in multiple occupation.[21]

Within six months of receiving the summary, you can require your landlord to allow you to inspect accounts and receipts.[22] This is particularly useful if you suspect you are being overcharged.

It may be more effective to exercise these rights through a tenants' association. If members' tenancies require them to contribute to the same costs, a tenants' association may apply to the landlord to become a 'recognised tenants' association'.[23] If the landlord does not agree to this, the association can apply to the local rent assessment committee for a certificate requiring the landlord to recognise it. It can then exercise the rights to information (see above) on behalf of its members.

Variable service charges in Scotland

The legislation mentioned in the previous section does not apply in Scotland. To find out if there is any limit on your landlord's discretion to increase charges for fuel or fuel-related services, you should look at your written tenancy agreement, if any. If there is a term which covers how service charges can be increased, then that will apply.

If there is no such term or it is unclear, then the courts may be prepared to introduce an implied term (see p155) into the tenancy agreement. In one case,[24] the court introduced an implied term that any service charge had to be 'fair and reasonable'. The court also decided that a surveyors' certificate claiming that the charges were reasonable was not valid because it was the landlord himself who signed the certification in his role as the surveyor.

Rent control

Note: If it is not clear what kind of tenancy you have, please refer to any standard text on the law of landlord and tenant (see Appendix 9).

Rent control is relevant to payments made to a landlord for fuel and fuel-related services, because such payments will normally be part of the rent; therefore, the payments can be increased only if the rent can be increased.

The Rent Act 1977 and the Rent (Scotland) Act 1984 used to provide a comprehensive system of rent control. However, they do not apply to most tenancies which started after 15 January 1989 in England and Wales, or 2 January 1989 in Scotland, as these are covered by the Housing Act 1988 or the Housing (Scotland) Act 1988. The new system of rent control under these later Acts is so loose that it is virtually useless as a tool for limiting rises in charges for fuel or fuel-related services. Therefore, it will not be covered in this book.

For tenancies granted before 15 January 1989 (England and Wales) or 2 January 1989 (Scotland)

There are different rent control systems for:

- tenancies which are regulated (ie, protected or statutory); *and*

- those which are restricted/Part VII contracts. It is outside the scope of this book to discuss the different types of tenancy, but a restricted/Part VII contract can be said to include most tenancies where the landlord is resident.

Tenancies starting after 15 January 1989 or 2 January 1989 are also regulated if they were granted:

- to an existing protected or statutory tenant (ie, regulated under the Rent Act 1977 or the Rent (Scotland) Act 1984);

- as a result of a possession order made against an existing statutory tenant in 'suitable alternative accommodation' proceedings; *or*

- in accordance with an agreement made before 15 January 1989 or 2 January 1989.

Regulated tenancies
If you are a regulated tenant under the Rent Act 1977, your position will depend on whether or not there is a registered fair rent and whether the tenancy is in a contractual or statutory phase. Once a tenancy has been granted, it is contractual until the agreed period ends (usually by a notice to quit). When this happens, a statutory tenancy arises so long as you continue to occupy the premises as your residence.

Unregistered rent
Contractual: if, at the time you were granted a tenancy, no rent had been registered, then there was no restriction on what rent might be agreed. Once agreed, the rent – including any charges for fuel or fuel-related services – can only be raised if:

- there is a rent review clause (unusual in a residential tenancy); *or*

- it is done on an application to register the rent; *or*

- you enter with your landlord into a 'rent agreement with a tenant having security of tenure'[25] – essentially this is a new tenancy agreement so that you are effectively starting from scratch.

Statutory: When the statutory phase begins, the last contractual rent applies, but may be changed in accordance with changes in the provision or costs of services (including payments for fuel or fuel-related services) or furniture.[26] There is no set form for giving notice of any change. If you do not agree in writing to any such proposed changes, you or your landlord can apply to the county court (the Sheriff Court in Scotland) to determine the change.[27] The court can take into account past changes when deciding on any increases.

Rather than bothering with applications to the court, if you have a serious disagreement with your landlord, it is more sensible to apply for a fair rent to be registered (see below). Alternatively, you and your landlord can enter into a 'rent agreement with a tenant having security of tenure' and the tenancy will revert to being contractual.

Registered rent

You, your landlord or both of you together can apply for a fair rent to be registered.[28] The registered rent must include any sums which are payable for services, including payments for fuel or fuel-related services.[29] It does not matter whether you make such payments to your landlord at the same time as payments for rent, at different times, or under separate agreements.

The rent officer must include service payments in the total figure for the registered rent but must state them as a separate figure.[30] Rent officers should also note separately costs in rent which are ineligible for housing benefit – this includes gas and electricity costs, heating, hot water, lighting and cooking.[31]

The rent that is registered for fuel and fuel-related services should reflect not the cost to your landlord, but their value to you. For example, if your central heating system works poorly, the payments to your landlord can be reduced – by 50% in one reported case.[32] You can argue that if your heating system runs efficiently, but is expensive because of the type of fuel used (eg, underfloor heating), your rent should be reduced to the level of a system which provides the same heat at a cheaper rate. Similarly, if the premises are poorly insulated or use energy inefficiently, this could be reflected in your rent.

The amount specified for services in the registered rent will be a fixed sum unless your tenancy has a variation clause relating to payments for services, and the mechanism for variation is reasonable.[33] (Again, there is no definition of 'reasonable'.) If there is such a clause, the amount entered in the rent register can be a sum which varies in accordance with the terms of the clause. You are then protected by the rules governing variable service charges (see p158).

Restricted contracts

Note: These are known as 'Part VII contracts' in Scotland.

The level of rent is fixed by the terms of your tenancy contract, which may be oral or written. However, you or your landlord can refer the contract to a rent assessment committee.[34] The rent assessment committee then has the power to increase or reduce the rent to a level which it considers reasonable in all the circumstances.[35] There is no definition of 'reasonable', but a 'reasonable rent' is not the same as a 'fair rent' under the same Act and will normally be higher.

The rent set by the rent assessment committee includes an assessment of any payments for services including fuel or fuel-related services. Once the rent is set, this stands for two years unless you and your landlord agree to a new application, or apply on the basis of a change in circumstances.[36] A change in the services provided would be a change in circumstances; a simple increase in fuel tariff would probably not be a sufficient change unless it was entirely unforeseen when the rent was set.

3. RESALE OF FUEL BY LANDLORD TO TENANT

As well as the variable service charge scheme and control on rents outlined above, there are specific controls on the maximum charge for gas or electricity supplied to landlords and resold to tenants. (See p153 for more information on resale of fuel.) The basis on which you can be recharged for fuel sold will be a term of your tenancy agreement – in practice, this will not normally be set out in writing. However, it is subject to an upper limit – a landlord re-selling fuel cannot recover more than the maximum charge.

Maximum Permitted Charges

OFFER has the power to fix maximum charges for the resale of electricity, and must publish details of any charges fixed.[37] Charges have two elements: a charge for each unit consumed and a 'daily availability charge' to cover the standing charge.

OFGAS has a duty to fix maximum charges for resale of gas and to publish details of the charges fixed.[38] Gas charges also have two elements: a charge per therm of gas used and a daily availability charge to cover the standing charge.

If your landlord overcharges for gas or electricity, you can recover the excess through legal action. OFFER and OFGAS each publish a leaflet setting out the latest maximum resale price and guidance on how to check the accuracy of what you are being charged (see also Appendices 9 and 10).[39]

If your landlord undercharges, you may have to make an additional payment, but this depends on your tenancy agreement. There is no implied term (see p155) that the tenant should pay the maximum charge.

Approval of Meters

Electricity meters cannot be used unless the pattern and the method of installation are as approved by regulations.[40] The meter must be tested and approved by a meter examiner appointed by OFFER. OFFER has the power to prosecute your landlord for failure to comply with these provisions, and she/he can be fined.

Gas meters must be of a pattern approved by the Secretary of State for Trade and Industry and stamped by, or on behalf of, a meter examiner appointed by her/him.[41] A supply of gas through an unstamped meter is an offence subject to a fine. The Gas Act does not state who would prosecute, but presumably it would be the meter examiners' service or, possibly, OFGAS. There is a power to make regulations for re-examining meters already stamped and for their periodic overhaul, but none has yet been made.

Problems with Landlords' Coin Meters

There is no recommended way of setting of coin meters to recoup 'resale' prices. Because there are two elements to the charge – one fixed and one variable – it is impossible, unless the fixed charge is collected separately, to know in advance how to set the meter. This means that your landlord may exceed the maximum permitted charge and may have to refund you when the meter is emptied.

Payment through a coin meter will also normally be a variable service charge, in which case 18 months' back payment is allowed under the rules on service charges (see p159).

Keep records

You should keep a record of how much has been put into the meter, and/or taken out of it, and of meter readings and their dates. You should try to be present when the meter is emptied so that you can compare the amount of fuel consumed with the money collected. To check how much your landlord is charging for fuel, follow the method explained on pp85-6. Compare the result with the maximum resale price set by OFGAS or OFFER (see p163).

Landlords' right to read or empty a meter

Your landlord has the right to enter your premises, if she/he gives reasonable notice, to read or empty a meter if it is provided as part of your tenancy agreement. If the meter is kept in a part of the building which you share with others – eg, the hallway entrance to flats – your landlord will be able to enter without giving notice to read it or empty it.

If your landlord fails to empty the meter, you will not be able to fit in any more coins and your supply will effectively be cut off. If you are deprived of a supply in this way, you can sue your landlord for breach of the implied covenant granting you 'quiet enjoyment' (see p155) or, in Scotland, for having been deprived of full possession.

Obtaining a Meter Direct from a Supplier

If you encounter continual problems over your landlord's approach to re-selling electricity or gas, you could obtain your own supply direct from a supplier. Both gas and electricity suppliers are under a duty to provide a supply, with your own meter, if required to do so by a consumer (see Chapter 2), although you may have to pay rewiring charges.[42] If you are getting the meter because of persistent breaches of the tenancy agreement by your landlord, you may be able to re-cover the charges from the landlord as damages (ie, money in compensation) for the breaches.

If you have a meter put in, this would be a tenant's 'improvement' – ie, an 'alteration connected with the provision of services to a dwelling house'. A tenant of a secure or regulated tenancy is not allowed to make any improvement without the consent of the landlord.[43] Landlords cannot withhold their consent unreasonably; if it is unreasonably withheld, it is treated as given. If suppliers are reluctant to co-operate with you, you can remind them that you have these rights.

Landlords' Failure to Pay Bills

If you pay for fuel with your rent, of if your landlord empties the coin meter, you can be disconnected if your landlord does not pay the bill. The electricity and gas suppliers' respective Codes of Practice should lay down a period during which disconnection action will not proceed in such circumstances – eg, London Electricity allows 15 working days and British Gas allows 21 days. There are a number of legal remedies dealing with conflicts in this area (see Chapter 13).

Local Councils' Powers in England and Wales

If you are seeking the help of the local authority in an emergency – eg, because the supplier is threatening disconnection – then you should tell the supplier. Suppliers' Codes of Practice allow for a delay in disconnecting while the local authority investigates whether it can help, but the delay will only come into effect if the supplier *knows* that the local council is involved.

Outside London

Local councils outside London have the power to protect occupiers if the supply is threatened or cut off as a result of an owner's failure to pay fuel charges.[44] Once a request is made in writing, the local council can make arrangements with the supplier to reconnect the supply; such arrangements can include payment of arrears and disconnection or reconnection charges.

Having arranged reconnection, the local council can recover expenses (plus interest) from the person who should have paid in the first place. If you have an arrangement where the owner, your landlord, pays the fuel bills, the local council can also serve notice on you to pay your rent direct to it to set off against its expenses.

Within London

London boroughs have powers to protect occupiers where an owner, usually a landlord, fails to pay a bill.[45] They can pay the expenses of reconnecting the supply of gas or electricity. After reconnection, they have a duty, as long as they think it is necessary, to pay the suppliers' charges for future consumption.

However, the boroughs have no power to pay arrears – ie, for past consumption. This can be a stumbling block as suppliers are under no obligation to reconnect the supply while money is owed. The supplier cannot chase you for the arrears because your landlord is the customer, not you. While such arrears are outstanding, a supplier may be reluctant to reconnect a supply.

You can get round this by getting the borough to recover the arrears itself – the borough has the power to take proceedings to recover money owing at the time fuel was reconnected,[46] and these proceedings can be taken against either the occupier (ie, you) or the defaulting owner. If you pay your rent to the borough under these provisions, you are treated as meeting your obligation to pay rent to the owner – you cannot be required to pay more than the rent that you would otherwise be paying to your landlord.

Suppliers should be keen on this kind of arrangement and prepared to reconnect as it means the borough does the suppliers' debt-collecting and, provided you pay your rent to the borough, payment is guaranteed. Boroughs can protect themselves by 'registering a charge'[47] on the affected property to recover their expenses (including administrative costs). Local councils usually appoint a particular officer – such as an environmental health officer or tenancy relations officer – to deal with these matters. If they are reluctant to become involved, you can point out that they can put a charge on the property to cover their expenses and protect themselves. It would be unlawful to have a blanket policy not to exercise these powers; they must consider each case individually. If you are told, 'We don't do that', you can consider judicial review (see Chapter 13).

Note: Although this section on local authorities' powers has been written for landlord and tenant, it applies where any 'occupier' has been affected by the failure of an 'owner' to pay a bill. 'Owner' has a wide definition[48] and might cover the position where one of a number of flat-sharers is both tenant and the person responsible for paying the fuel bills.

Local council powers in Scotland

There are no equivalent powers in Scotland to those in England and Wales. However, local councils throughout Great Britain do have powers to make 'Control Orders' in extreme cases.[49] This means the local council can take over a house in multiple occupation from a bad landlord and collect the rent in order to pay for any necessary repairs and to pay bills such as fuel bills. Unfortunately, it is unlikely that a Control Order would be made on the basis of unpaid fuel bills alone; these powers are more typically used if there is substantial disrepair.

Disconnection of a landlord

Gas can only be disconnected at the premises for which there are arrears. However, electricity can be disconnected at any premises which your landlord occupies and for which she/he is registered as the consumer (eg, at the landlord's home or workplace) for failure to pay a bill incurred at other premises.[50] This provision is difficult to use if the two premises in question are supplied by different companies, but if it is the same company, your electricity supply may be at risk of disconnection if your landlord has arrears elsewhere. Remember that the supplier may not be aware that your landlord is not the occupier unless you, as tenant, tell them. Always press for disconnection of your landlord, rather than you, if disconnection cannot be avoided.

What a tenant can do

If you pay for fuel through a coin meter or with the rent, it will be a term of your tenancy that your landlord maintains the supply. If your landlord fails to pay a bill and the supply is threatened or cut off, you could seek a court order to restore the supply and for damages for loss and suffering. You could also claim breach of the implied covenant of 'quiet enjoyment' (see p155),[51] or, in Scotland, of the right to full possession.

Also, if two or more tenants contribute to the same costs by paying a variable service charge, the sums paid to the landlord are held 'on trust' by her/him. This imposes strict obligations on the landlord as 'trustee'. Failure to pay fuel bills with this money would be a 'breach of trust'. Legal advice would be essential before taking legal action.

Harassment

Your landlord is committing a criminal offence if she/he harasses you in order to make you give up your tenancy or prevent you from exercising your rights. Harassment means action likely to interfere with your peace or comfort, including the withdrawal of services such as the supply of gas or electricity.[52] You can also sue for damages, which can be very large if you have to give up occupation.[53] Your landlord has a defence if she/he can show that she/he had reasonable grounds for interfering with your peace or comfort, or for withdrawing services – eg, they turned off the gas in an emergency such as a nearby fire.

Local councils are often prepared to prosecute landlords for harassment. You can ask the tenancy relations officer to intervene. In England and Wales, if a local council refuses to prosecute, you can take out a summons yourself in the magistrates' court. However, legal aid is available only for advice, not for representation. If a prosecution is unsuccessful, there is a risk of being ordered to pay costs.[54]

Transfer of Account from Landlord to Tenant

If your landlord consistently fails to pay bills, the simplest solution may be for you to open an account and get the supply in your own name (see Chapter 2).

Rewiring work might be necessary if a meter is moved or a new one installed. For example, in houses in multiple occupation, considerable work would be needed to replace one main meter with separate meters for each tenant – in most cases, you would only have to pay for the costs of work to the premises you yourself occupy.

If a supply is being transferred because of a breach of the terms of the tenancy, you can claim the costs of the work as damages in a court action. Otherwise this work would be an 'improvement' (see 170).

4. DEFECTIVE HOUSING AND HEATING SYSTEMS: TENANTS' RIGHTS

A full discussion of legal remedies for defective housing is outside the scope of this book. However, defective heating systems, structural disrepair, use of poor materials, inadequate insulation and draught-proofing can all contribute to high heating bills. Tackling these problems can be expensive and would rarely be a tenant's responsibility. Therefore, this section looks briefly at the legal remedies available to a tenant, dividing them into three main categories:

• repairing obligations;

• negligence;

• premises prejudicial to health.

Condensation is a particular problem and is dealt with separately.

There are different forms of action which can be taken against a landlord, but the purpose will always be to get work carried out and/or to get compensation. Good records are important evidence and can make a big difference to the level of any compensation. Therefore, in any potential dispute with your landlord over disrepair, it is important that you keep proper records of what is in disrepair and:

• when the problems started;

• when your landlord was first told of the disrepair;

• all other occasions on which your landlord has been told about the disrepair;

• what has been done, if anything, to put things right.

If you incur extra expenses (eg, to keep warm, eating out or for replacement heaters), you should make notes and, if possible, keep any receipts. If heating bills are higher than normal, you should also keep these.

Repairing Obligations

Your landlord's repairing obligations may be set out in a written tenancy agreement. Tenants of councils and housing associations in Scotland have a right to a formal written lease.[55] Whether or not you have a written agreement and whatever is stated in any such written agreement, there is legislation which puts a wide range of obligations on landlords. It is unusual for written agreements to be better than the responsibilities required by legislation. The law in Scotland is dealt with first because a Scottish tenant has additional rights which a tenant South of the border does not.

Scotland

The landlord's obligation is to make sure that any property they rent out is in a 'tenantable and habitable condition'[56] or 'reasonably fit for human habitation'.[57] These two phrases almost certainly mean the same thing – the property must be safe, free from damp and generally in a suitable condition for you and your family to live in.

This obligation applies from the very start of the tenancy and cannot be excluded by anything in the tenancy agreement if the rent is less than £300 per week.[58] The landlord should inspect the property and bring it up to standard before any tenancy starts. If this is not done you can sue for damages and/or an order of 'specific implement' to force the landlord to carry out any necessary works (see Chapter 13). Unlike in England and Wales, your landlord's duty may include carrying out works which improve the property, rather than merely repair it, if that is necessary to comply with her/his duty. However, in Scotland it is it is much more difficult to get an order ('specific implement') which enforces that duty (see *Note* below).

If any problems arise after the tenancy starts, the landlord is only obliged to deal with them if she/he knows or should know about them. This means you should report any problems as soon as they arise, preferably in writing. Again, if your landlord does not carry out necessary works within a reasonable time, you can take her/him to court.

Right to Warmth has produced a useful booklet, *Warm Homes: the Law*, which summarises the position for tenants (see Appendix 10).

Note: The problem for Scottish tenants is how to enforce these rights. The rights themselves are better than those in England and Wales but enforcement is much more difficult. An order for 'specific implement' is very difficult to obtain because you are required to specify in great detail exactly what you want the court to order your landlord to do.[59] The law in England and Wales does not require such precision. Therefore, legal advice is essential before you consider taking legal action.

England, Wales and Scotland

For England and Wales generally and in Scotland, in connection with the following rights, it is important to distinguish between 'repairs' and 'improvements'. Under these rights, a landlord has no obligation to improve a home as such – if the works which are needed constitute improvements, rather than just repairs (and the case cannot be brought under the headings of 'Negligence' or 'Premises prejudicial to health' – see below), then a tenant has no rights.[60]

Also, you can take legal action against your landlord for disrepair only if she/he knows about it or should have known about it.[61] It is best to tell your landlord in writing (keeping copies of any letters) about the disrepair so that there can be no dispute about whether it has been given.

Your rights are set out in the Landlord and Tenant Act 1985 or the Housing (Scotland) Act 1987 (these provisions do not apply to tenancies for a fixed period of seven years or more). The rights of Scottish tenants set out in the previous section are more wide-ranging so it will not normally be necessary for them to rely on these rights.

Structure and exterior

Your landlord must keep in repair 'the structure and exterior of the dwelling-house (including drains, gutters and external pipes)'.[62] This includes walls, roofs, windows and doors. If these are not kept in good repair, a house can become damp and hard to heat.

Installations for heating and for the supply of gas and electricity

Your landlord must keep in repair and proper working order installations for space heating (ie, central heating, gas and electric fires), for heating water and for the supply of gas and electricity.[63] This does not include fittings or appliances making use of the supply – ie, wiring and pipes would be included but not cookers or refrigerators. For tenancies which started after 15 January 1989 (2 January 1989 in Scotland), a central heating boiler in the basement of a block of flats would normally come within the repairing obligation.[64]

What the tenant can do

If your landlord does not keep the structure, etc, in good repair, you have two options:

- You can bring an action for damages and for a court order requiring your landlord to do the repair. Damages are calculated by assessing how much the value of the premises to you has been reduced so as to put you, as far as possible, in the same position as if there had been no breach.[65] This may involve calculating the costs of alternative accommodation, redecoration, eating out, using public baths or launderettes, together with an amount for discomfort and inconvenience arising from the disrepair. Keep a record of all expenses as far as you can. Most claims are made in the county court or, in Scotland, the Sheriff Court. You will need the help of a solicitor – legal aid is available.

• In some cases, rather than taking your landlord to court, it would be easier to do the repair work yourself and recover the costs by withholding rent to the same value. You should write to your landlord to warn her/him of what you are doing – you cannot recover the costs unless the works fall within your landlord's repairing obligations, so you must give her/him an opportunity to object or comment. You should send estimates for the cost of the work to your landlord and give her/him time for any observations she/he has on what is being suggested – eg, 21 days. After the work has been done, you should write to your landlord to warn that, unless she/he pays the costs, rent to the same value will be withheld. These costs are a 'set-off' against rent due and will not be treated by a court as rent arrears, provided the court agrees that the costs were reasonable.[66] The consequences of getting this procedure wrong can be serious, so you should get legal advice.

Note: In Scotland, this way of retaining your rent is not available to statutory tenants.

Negligence

Electricity and gas are, or can be, dangerous. Consumers are protected by safety regulations which prescribe standards and methods of installation of meters and other equipment for the supply of gas or electricity. If landlords carry out work on the premises, they must comply with such standards and are also under a duty to use reasonable care for the safety of those who might be affected by the work.[67] If a landlord has repairing obligations (see above), she/he is also under a duty to make sure that anyone who could be expected to be in the premises will not suffer harm from any disrepair.[68]

This is also the case if the works are carried out before a tenancy is granted.[69] Architects, surveyors and others may be liable if they are responsible for defective work on premises.

Failure to meet the appropriate standards may be negligence. The main remedy for negligence is to claim damages in a court action. These are assessed so as to put the injured party, so far as possible, in the position they would have been in had there been no negligence. Legal advice is essential; legal aid may be available.

Premises Prejudicial to Health

In England and Wales, the Environmental Protection Act 1990 gives a remedy to any person 'aggrieved' by a 'statutory nuisance'. In Scotland, there are similar, although more limited, rights under the Public Health (Scotland) Act 1897.

The two Acts define 'statutory nuisance' to cover a range of matters. For people who live in defective premises, the most relevant of these is 'any premises in such a state as to be prejudicial to health or a nuisance'.[70]

Severe damp, including condensation, is generally accepted as being prejudicial to health for the purposes of the Acts – it encourages growth of mould spores, an increase in the number of dust mites and is associated with respiratory infection and rheumatism. Loose or exposed wiring and draughty windows and doors are other examples of problems which make a home prejudicial to health.

Local councils have a duty to investigate complaints of statutory nuisance, including at their own properties, and to serve a notice requiring the nuisance to be abated – ie, it must be put right. If the notice is not appealed against or complied with, the local authority can prosecute the person who was sent the notice and/or do the works itself.

Alternatively, you yourself can take your landlord to the magistrates' court.[71] In Scotland, you can only do this if the local authority fails to do so and ten local taxpayers jointly apply. These can be any ten local taxpayers, not just those living in the house.

In England and Wales, you must give 21 days' written warning to your landlord that you are going to take proceedings. You then 'lay an information' at your local magistrate's court giving details of the defective premises and why they are prejudicial to your health and/or any other occupier of the premises. In Scotland, the procedure is by Summary Application at the local Sheriff Court. At the subsequent hearing, you must prove the existence of the statutory nuisance and that the person you are prosecuting, your landlord, is responsible. Environmental health officers can give evidence of the existence of a statutory nuisance.

The court can make an order that your landlord must abate the nuisance. The court has wide discretion over what work it may order a landlord to do,[72] although it must be for abating the nuisance. As explained above, the repairing obligations are limited, so this kind of action can be useful if something additional, including improvements, is needed to abate the nuisance – in some cases courts have ordered the installation of central heating, double glazing and mechanical ventilators.

In England and Wales, the magistrates' court can also make a compensation order[73] for up to £5,000 for things such as damaged belongings and discomfort and inconvenience. If a court refuses to make a compensation order, it must give reasons. There is a small risk that you might have to pay the defendant's legal costs if you lose,[74] so you should take legal advice before starting a prosecution.

Condensation

Condensation dampness causes severe problems for many people, particularly those living in post-war system-built flats. The dampness and consequent mould growth can be damaging to health and can destroy clothing and furnishing. Attempts to heat damp premises can lead to high fuel bills. The causes of, and remedies for, condensation are complex. Most remedies are beyond the means or control of weekly tenants, involving substantial expenditure on, for example, structure and heating systems.

The existence of cold surfaces on which condensation forms depends on the level of:

• heating

• insulation *and*

• ventilation.

Avoiding condensation depends on establishing a balance between these inter-related factors. None is a solution by itself. A well-insulated building with no heating will be cold. A well-heated building with poorly insulated surfaces will be cold, particularly on the external walls where condensation occurs. If there is good ventilation, more heat is needed. If there is poor ventilation, less heat is necessary but there will be more moisture in the air.

Modern flats made from materials with poor insulatory qualities (eg, concrete instead of brick), with 'efficient' well-fitting windows (no draughts: poor ventilation) have the worst condensation problems. Remedying condensation may involve installing low-level background heating (so that the structure is warmed), installing electric extractor fans, increasing thermal insulation and double glazing. It may involve reducing or changing high moisture-producing activities. Most of these matters relate to the original design of a building and remedying them is not a tenant's responsibility.

Legal remedies for condensation

Disrepair: In Scotland, the obligations on a landlord discussed above (see p170) are wide enough to cover condensation. This means your landlord has to make sure that there is no condensation problem when your tenancy starts and that, if it arises during the tenancy and you tell her/him about it, she/he must do whatever works are necessary to solve the problem.

However, in England and Wales, for condensation to come within a landlord's repairing obligations, you must show that there has been 'damage to the structure and exterior which requires to be made good'.[75] This has to relate to the physical condition of the structure or exterior. Unless condensation has occurred over a long time and plaster has perished or window frames are rotten as a result, it may be hard to show this.

If the condensation damage is caused by inherent defects in the building (eg, because of defective materials), and if the only way to correct this is to carry out improvements, then this can be ordered by the court. A landlord will not, however, be ordered to renew a building completely or to change it substantially – what will be required is a question of degree.[76] But it is unlikely that a court would order installation of a different heating system or the full range of works necessary to remedy condensation.

Statutory nuisance

Therefore, in England and Wales, it will normally be more effective to prosecute under the Environmental Protection Act 1990 for a statutory nuisance' (see p173). It is not necessary to prove a breach of any contractual or statutory duty to use this remedy.[77] This means that a court can hold landlords liable even if they are not in breach of their responsibilities for repairs. A court can also order works of improvement if these are necessary to abate a nuisance.[78]

Landlords sometimes argue that tenants could avoid the nuisance by changing their lifestyle or by heating premises properly. This is rarely correct. If your landlord provides ventilation or a heating system, you would be expected to use it,[79] but you would not be required to use 'wholly abnormal quantities of fuel'.[80]

Remedies

This chapter covers:

I. INTRODUCTION

Various problems have been brought out in other parts of this book and the remedies in each instance have been touched on. This chapter aims to give a round-up of the remedies available if you are in dispute with a supplier of gas or electricity.

The powers of OFFER and OFGAS will be dealt with, followed by the individual remedies of taking a supplier to court for an injunction/interdict and/or damages and judicial review. But it is also possible to get what you want by approaching the supplier itself first, and the first section deals with such negotiations.

2. NEGOTIATIONS

Negotiating with the supplier can be the most appropriate way of resolving a problem or dispute. To negotiate effectively, you will need to rely on a range of documents which, in their different ways, provide 'rules' about how suppliers should behave. You may also want to involve OFFER or OFGAS. This book's introductory chapter gives background information on sources of law, and on OFFER and OFGAS, and it may be useful to read it first.

Using This Book for Legal Remedies

You can quote any part of this book in support of anything you might want to say, including the detailed references in the notes at the back (see pp284-294). Quoting the law can show that you know what you are talking about and that you are serious. However, suppliers' staff are more likely to be familiar with what their own Codes of Practice and policy statements say.

Using Codes of Practice and Policy Statements

Every supplier has to produce a Code of Practice on handling complaints.[1] You should get hold of a copy from your local showroom or regional office so that you know the procedure beforehand. British Gas has a customer relations manager in each region who should act like a kind of ombudsman, taking up your complaint and trying to resolve it before it goes anywhere else – OFGAS thinks that this system is working well.

The suppliers have also produced other Codes of Practice, as required by their Authorisation to Supply or Licence. Their staff will be more familiar with these than the precise provisions of the law. So long as the provisions of a Code of Practice support your case, it will normally be easier and more effective to quote them, rather than sections of Acts of Parliament. Each Code of Practice has been approved by OFFER or OFGAS before being used.

Each supplier should have Codes of Practice on:

• payment of bills;

• services for elderly or disabled people;

• using fuel efficiently;

• complaints procedures.

Each supplier also produces various documents setting out, or summarising, its policies, and giving other useful information. They are obliged to publish information regularly about their performance compared with targets set by OFGAS and OFFER and by themselves.[2] You should, of course, use these if they support your case, but you should always be cautious – as a summary of the law, they will not always be accurate.

Involving OFFER/OFGAS

Always remember that any negotiations you have with a supplier are carried out with the shadow of OFFER or OFGAS in the background. In general, the Gas Act and the Electricity Act do not set out individual remedies, but rather set out the powers of OFFER and OFGAS to enforce the provisions of the Acts. You can enforce those provisions directly in the ways discussed below, but it will often be worth involving OFFER or OFGAS before doing so.

You do not have to pay for their services. Also, the suppliers are very conscious of the presence of OFFER and OFGAS and will do their utmost not to trigger their statutory enforcement powers. The suppliers prefer to decide for themselves how to treat their customers, but each case in which OFFER or OFGAS is involved can lead to the setting out of general principles which will limit the suppliers' discretion on future cases. They may often concede an individual case before any formal procedure starts in order to avoid such a thing happening.

Standards of Performance

Each electricity supplier also has to comply with certain standards of performance.[3] There is now a power to set similar standards for gas,[4] but this has not yet been used. Instead, OFGAS has pressurised British Gas into devising a similar scheme. If the supplier fails to meet the standards laid down, then you are automatically entitled to payment of a fixed sum, although British Gas has kept a discretion to refuse payments under its scheme.

Electricity

The standards and the payments are virtually identical for each supplier. Your local showroom or regional office should provide a leaflet which sets them out – some leaflets may also describe additional standards which the supplier has set for itself. The standards set down by the law cover:

- failure of the supplier's fuse;
- restoring supply where disconnection was the supplier's fault;
- providing a supply;
- providing an estimate of charges for connection of a supply or moving a meter;
- giving notice when the supplier has to interrupt a supply;
- dealing with voltage complaints;

- dealing with meter disputes;
- responding to requests or queries about charges or payments;
- making and keeping appointments; *and*
- giving notice to consumers of their rights under this scheme.

The standards require the suppliers to carry out functions under each of these headings within a certain number of working days. Failure to do so means they have to pay you a sum of money, normally £20 or £40. There is a list of the normal time periods and compensation payments in Appendix 6.

However, these payments are not maximum payments. If failure to meet the standards causes you to lose more than £20 or £40, you can still claim the larger amount. If necessary, you can go to court over it (see p185). If there is any dispute between you and the supplier over these standards or the payments under them, you can refer the dispute to OFFER.

Gas

There are no standards laid down in law for gas (see above). However, OFGAS has persuaded British Gas to introduce similar standards of its own, backed up by a new Condition 13A inserted in their 'Authorisation to Supply'. Condition 13A is set out in Appendix 6. Again, you can get the appropriate leaflet from your local showroom or regional office setting out the standards.

There are some automatic levels of compensation, although fewer than for electricity, but the customer relations manager in each British Gas region does have the authority to settle claims for breach of these standards, up to £5,000.

You cannot sue directly for breach of these standards, but such a breach is an enforcement matter which OFGAS can take up by enforcing Condition 13A.

3. OFFER AND OFGAS

The statutory remedies described in this section have limitations. OFFER/OFGAS are independent, not acting on behalf of you or the supplier, so you cannot tell them what to do and it is possible for them to act in ways which are not in your best interests, however good their intentions. Despite the fact that it will almost certainly involve more time, effort and, if you do not qualify for legal aid, money, taking

your own legal action will sometimes be a better way of asserting
your rights (see p185).

Enforcement Matters

OFFER and OFGAS have powers to order the suppliers to do anything they think is needed to get them to comply with certain provisions of the Acts or any conditions in their Authorisation to Supply or
Licence.[5] The matters covered by these powers are called 'enforcement matters'.[6]

Enforcement matters include:

- giving and continuing to supply electricity/gas;[7]

- paying interest on security deposits for meters and supply;[8]

- publicising tariffs;[9]

- providing meters;[10]

- producing Codes of Practice on dealing with customers in default.[11]

The list of enforcement matters seems more limited than it really is.
For instance, disputes about responsibility for bills are not specifically
mentioned but may be covered indirectly, because one remedy for a
supplier in a dispute is to disconnect you and disconnection is an
enforcement matter.

Both OFFER and OFGAS can intervene in a dispute if it is likely to
end up being an enforcement matter.[12]

The Conditions in gas suppliers' Authorisations to Supply and electricity suppliers' Licences are not enforceable by individual consumers
because they are obligations arising between the respective supplier
and OFFER/OFGAS. Most disputes will arise directly under the Acts;
but those that only involve breaches of Licence Conditions will have
to be referred to OFFER or OFGAS. If necessary, OFFER or OFGAS's
exercise of their powers can be judicially reviewed;[13] in certain circumstances the suppliers themselves may be judicially reviewed also
(see p188).

Orders

When an enforcement matter arises, OFFER or OFGAS can make one
of two kinds of order: a 'Provisional Order' or a 'Final Order'. The
making of a Provisional Order[14] is quicker than that of a Final Order[15] so you should always press for the former.

Procedure

If you think a supplier is in breach of an enforcement matter, you should write to OFFER/OFGAS, specifically referring to an 'enforcement matter'. Unless the matter is considered 'frivolous', OFFER/OFGAS must investigate it.[16] If satisfied that there has been a breach, OFFER/OFGAS must make either a Provisional or Final Order.[17]

OFFER/OFGAS cannot make an order if:

- they think that the general duties laid on them by the Acts do not allow it;

- the supplier's breaches of its obligations are trivial;[18] *or*

- they are satisfied that the supplier has agreed to and is taking all steps necessary to comply with their obligations anyway.[19]

OFFER/OFGAS must tell you if they decide not to make an Order.[20]

In deciding whether to make an Order, OFFER/OFGAS must take into account, in particular, your lack of other remedies and the loss or damage which you might suffer during the consultation period which has to take place before a Final Order is made.[21] If you would otherwise be without a supply, a Provisional Order will normally be appropriate.

If a Provisional Order is made and complied with, OFFER/OFGAS will only go on to confirm it as a Final Order if further breaches might happen.

Before making a Final Order or confirming a Provisional Order, OFFER/OFGAS must serve you and the supplier with a copy of the proposed Order and allow 28 days for representations.[22] If they want to modify the original proposal, OFFER/OFGAS must either get the consent of the supplier or serve copies and allow 28 days again.[23] They must go through a similar procedure to revoke a Final Order.[24]

OFFER/OFGAS must also comply with the ordinary legal rules about natural justice which govern public or government organisations (see p188 for information on judicial reviews). In one case, a decision by OFGAS was quashed by the High Court because they did not tell a consumer that they had interviewed an important witness, nor did they give the consumer a chance to reply to what the witness had said.[25]

You are entitled to a copy of any Order when it is made.[26]

A supplier can appeal to the High Court (or the Court of Session in Scotland) against the making of an Order.[27] Although you would not necessarily be directly involved, you can be added as a third party – this is a technical procedure for which you will have to get legal advice.

The duty to obey any Order is owed by the supplier not only to OFFER/OFGAS, but also to you and anyone else who might be affected by a breach of it by the supplier.[28] This means you can sue for a breach if OFFER/OFGAS do not enforce their own Order.[29] OFFER/OFGAS can also enforce their own Orders by ordinary civil action against the supplier – if you cannot obtain legal aid to do this yourself, this way may be easier and cheaper.

Neither OFFER nor OFGAS has devised any guidelines about their use of Provisional and Final Orders so each case is decided on its merits. As mentioned above, cases will rarely reach this stage because suppliers want to avoid formal (and public) action against themselves.

Content of Orders

The Order must set out what the supplier is required to do in order to comply with its obligations – eg, reconnect the supply. The Acts do not go any further than to say that what is ordered must not be outside what is allowed under the general duties and powers of the respective Director General.[30] Neither OFFER nor OFGAS believes that they have the power to order a supplier to pay any money in compensation. If you have suffered a loss which you have to pay out for, you will have to rely on informal pressure by OFFER/OFGAS on the supplier or on your own legal action.

The Order must also say when it is to take effect and it must be the earliest practicable time.[31] A Provisional Order must also say when it will cease to have effect and that must be not more than three months after it comes into effect.[32]

Breach of Conditions 12A and 19

Condition 12A in British Gas's Authorisation to Supply and Condition 19 in the electricity companies' Licences require them to compile methods to deal with customers in default. These matters are dealt with elsewhere in this book but it is worth pointing out that a supplier's failure to comply with these 'methods' is an enforcement matter because it is a breach of the relevant Condition. Normally, the methods for dealing with customers in default are kept a commercial secret which only OFFER/OFGAS and the relevant company know. Therefore, if you think you have not been dealt with properly, it is worth referring the matter to OFFER or OFGAS so that they can see if the methods have not been followed correctly. On the other hand, some suppliers are willing to allow advice agencies to see their methods on a confidential basis – you should ask the local company or region if your adviser can have a look.

Non-Enforcement Matters – Consumers' Councils and Committees

Non-enforcement matters are those for which OFFER/OFGAS cannot use their enforcement powers. OFFER/OFGAS can still be involved, particularly if a non-enforcement matter might turn into an enforcement matter, but this is more the area covered by the Gas Consumers' Council and the various electricity consumers' committees.

The Council and the committees have to investigate certain matters referred to them, mainly to do with problems arising where the supplier is not actually breaking the law.[33] This includes disputes about arrangements for paying off arrears, or about the amount of a deposit where the amount is reasonable but you cannot afford it.

You can write direct to the Council or committee, or OFFER/-OFGAS can refer the matter to them. When a complaint is received, the first thing that has to be decided is whether it relates to an enforcement matter. If it does, it is referred back to OFFER/OFGAS; if not, the Council or committee should investigate it. If appropriate, the Council or committee can refer the matter to OFFER/OFGAS even if it is a non-enforcement matter.[34]

If there is a dispute about something which is technically a non-enforcement matter (eg, a potential breach of a supplier's Code of Practice) but one which will become an enforcement matter if the supplier acts as it threatens, you should ask the Council or committee to refer the dispute to OFFER/OFGAS straight away, if that has not already been done.

Neither the Gas Act nor the Electricity Act says what the Council or committee should do once they have finished their investigations. They have no powers of enforcement but have general powers to report and publicise their work.[35] In practice, the suppliers do co-operate with their respective Council or committee, appearing in front of them when asked to do so and answering questions which are asked. Obviously, however, when there is conflict, the Council and committees have no teeth to back up their bark and you may end up relying on your individual remedies.

The Gas Consumers' Council also has the power to investigate and report on matters concerning gas fittings supplied by a gas supplier.[36]

Determinations

The Directors General of OFFER and OFGAS also have the power to 'determine' certain disputes between suppliers and consumers.[37] A Determination binds the parties and cannot be appealed.[38] However, anything done by OFFER/OFGAS is subject to judicial review (see p188).

OFFER/OFGAS are limited to determining disputes arising under a few sections of the respective Acts.[39] This includes the duty to supply electricity or gas, the power to recover charges or require security and special agreements. However, as with enforcement powers, this list is not quite as limited as it seems – eg, a disconnection is a failure of the duty to supply electricity or gas.

There are provisions for disputes about gas or electricity bills to be determined by OFFER/OFGAS.[40] However, the required regulations, setting out when and how such a decision can be made, have not yet been issued and are not likely to be issued. Most billing disputes can come within the other determination and enforcement powers anyway.

Procedure

You or the supplier can refer a dispute to OFFER/OFGAS.[41] The supplier is unlikely to do this because a decision of this kind reads like a court judgment, setting out OFFER/OFGAS's opinion of the law, and will restrict what the supplier can do in future in a similar way as any rule of law.

Once the dispute has been referred, OFFER/OFGAS are obliged to go through with the Determination.[42] In fact, although this is what the law says, OFFER/OFGAS's practice is to try to settle a dispute rather than go through with a Determination if it thinks that this is the best way of dealing with it from its point of view. If you did not approach the supplier to try to settle the matter before referring it to OFFER/OFGAS, its first step would be to ask you to do so. OFGAS in particular wants to reserve its determination powers for test cases where it will have an opportunity to set out a new legal opinion.

The procedure by which OFFER/OFGAS go about making the Determination can be whatever they think is appropriate.[43] However, OFFER/OFGAS will have to comply with the rules of natural justice and are subject to judicial review (see p188).

If the supplier is threatening to disconnect you, OFFER/OFGAS do have the power to order that the supply should restart or continue, as appropriate, until they have finished determining the dispute.[44] If OFFER/OFGAS refuse to exercise this power and the supplier will not voluntarily refrain from disconnection, it may be best to abandon the Determination procedure and pursue your normal rights through the courts or to challenge OFFER/OFGAS by judicial review (see p188).

If the dispute is about providing security, OFFER/OFGAS also have the power to require you to provide security pending the Determination.[45]

OFFER/OFGAS must give reasons for reaching their decisions under this procedure.[46]

Costs

A danger in this procedure is that OFFER/OFGAS have the power to order either side (presumably the 'losing' side) to pay the costs of making the determination.[47] In a court case, if you have legal aid, you can be protected against a costs order, but legal aid is not available for a Determination. In fact, this danger is likely to be extremely small, particularly as OFFER/OFGAS must take into account your financial circumstances before making any such order.[48]

OFFER has now made a small number of Determinations. OFGAS has not, although, before its power to make determinations was brought in, it did decide on a number of cases involving tampering – these decisions had the same effect as Determinations but were not published. With its emphasis on settling cases rather than using determination powers, OFGAS may still follow this procedure in the future if it thinks it is appropriate. If it is not appropriate to your case, you can challenge OFGAS through judicial review (see p188).

The relevant findings and opinions of the law in any Determinations are included, where appropriate, in the text of the relevant preceding chapters. Copies of Determinations are available from OFFER (see Appendix 10 for addresses).

4. USING THE COURTS

There are two possible relevant types of court action in the field of fuel rights – ordinary court action or judicial review. It has already been said that Scotland has a different legal system from that in England and Wales; the availability of each of the two court procedures is therefore different.

Appendix 7 gives an example of how an ordinary court claim would look in England and Wales when suing a supplier. However, a Scottish Sheriff Court would probably not allow such an action so that you would be left with pursuing your remedies through OFFER/OFGAS. On the other hand, OFFER and OFGAS are subject to judicial review. The procedure for judicial review is more flexible and easier to use in Scotland than in England and Wales so you should still have an effective remedy.

Legal aid is available for suing a supplier or for judicial review, if you have a strong enough case and qualify on financial grounds. This will cover all your legal costs and protect you against an order to pay the other side's legal costs if you lose. If your income is above a certain level, you will have to make a contribution to these costs.

Injunctions/Interdicts and Damages

This section sets out the remedies you can get through the ordinary courts and so is more relevant to English and Welsh readers. Firstly, it is necessary to know how they relate to the remedies available from OFFER/OFGAS.

Determinations by OFFER/OFGAS are final, and once a determination has been made you cannot sue a supplier over the same matters.[49] Whether you can sue a supplier at the same time as OFFER/OFGAS is using its enforcement powers is not so clear.[50]

In practice, it should rarely, if ever, be necessary to duplicate proceedings in this way. However, in theory, for example, OFFER/OFGAS could refuse to make an order to reconnect your supply so that you need to get your own court order while they continue to consider what else they might order the supplier to do or not to do. Also a court could, and almost certainly would, refuse to consider a case if it felt that OFFER/OFGAS were dealing with it in a way which seemed to be adequate at the time.

In practice, you will have to consider at the very start which route you should take: Determination, enforcement or your own legal action. Whether or not to use the enforcement powers is OFFER/OFGAS's own decision (subject to judicial review) but you can take the lead on the other two routes.

Injunctions/interdicts

An injunction is an order made by a court which either prohibits someone from doing something (a 'prohibitory' injunction) or instructs someone to do something (a 'mandatory' injunction). (The Scottish equivalent is an interdict.) For example, if a supplier cuts off your supply you could ask for an injunction to get it reconnected. Failure to obey an injunction is contempt of court, punishable by fines or even imprisonment in extreme cases.

Although there are some situations in which an injunction is granted almost as a matter of course (eg, illegal eviction), you have no 'right' to an injunction. Injunctions are within a court's discretion and whether or not they are granted depends on the overall circumstances of the case.

The most common situation in a dispute with a supplier is where you will be asking for an 'interlocutory injunction' (or interim interdict in Scotland). You go for an interlocutory injunction when you need a court order quickly which will only apply for a limited time, usually until the whole case can be put properly before the court in a fully prepared trial. In this situation, neither you nor the supplier will have time to present your case fully and the court will have to make up its mind without hearing the evidence in full. The court will consider the 'balance of convenience' – ie, whether you or the supplier has more to lose or gain from the refusal or granting of an interlocutory injunction, including whether a later award of damages will make up for any such loss.[51] For example, where a supplier threatens disconnection, the court will balance the inconvenience to you of being disconnected against the inconvenience to the supplier of having to continue to supply someone regarded as a bad customer. Legal advice will be essential.

Damages

As well as, or instead of, an injunction, you can claim damages – ie, monetary compensation – for a supplier's abuse of its powers or failure to comply with its duties. If a supplier accidentally cuts off your supply, you may be able to claim damages for negligence. If a supplier deliberately cuts off your supply but without legal justification, you may be able to claim damages for breach of statutory duty.

In a case of failure to supply, damages would cover compensation not only for the distress and discomfort of being without a supply, but also for additional expenses (eg, take-away meals) and the loss of specific items (eg, fridge/freezer contents).

The duty to supply you with electricity or gas is statutory, not contractual, and failure to supply you would be a clear breach of that duty. The authors of the seventh edition of this book expressed doubts as to whether the courts would allow an individual to sue for damages for such a breach. The argument would be that Parliament has provided other remedies – ie, the enforcement powers of OFGAS and OFFER – and that these are meant to be the only remedies.[52] This argument was stronger under the old law which provided for criminal prosecution when certain duties were breached. The current authors believe that there can now be little doubt that individuals can, in principle, recover damages for breach of suppliers' present legal duties. The fact that OFFER and OFGAS have no power to order monetary compensation supports this.

Enforcing an Order Made by OFFER/OFGAS

Despite the limitations discussed above, it will, more often than not, be easier and cheaper if OFFER or OFGAS take action first. A Determination has the same status as a court judgment ('an extract registered decree arbitral bearing a warrant for execution issued by a sheriff' in Scotland)[53] so you can enforce it yourself, if necessary. If a final or provisional order is made, you can sue a supplier in England and Wales for failure to comply with any part of it, including a claim for damages, as described in the previous section.[54]

Judicial Review

Public bodies such as OFFER or OFGAS have both statutory duties, which must be performed, and powers, which allow for a large element of discretion. There is usually no right of appeal against a failure to perform a 'power',[55] or as to how that discretion is exercised. However, this does not mean that nothing can be done. Such administrative matters are subject to control by judicial review[56] on the grounds of illegality, irrationality or procedural impropriety (see below).[57]

The exercise of any 'public' powers by any of the principal bodies discussed in this book will be subject to judicial review. This includes not only OFFER, OFGAS and the various consumers' councils and committees, but also the suppliers themselves. That the suppliers should be subject to judicial review in appropriate circumstances is probably a radical suggestion but is in line with the latest decisions by the courts.[58] Legal advice will be essential.

- An *illegal* decision is one where the decision-making body has not been given the legal power to do what it has done – ie, if it has gone outside its remit or what it was set up to do.

- An *irrational* decision is one which is so unreasonable that no reasonable authority could make it (in legal jargon this is 'Wednesbury' unreasonableness, named after the court case in which the principle was established).

- *Procedural impropriety* means procedural unfairness – ie, breaches of the rules of natural justice.

Breach of one or more of these principles gives the court the power to overturn an authority's decision. It is important to realise that a court cannot overturn a decision simply because it thinks it would have come to a different decision. The court does not put itself in the place of the decision-maker but merely ensures she/he has kept within the boundaries of the law. It is possible for two different, even contradictory, decisions to lie within those boundaries so that it would be equally lawful for the decision-maker to choose either.

In England and Wales, the court can make an order overturning a decision ('certiorari') or requiring the body which is being judicially reviewed to do or not to do something ('mandamus' and 'prohibition'), in the same way as an injunction described above. In Scotland, a decision can be quashed by 'reduction' and a 'declarator' ('declaration' in England and Wales) can be issued establishing the legal position. If damages could be claimed on ordinary principles, the court in judicial review proceedings may also award them.

Applications for judicial review in England and Wales must be made promptly to the High Court and, in any event, within three months of the relevant decision.[59] In Scotland, applications must be made to the Court of Session; there is no specific time limit but applications must not be unduly delayed.

Small Claims

If you have a dispute which only involves a money claim of less than £1,000 (£750 in Scotland), you can use the small claims procedure in the county court/Sheriff Court. This might be appropriate if an unlawful disconnection has caused you a relatively small loss or your landlord has been charging more than the maximum resale price for gas or electricity.

Legal aid is not available and a more informal procedure is used, suitable for people who are not represented by a solicitor. The court staff should always be willing to help you with the procedure (Citizens' Advice Bureaux or other local advice agencies may also help). When you issue the summons you will have to pay a court fee (normally 10% of the amount you are claiming up to a limit of £60, although in England and Wales the fee can be waived in cases of hardship on application to the Lord Chancellor's Department).

If you win your case, this fee is added to the amount which the other side have to pay you. In England and Wales, unlike other court proceedings, no other costs can be reclaimed. This means that, even if you lose, you will not have to pay the other side's own legal costs. In Scotland, no costs are payable if the claim is under £200, but costs can be awarded up to £75 if the claim is over £200.

Legal Advice

In any application for an injunction or damages or for judicial review, legal advice is essential. However, it is not always easy to find a solicitor willing to take up a fuel rights case. There are a number of reasons for this, including that fuel law is complicated and not widely known.

This book has been designed, with all the legal references at the back, to be just as useful for a lawyer as anyone else and can be used as a full legal reference work. In order to help advisers in England and Wales, Appendix 7 gives an example for a legal action concerning a threat of disconnection over a damaged meter. When you go to a solicitor you can refer her/him to this book, including the Appendix; it could also be used when drafting an application for legal aid.

Legal References

This appendix contains extracts of legislation and notes of court decisions that are referred to in the text and footnotes. The legislation appears first and the notes of court decisions follow.

The extracts do not include social security law (which is more readily available) nor laws whose bearing on the text is of a more marginal or general nature.

GAS ACT 1986

General duties of Secretary of State and Director

4(1) The Secretary of State and the Director shall each have a duty to exercise the functions assigned to him by this Part in the manner which he considers is best calculated

    (a) to secure that persons authorised by or under this Part to supply gas through pipes satisfy, so far as it is economical to do so, all reasonable demands for gas in Great Britain; and

    (b) without prejudice to the generality of paragraph (a) above, to secure that such persons are able to finance the provision of gas supply services.

(1A) In relation to the conveyance and storage of gas the Secretary of State and the Director shall, in addition, each have a duty to exercise the functions assigned to him by this Part in the manner which he considers is best calculated to secure effective competition between persons whose business consists of or includes the supply of gas.

(2) Subject to subsection (1) above, the Secretary of State and the Director shall each have a duty to exercise the functions assigned to him by this Part in the manner which he considers is best calculated

    (a) to protect the interests of consumers of gas supplied through pipes in respect of the prices charged and the other terms of supply, the continuity of supply and the quality of the gas supply services provided;

    (b) to promote efficiency and economy on the part of persons authorised by or under this Part to supply gas through pipes and the efficient use of gas supplied through pipes;

    (c) to protect the public from dangers arising from the transmission or distribution of gas through pipes or from the use of gas supplied through pipes;

    (d) to enable persons to compete effectively in the supply of gas through pipes at rates which, in relation to any premises, exceed 2,500 therms a year.

(3) In performing his duty under subsection (2) above to exercise functions assigned to him in the manner which he considers is best calculated to protect

the interests of consumers of gas supplied through pipes in respect of the quality of the gas supply services provided, the Secretary of State or, as the case may be, the Director shall take into account, in particular, the interests of those who are disabled or of pensionable age.

(4)   Subsections (1) and (2) above do not apply in relation to the determination of disputes by the Director under or by virtue of section 14A, 15A or 33A below.

General powers and duties

9(1)   It shall be the duty of a public gas supplier
(a)   to develop and maintain an efficient, co-ordinated and economical system of gas supply; and
(b)   subject to paragraph (a) above, to comply, so far as it is economical to do so, with any reasonable request for him to give a supply of gas to any premises.

(2)   It shall also be the duty of a public gas supplier to avoid any undue preference in the supply of gas to persons entitled to a supply in pursuance of section 10(1) below.

(3)   The following provisions shall have effect, namely
(a)   Schedule 3 to this Act (which provides for the acquisition of land by public gas suppliers); and
(b)   Schedule 4 to this Act (which relates to the breaking up of streets and bridges by such suppliers).

Duty to supply certain premises

10(1)   Subject to the following provisions of this Part and any regulations made under those provisions, a public gas supplier shall, upon being required to do so by the owner or occupier, give and continue to give a supply of gas to any premises which
(a)   are situated within 25 yards from a relevant main of the supplier; or
(b)   are connected by a service pipe to any such main, and in the case of premises falling within paragraph (a) above, shall also provide and lay any pipe that may be necessary for that purpose.

(2)   Where any person requires a supply of gas in pursuance of subsection (1) above, he shall serve on the public gas supplier a notice specifying
(a)   the premises in respect of which the supply is required; and
(b)   the day (not being earlier than a reasonable time after the service of the notice) upon which the supply is required to commence.

(3)   Where any pipe is provided and laid by a public gas supplier in pursuance of subsection (1) above, the cost of providing and laying
(a)   so much of the pipe as is laid upon property owned or occupied by the person requiring the supply, not being property dedicated to public use; and
(b)   so much of the pipe as is laid for a greater distance than 30 feet from any pipe of the supplier, although not on such property as is mentioned in paragraph (a) above, shall, if the supplier so requires, be defrayed by that person.

(4)   The Secretary of State may, after consultation with the Director, make provision by regulations for entitling a public gas supplier to require a person requiring a supply of gas in pursuance of subsection (1) above to pay to the

supplier an amount in respect of the expenses of the laying of the main used for the purpose of giving that supply if

(a) the supply is required within the prescribed period after the laying of the main;

(b) a person for the purpose of supplying whom the main was laid has made a payment to the supplier in respect of those expenses;

(c) the amount required does not exceed any amount paid in respect of those expenses by such a person or by any person previously required to make a payment under the regulations; and

(d) the supplier has not recovered those expenses in full.

(5) Nothing in subsection (1) above shall be taken as requiring a public gas supplier to supply gas to any premises in excess of [2,500] therms in any period of twelve months.

(6) Nothing in subsection (1) above shall be taken as requiring a public gas supplier to give or continue to give a supply of gas to any premises if

(a) he is prevented from doing so by circumstances not within his control; or

(b) circumstances exist by reason of which his doing so would or might involve danger to the public, and he has taken all such steps as it was reasonable to take both to prevent the circumstances from occurring and to prevent them from having that effect.

(7) Where any person requires a new or increased supply of gas in pursuance of subsection (1) above for purposes other than domestic use, and the supply cannot be given without the laying of a new main, or the enlarging of an existing main, or the construction or enlarging of any other works required for the supply of gas by the public gas supplier, the supplier may, if he thinks fit, refuse to give the supply unless that person enters into a written contract with him

(a) to continue to receive and pay for a supply of gas of such minimum quantity and for such minimum period as the supplier may reasonably require, having regard to the expense to be incurred by him in laying or enlarging the main or constructing or enlarging the other works; or

(b) to make such payment to the supplier (in addition to any payments to be made from time to time for gas supplied) as the supplier may reasonably require having regard to the matters aforesaid.

(8) Where any person requires a supply of gas in pursuance of subsection (1) above for the purposes only of a stand-by supply for any premises having a separate supply of gas, or having a supply (in use or ready for use for the purpose for which the stand-by supply is required) of electricity, steam or other form of energy, the supplier may, if he thinks fit, refuse to give or discontinue the supply unless that person enters into a written contract with him to pay him such annual sum in addition to any charge for gas supplied as

(a) will give him a reasonable return on the capital expenditure incurred by him in providing the stand-by supply; and

(b) will cover other expenditure incurred by him in order to meet the maximum possible demand for those premises.

(9) In this section 'relevant main' has the same meaning as in section 7 above.

Power to require security

11(1) Where any person requires a supply of gas in pursuance of subsection (1) of section 10 above

(a) the public gas supplier may require that person to give him reasonable security for the payment to him of all money which may become due to him in respect of the supply or, where any pipe falls to be provided and laid in pursuance of that subsection, the provision and laying of the pipe; and

(b) if that person fails to give such security, the supplier may if he thinks fit refuse to give the supply, or to provide and lay the pipe, for so long as the failure continues.

(2) Where any person who requires a supply of gas in pursuance of subsection (1) of section 10 above enters into such a contract as is mentioned in subsection (7) or (8) of that section

(a) the public gas supplier may require that person to give him reasonable security for the payment to him of all money which may become due to him under the contract; and

(b) if that person fails to give such security, the supplier may if he thinks fit refuse to give the supply for so long as the failure continues.

(3) Where any person has not given such security as is mentioned in subsection (1) or (2) above, or the security given by any person has become invalid or insufficient

(a) the public gas supplier may by notice require that person within seven days after the service of the notice, to give him reasonable security for the payment of all money which may become due to him in respect of the supply or, as the case may be, under the contract; and

(b) if that person fails to give such security, the supplier may if he thinks fit discontinue the supply for so long as the failure continues.

(4) Where any money is deposited with a public gas supplier by way of security in pursuance of this section, the supplier shall pay interest, at such rate as may from time to time be fixed by the supplier with the approval of the Director, on every sum of 50p so deposited for every three months during which it remains in the hands of the supplier.

Fixing of tariffs

14(1) Subject to the following provisions of this section, the prices to be charged by a public gas supplier for the supply of gas by him shall be in accordance with such tariffs as may be fixed from time to time by him, and those tariffs, which may relate to the supply of gas in different areas, cases and circumstances, shall be so framed as to show the methods by which and the principles on which the charges are to be made as well as the prices which are to be charged and shall be published in such manner as in the opinion of the supplier will secure adequate publicity for them.

(2) A tariff fixed by a public gas supplier under subsection (1) above may include a standing charge in addition to the charge for the actual gas supplied, and may also include a rent or other charge in respect of any gas meter or other gas fittings provided by the supplier on the premises of the consumer.

(3) In fixing tariffs under subsection (1) above, a public gas supplier shall not show undue preference to any person or class of persons, and shall not exercise any undue discrimination against any person or class of persons; but this subsection shall not apply in relation to tariffs fixed under that subsection with respect to the prices to be charged for therms supplied to any premises in excess of 2,500 therms in any period of twelve months.

(4) Notwithstanding anything in section 12 or 13 above or the preceding provisions of this section, a public gas supplier may enter into a special

agreement with any consumer for the supply of gas to him on such terms as may be specified in the agreement if either

  (a)   the tariffs in force are not appropriate owing to special circumstances; or

  (b)   the agreement provides for a minimum supply of gas to any premises in excess of 2,500 therms in any period of twelve months.

  (5)   In this Part 'tariff customer' means a person who is supplied with gas by a public gas supplier otherwise than in pursuance of such an agreement as is mentioned in subsection (4) above.

Determination of disputes

14A(1)   Any dispute arising under section 9(1)(b), 10, 11 or 14 above, or any provision of paragraphs 1 to 4 of Schedule 5 to this Act ('the relevant provisions'), between a public gas supplier and a person who is, or wishes to become, a tariff customer of that supplier

  (a)   may be referred to the Director by either party, or with the agreement of either party, by the Council; and

  (b)   on such a reference, shall be determined by order made either by the Director, or if he thinks fit by an arbitrator (or in Scotland arbiter), appointed by him.

  (2)   Any person making an order under subsection (1) above shall include in the order his reasons for reaching his decision with respect to the dispute.

  (3)   The practice and procedure to be followed in connection with any such determination shall be such as the Director may consider appropriate.

  (4)   Where any dispute between a public gas supplier and a person requiring a supply of gas falls to be determined under this section, the Director may give directions as to the circumstances in which, and the terms on which, the supplier is to give or (as the case may be) to continue to give the supply pending the determination of the dispute.

  (5)   Where any dispute arising under section 11(1) above falls to be determined under this section, the Director may give directions as to the security (if any) to be given pending the determination of the dispute.

  (6)   Any direction under subsection (4) or (5) above may be expressed to apply either in relation to a particular case or in relation to a class of case.

  (7)   An order under this section

  (a)   may include such incidental, supplemental and consequential provision (including provision requiring either party to pay a sum in respect of the costs or expenses incurred by the person making the order) as that person considers appropriate; and

  (b)   shall be final and

  (i)   in England and Wales enforceable, in so far as it includes such provision as to costs or expenses, as if it were a judgment of a county court; and

  (ii)   in Scotland, enforceable as if it were an extract registered decree arbitral bearing a warrant for execution issued by the sheriff.

  (8)   In including in an order under this section any such provision as to costs or expenses, the person making the order shall have regard to the conduct and means of the parties and any other relevant circumstances.

Billing disputes

15A(1)   The Secretary of State may by regulations make provision for billing disputes to be referred to the Director for determination in accordance with the regulations.

(2)   In this section 'billing dispute' means a dispute between a public gas supplier and a tariff customer of his concerning the amount of the charge which the supplier is entitled to recover from the customer in connection with the provision of gas supply services.

(3)   Regulations under this section may only be made after consulting
(a)   the Director; and
(b)   persons or bodies appearing to the Secretary of State to be representative of persons likely to be affected by the regulations.

(4)   Regulations under this section may provide that, where a billing dispute is referred to the Director, he may either
(a)   determine the dispute, or
(b)   appoint an arbitrator (or in Scotland an arbiter) to determine it.

(5)   Any person determining any billing dispute in accordance with regulations under this section shall, in such manner as may be specified in the regulations, give his reasons for reaching his decision with respect to the dispute.

(6)   Regulations under this section may provide
(a)   that disputes may be referred to the Director under this section only by prescribed persons; and
(b)   for any determination to be final and enforceable
(i)   in England and Wales, as if it were a judgment of a county court; and
(ii)   in Scotland, as if it were an extract registered decree arbitral bearing a warrant for execution issued by the sheriff.

(7)   Except in such circumstances (if any) as may be prescribed
(a)   the Director or an arbitrator (or in Scotland an arbiter) appointed by him shall not determine any billing dispute which is the subject of proceedings before, or with respect to which judgment has been given by, any court; and
(b)   neither party to any billing dispute which has been referred to the Director for determination in accordance with regulations under this section shall commence proceedings before any court in respect of that dispute pending its determination in accordance with the regulations.

(8)   No public gas supplier may commence proceedings before any court in respect of any charge in connection with the provision by him of gas supply services unless, not less than 28 days before doing so, the tariff customer concerned was informed by him, in such form and manner as may be prescribed, of
(a)   his intention to commence proceedings;
(b)   the customer's rights by virtue of this section; and
(c)   such other matters (if any) as may be prescribed.

(9)   The powers of the Director under section 38 below shall also be exercisable for any purpose connected with the determination of any dispute referred to him in accordance with regulations made under this section.

Meter testing and stamping

17(1)   No meter shall be used for the purpose of ascertaining the quantity of gas supplied through pipes to any person unless it is stamped either by, or on the authority of, a meter examiner appointed under this section or in such other manner as may be authorised by regulations.

(2) Subject to subsections (3) and (4) below, it shall be the duty of a meter examiner, on being required to do so by any person and on payment of the prescribed fee, to examine any meter used or intended to be used for ascertaining the quantity of gas supplied to any person, and to stamp, or authorise the stamping of, that meter.

(3) A meter examiner shall not stamp, or authorise the stamping of, any meter unless he is satisfied that it is of such pattern and construction and is marked in such manner as is approved by the Secretary of State and that the meter conforms with such standards as may be prescribed.

(4) A meter examiner may stamp, or authorise the stamping of, a meter submitted to him, notwithstanding that he has not himself examined it, if
(a) the meter was manufactured or repaired by the person submitting it;
(b) that person has obtained the consent of the Secretary of State to the submission; and
(c) any conditions subject to which the consent was given have been satisfied.

(5) The Secretary of State shall appoint competent and impartial persons as meter examiners for the purposes of this section.

(6) There shall be paid out of money provided by Parliament to meter examiners such remuneration and such allowances as may be determined by the Secretary of State with the approval of the Treasury, and such pensions as maybe so determined may be paid out of money provided by Parliament to or in respect of such examiners.

(7) All fees payable in respect of the examination of meters by meter examiners shall be paid to the Secretary of State; and any sums received by him under this subsection shall be paid into the Consolidated Fund.

(8) Regulations may make provision
(a) for re-examining meters already stamped, and for the cancellation of stamps in the case of meters which no longer conform with the prescribed standards and in such other circumstances as may be prescribed;
(b) for requiring meters to be periodically overhauled;
(c) for the revocation of any approval given by the Secretary of State to any particular pattern or construction of meter, and for requiring existing meters of that pattern or construction to be replaced within such period as may be prescribed; and
(d) for determining the fees to be paid for examining, stamping and re-examining meters, and the persons by whom they are to be paid.

(9) If any person supplies gas through a meter which has not been stamped under this section, he shall be guilty of an offence and liable on summary conviction to a fine not exceeding level 3 on the standard scale.

(10) Where the commission by any person of an offence under subsection (9) above is due to the act or default of some other person, that other person shall be guilty of the offence; and a person may be charged with and convicted of the offence by virtue of this subsection whether or not proceedings are taken against the first-mentioned person.

(11) In any proceedings for an offence under subsection (9) above it shall be a defence for the person charged to prove that he took all reasonable steps and exercised all due diligence to avoid committing the offence.

(12) The preceding provisions of this section shall not have effect in relation to the supply of gas to a person under any agreement providing for the quantity

of gas supplied to him to be ascertained by a meter designed for rates of flow which, if measured at a temperature of 15°C and a pressure of 1013.25 millibars, would exceed 1,600 cubic metres an hour.

Orders for securing compliance with certain provisions

28(1)   Subject to subsections (2) and (5) and section 29 below, where the Director is satisfied that a public gas supplier is contravening, or is likely to contravene, any relevant condition or requirement, the Director shall by a final order make such provision as is requisite for the purpose of securing compliance with that condition or requirement.

(2)   Subject to subsection (5) below, where it appears to the Director
   (a)   that a public gas supplier is contravening, or is likely to contravene, any relevant condition or requirement; and
   (b)   that it is requisite that a provisional order be made, the Director shall (instead of taking steps towards the making of a final order) by a provisional order make such provision as appears to him requisite for the purpose of securing compliance with that condition or requirement.

(3)   In determining for the purposes of subsection (2)(b) above whether it is requisite that a provisional order be made, the Director shall have regard, in particular
   (a)   to the extent to which any person is likely to sustain loss or damage in consequence of anything which, in contravention of the relevant condition or requirement, is likely to be done, or omitted to be done, before a final order may be made; and
   (b)   to the fact that the effect of the provisions of this section and section 30 below is to exclude the availability of any remedy (apart from under those provisions or for negligence) in respect of any contravention of a relevant condition or requirement.

(4)   Subject to subsection (5) and section 29 below, the Director shall confirm a provisional order, with or without modifications, if
   (a)   he is satisfied that the public gas supplier is contravening, or ... is likely ...to contravene, any relevant condition or requirement; and
   (b)   the provision made by the order (with any modifications) is requisite for the purpose of securing compliance with that condition or requirement.

(5)   The Director shall not make a final order or make or confirm a provisional order if he is satisfied
   (a)   that the duties imposed on him by section 4 above preclude the making or, as the case may be, the confirmation of the order; or
   (aa)   that the public gas supplier has agreed to take and is taking all such steps as it appears to the Director for the time being to be appropriate for the supplier to take for the purpose of securing or facilitating compliance with the condition or requirement in question;
   (b)   that the contraventions were or the apprehended contraventions are of a trivial nature.

(6)   Where the Director is satisfied as mentioned in subsection (5) above, he shall
   (a)   give notice that he is so satisfied to the public gas supplier; and
   (b)   publish a copy of the notice in such manner as the Director considers appropriate for the purpose of bringing the matters to which the notice relates to the attention of persons likely to be affected by them.

(7) A final or provisional order
  (a) shall require the public gas supplier (according to the circumstances of the case) to do, or not to do, such things as are specified in the order or are of a description so specified;
  (b) shall take effect at such time, being the earliest practicable time, as is determined by or under the order; and
  (c) may be revoked at any time by the Director.
(8) In this section and sections 29 and 30 below
  'final order' means an order under this section other than a provisional order;
  'provisional order' means an order under this section which, if not previously confirmed under subsection (4) above, will cease to have effect at the end of such period (not exceeding three months) as is determined by or under the order;
  'relevant condition', in relation to a public gas supplier, means any condition of his authorisation;
  'relevant requirement', in relation to a public gas supplier, means any requirement imposed on him by or under section 9(1) or (2), 10(1), 11(4), 12(1), 14(1) or (3), 14A(4) or 15B above or section 33B, 33D or 33E below or any provision of paragraphs 1 to 4 and 14 of Schedule 5 to this Act.

Procedural requirements

29(1) Before making a final order or confirming a provisional order, the Director shall give notice
  (a) stating that he proposes to make or confirm the order and setting out its effect;
  (b) stating the relevant condition or requirement, the acts or omissions which, in his opinion, constitute or would constitute contraventions of it and the other facts which, in his opinion, justify the making or confirmation of the order; and
  (c) specifying the time (not being less than 28 days from the date of publication of the notice) within which representations or objections to the proposed order or confirmation of the order may be made, and shall consider any representations or objections which are duly made and not withdrawn.
(2) A notice under subsection (1) above shall be given
  (a) by publishing the notice in such manner as the Director considers appropriate for the purpose of bringing the matters to which the notice relates to the attention of persons likely to be affected by them; and
  (b) by sending a copy of the notice, and a copy of the proposed order or of the order proposed to be confirmed, to the public gas supplier.
(3) The Director shall not make a final order, or confirm a provisional order, with modifications except with the consent of the public gas supplier or after complying with the requirements of subsection (4) below.
(4) The said requirements are that the Director shall
  (a) give to the public gas supplier such notice as appears to him requisite of his proposal to make or confirm the order with modifications;
  (b) specify the time (not being less than 28 days from the date of the service of the notice) within which representations or objections to the proposed modifications may be made; and

(c)   consider any representations or objections which are duly made and not withdrawn.

(5)   Before revoking a final order or a provisional order which has been confirmed, the Director shall give notice

(a)   stating that he proposes to revoke the order and setting out its effect; and

(b)   specifying the time (not being less than 28 days) from the date of publication of the notice within which representations or objections to the proposed revocation may be made, and shall consider any representations or objections which are duly made and not withdrawn.

(6)   A notice under subsection (5) above shall be given

(a)   by publishing the notice in such manner as the Director considers appropriate for the purpose of bringing the matters to which the notice relates to the attention of persons likely to be affected by them; and

(b)   by sending a copy of the notice to the public gas supplier.

(7)   As soon as practicable after a final order is made or a provisional order is made or confirmed, the Director shall

(a)   serve a copy of the order on the public gas supplier; and

(b)   publish such a copy in such manner as he considers appropriate for the purpose of bringing the order to the attention of persons likely to be affected by it.

Validity and effect of orders

30(1)   If the public gas supplier is aggrieved by a final or provisional order and desires to question its validity on the ground that the making or confirmation of it was not within the powers of section 28 above or that any of the requirements of section 29 above have not been complied with in relation to it, he may within 42 days from the date of service on him of a copy of the order make an application to the court under this section.

(2)   On any such application the court may, if satisfied that the making or confirmation of the order was not within those powers or that the interests of the public gas supplier have been substantially prejudiced by a failure to comply with those requirements, quash the order or any provision of the order.

(3)   Except as provided by this section, the validity of a final or provisional order shall not be questioned by any legal proceedings whatever.

(4)   No criminal proceedings shall, by virtue of the making of a final order or the making or confirmation of a provisional order, lie against any person on the ground that he has committed, or aided, abetted, counselled or procured the commission of, or conspired or attempted to commit, or incited others to commit, any contravention of the order.

(5)   The obligation to comply with a final or provisional order is a duty owed to any person who may be affected by a contravention of it.

(6)   Where a duty is owed by virtue of subsection (5) above to any person any breach of the duty which causes that person to sustain loss or damage shall be actionable at the suit or instance of that person.

(7)   In any proceedings brought against any person in pursuance of subsection (6) above, it shall be a defence for him to prove that he took all reasonable steps and exercised all due diligence to avoid contravening the order.

(8) Without prejudice to any right which any person may have by virtue of subsection (6) above to bring civil proceedings in respect of any contravention or apprehended contravention of a final or provisional order, compliance with any such order shall be enforceable by civil proceedings by the Director for an injunction or interdict or for any other appropriate relief.

(9) In this section 'the court' means
    (a)   in relation to England and Wales, the High Court;
    (b)   in relation to Scotland, the Court of Session.

Duty of Director to investigate certain matters

31(1) It shall be the duty of the Director to investigate any matter which appears to him to be an enforcement matter and which
    (a)   is the subject of a representation (other than one appearing to the Director to be frivolous) made to the Director by or on behalf of a person appearing to the Director to have an interest in that matter; or
    (b)   is referred to him by the Council under subsection (2) below.

(2) It shall be the duty of the Council to refer to the Director any matter which appears to the Council to be an enforcement matter and which is the subject of a representation (other than one appearing to the Council to be frivolous) made to the Council by or on behalf of a person appearing to the Council to have an interest in that matter.

(3) In this section and section 32 below 'enforcement matter' means any matter in respect of which any functions of the Director under section 28 above are or may be exercisable.

Duty of Council to investigate certain matters

32(1) It shall be the duty of the Council to investigate any matter which appears to it to be a matter to which subsection (2) below applies and which
    (a)   is the subject of a representation (other than one appearing to the Council to be frivolous) made to the Council by or on behalf of a person appearing to the Council to have an interest in that matter; or
    (b)   is referred to it by the Director under subsection (3) below.

(2) This subsection applies to
    (a)   any matter (not being an enforcement matter or a matter relating only to contract customers) in respect of which any functions of the Director under this Part are or may be exercisable; and
    (b)   any matter (not being an enforcement matter or a matter relating to tariff customers) which relates to the supply of gas through pipes and in respect of which any functions of the Director General of Fair Trading under the Fair Trading Act 1973 or the Competition Act 1980 are or may be exercisable.

(3) Subject to subsection (4) below, it shall be the duty of the Director to refer to the Council any matter which appears to the Director to be a matter falling within paragraph (a) of subsection (2) above and which is the subject of a representation (other than one appearing to the Director to be frivolous) made to the Director by or on behalf of a person appearing to the Director to have an interest in that matter.

(4) Nothing in subsection (3) above shall require the Director to refer to the Council any matter in respect of which he is already considering exercising functions under this Part.

(5) Where on an investigation under subsection (1) above any matter appears to the Council to be a matter falling within paragraph (a) of subsection (2) above in respect of which it would be appropriate for the Director to exercise any functions under this Part, the Council shall refer that matter to the Director with a view to his exercising those functions with respect to that matter.

(6) Where on an investigation under subsection (1) above any matter appears to the Council to be a matter falling within paragraph (b) of subsection (2) above in respect of which it would be appropriate for the Director General of Fair Trading to exercise any functions under the Fair Trading Act 1973 or the Competition Act 1980, the Council shall refer the matter to that Director with a view to his exercising those functions with respect to that matter.

(7) In this section 'contract customer' means a person who is supplied with gas by a public gas supplier in pursuance of such an agreement as is mentioned in section 14(4) above.

Preliminary investigation by Council of certain disputes

32A(1) This section applies where

(a) representations are made to the Council by or on behalf of a person who appears to the Council to have an interest in the matter to which the representations relate; and

(b) that matter appears to the Council to constitute a dispute of a kind which may be referred to the Director under section 14A above or 33A below, or under regulations made under section 1 SA above.

(2) It shall be the duty of the Council

(a) to inform the person by or on whose behalf the representations are made that he may have the right to refer his dispute to the Director; and

(b) to make such investigations with respect to the matter to which the representations relate as may be specified in a direction given by the Director.

(3) Any such direction may be given so as to apply generally or to a specified class of matter or particular matter and may, in particular, specify in relation to any investigation which the Council is required to make under this section

(a) the practice and procedure which it is to follow in conducting its investigation; and

(b) the information which it is to give to the Director with respect to the matter investigated.

Power of Council to investigate other matters

33(1) The Council shall have power to investigate any matter (not being a matter which it is its duty to investigate under section 32 above) which

(a) appears to it to be a matter to which subsection (2) below applies and not to be an enforcement matter within the meaning of that section; and

(b) is the subject of a representation (other than one appearing to the Council to be frivolous) made to the Council by or on behalf of a person appearing to the Council to have an interest in that matter.

(2) This subsection applies to

(a)   any matter relating to the design, manufacture, importation or supply (whether by sale, hire or loan or otherwise) of gas fittings used or intended to be used by persons supplied with gas by public gas suppliers;

(b)   any matter relating to the installation, maintenance or inspection of gas fittings used or intended to be used by such persons; and

(c)   any other matter relating to, or to anything connected with, the use by such persons of gas supplied by such a supplier or the use of such fittings.

(3)   Where the Council has investigated any matter under this section, it may prepare a report on that matter and (subject to section 42 below) shall send a copy of any such report to such (if any) of the following persons as it thinks appropriate, that is to say

(a)   any person to whom the report refers or who (whether or not he has made a representation to the Council) appears to the Council to have an interest in the matter to which the report relates;

(b)   the Director General of Fair Trading or any person whose functions under any enactment appear to the Council to be exercisable in relation to that matter;

(c)   any person who appears to the Council to be a person who ought to take account of the report in determining how to act in relation to that matter; but nothing in this subsection shall require the Council to send any such copy to the Director.

Procedures for dealing with complaints

33E(1) Each public gas supplier shall establish a procedure for dealing with complaints made by his tariff customers or potential tariff customers in connection with the provision of gas supply services.

(2)   No such procedure shall be established, and no modification of such a procedure shall be made, unless

(a)   the public gas supplier has consulted the Council; and

(b)   the proposed procedure or modification has been approved by the Director.

(3)   The public gas supplier shall

(a)   publicise the procedure in such manner as may be approved by the Director; and

(b)   send a description of the procedure, free of charge, to any person who asks for one.

(4)   The Director may give a direction to a public gas supplier requiring the supplier to review his procedure or the manner in which it operates.

(5)   A direction under subsection (4) above

(a)   may specify the manner in which the review is to be conducted; and (b) shall require a written report of the review to be made to the Director.

(6)   Where the Director receives a report under subsection (5)(b) above, he may, after consulting the public gas supplier, direct him to make such modifications of

(a)   the procedure; or

(b)   the manner in which the procedure operates, as may be specified in the direction.

(7)   Subsection (2) above does not apply to any modification made in compliance with a direction under subsection (6) above.

Fixing of maximum charges for reselling gas

37(1)   The Director shall from time to time fix maximum prices at which gas
supplied by public gas suppliers may be resold, and shall publish the prices
so fixed in such manner as in his opinion will secure adequate publicity
therefor.

(2)   Different prices may be fixed under this section in different classes of cases
which may be defined by reference to areas, tariffs applicable to gas supplied
by the suppliers or any other relevant circumstances.

(3)   If any person resells any gas supplied by a public gas supplier at a price
exceeding the maximum price fixed under this section and applicable
thereto, the amount of the excess shall be recoverable by the person to whom
the gas was resold.

Power to require information etc

38(1)   Where it appears to the Director that a public gas supplier may be
contravening, or may have contravened, any relevant condition or
requirement, the Director may, for any purpose connected with the exercise
of his functions under section 28, 31 or 33E above in relation to that matter,
by notice signed by him

(a)   require any person to produce, at a time and place specified in the
notice, to the Director or to any person appointed by him for the
purpose, any documents which are specified or described in the notice
and are in that person's custody or under his control; or

(b)   require any person carrying on any business to furnish to the Director
such information as may be specified or described in the notice, and
specify the time, the manner and the form in which any such
information is to be furnished; but no person shall be compelled for
any such purpose to produce any documents which he could not be
compelled to produce in civil proceedings before the court or, in
complying with any requirement for the furnishing of information, to
give any information which he could not be compelled to give in
evidence in such proceedings.

(2)   A person who without reasonable excuse fails to do anything duly required
of him by a notice under subsection (1) above shall be guilty of an offence
and liable on summary conviction to a fine not exceeding level 5 on the
standard scale.

(3)   A person who intentionally alters, suppresses or destroys any document
which he has been required by any such notice to produce shall be guilty of
an offence and liable

(a)   on summary conviction, to a fine not exceeding the statutory
maximum;

(b)   on conviction on indictment, to a fine.

(4)   If a person makes default in complying with a notice under subsection (1)
above, the court may, on the application of the Director, make such order
as the court thinks fit for requiring the default to be made good; and any
such order may provide that all the costs or expenses of and incidental to
the application shall be borne by the person in default or by any officers of
a company or other association who are responsible for its default.

(5)   In this section 'relevant condition' and 'relevant requirement' have the same
meanings as in section 28 above, 'the court' has the same meaning as in
section 30 above.

Service of notices etc

46(1) Subject to subsection (2) below, any notice or other document required or authorised to be given, delivered or served under this Part or regulations made under this Part may be given, delivered or served either

(a) by delivering it to the person to whom it is to be given or delivered or on whom it is to be served;

(b) by leaving it at the usual or last known place of abode of that person;

(c) by sending it in a prepaid letter addressed to that person at his usual or last known place of abode;

(d) in the case of a body corporate, by delivering it to the secretary or clerk of the body at their registered or principal office, or sending it in a prepaid letter addressed to the secretary or clerk of the body at that office; or

(e) if it is not practicable after reasonable inquiry to ascertain the name or address of a person to whom it should be given or delivered, or on whom it should be served, as being a person having any interest in premises, by addressing it to him by the description of the person having that interest in the premises (naming them) to which it relates and delivering it to some responsible person on the premises, or affixing it or a copy of it to some conspicuous part of the premises.

(2) Where this subsection applies in relation to a public gas supplier, subsection (1) above shall not apply to notices to be given to or served on the supplier under section 10 above or any provision of Schedule 5 to this Act but any such notice

(a) may be given or served by delivering it at, or sending it in a prepaid letter to, an appropriate office of the supplier; and

(b) in the case of a notice under paragraph 7(2) or 12(1) of that Schedule, shall be treated as received by the supplier only if received by him at an appropriate office.

(3) Subsection (2) above applies in relation to a public gas supplier if he divides his authorised area into such areas as he thinks fit and

(a) in the case of each area, fixes offices of his which are to be appropriate offices in relation to notices relating to matters arising in that area;

(b) publishes in each area, in such manner as he considers adequate, the addresses of the offices fixed by him for that area; and

(c) endorses on every demand note for gas charges payable to him the addresses of the offices fixed for the area in question.

Definitions

48(1) 'notice' means notice in writing;...

SCHEDULE 5
Public Gas Supply Code

Part I – Supply of Gas to Tariff Customers

Maintenance etc. of service pipes

1   A public gas supplier shall carry out any necessary work of maintenance, repair or renewal of any service pipe
   (a) by which a tariff customer is supplied with gas; and
   (b) which was provided and laid otherwise than at the expense of the supplier or a predecessor of his, and may recover the expenses reasonably incurred in so doing from the customer.

Consumption of gas to be ascertained by meter

3(1)   Every tariff customer of a public gas supplier shall, if required to do so by the supplier, take his supply through a meter, and in default of his doing so the supplier may refuse to give or discontinue the supply of gas.

(2)   A public gas supplier shall if so required by a tariff customer, supply to the customer, whether by way of sale, hire or loan, an appropriate meter (whether a prepayment meter or otherwise) for ascertaining the quantity of gas supplied by him; but in the case of a supply by way of hire or loan the customer shall, if so required by the supplier, before receiving the meter give to the supplier reasonable security for the due performance of his obligation to take proper care of it.

(3)   Where any money is deposited with a public gas supplier by way of security in pursuance of this paragraph, the supplier shall pay interest, at such rate as may from time to time be fixed by the supplier with the approval of the Director, on every sum of 50p so deposited for every three months during which it remains in the hands of the supplier.

Meters to be kept in proper order

4(1)   Every tariff customer shall at all times, at his own expense, keep all meters belonging to him, whereby the quantity of gas supplied by the public gas supplier is registered, in proper order for correctly registering the quantity of gas, and in default of his doing so the supplier may discontinue the supply of gas through that meter.

(2)   A public gas supplier shall at all times, at his own expense, keep all meters let for hire or lent by him to any tariff customer in proper order for correctly registering the quantity of gas supplied; but this sub-paragraph is without prejudice to any remedy the supplier may have against the customer for failure to take proper care of the meter.

(3)   A public gas supplier shall have power to remove, inspect and re-install any meter by which the quantity of gas supplied by him to a tariff customer is registered, and shall, while any such meter is removed, fix a substituted meter on the premises; and, subject to sub-paragraph (4) below, the cost of removing, inspecting and reinstalling a meter and of fixing a substituted meter shall be defrayed by the supplier.

(4)   Where such a meter is removed for the purpose of being examined by a meter examiner in accordance with section 17 of this Act, the expenses

incurred in removing, examining and re-installing the meter and fixing a substituted meter shall, if the meter is found in proper order, be defrayed by the person at whose request the examination is to be carried out but otherwise shall be defrayed by the owner of the meter.

(5) A meter is found in proper order for the purposes of sub-paragraph (4) above if it is found to register correctly or to register erroneously to a degree not exceeding the degree permitted by regulations under section 17 of this Act.

Meter as evidence of quantity of gas supplied

5(1) Subject to sub-paragraph (2) below, where gas is supplied to a tariff customer through a meter, the register of the meter shall be prima facie evidence of the quantity of gas supplied.

(2) Where a meter through which a tariff customer is supplied with gas is found, when examined by a meter examiner appointed under section 17 of this Act, to register erroneously to a degree exceeding the degree permitted by regulations under that section

(a) the meter shall be deemed to have registered erroneously to the degree so found since the relevant date, except in a case where it is proved to have begun to register erroneously as aforesaid on some later date; and

(b) the amount of allowance to be made to, or the surcharge to be made on, the customer by the supplier in consequence of the erroneous registration shall be paid to or by the customer, as the case may be.

(3) In sub-paragraph (2) above 'the relevant date' means the penultimate date on which, otherwise than in connection with the examination, the register of the meter was ascertained.

Installation of meters in new premises

6(1) This paragraph applies where a meter is to be used to register the quantity of gas supplied to a tariff customer and

(a) the building has not previously been supplied with gas by the public gas supplier; or

(b) a new or substituted pipe is to be laid between the public gas supplier's main and the meter.

(2) Subject to sub-paragraph (3) below, the meter shall be installed as near as practicable to the main, but within the outside wall of the building.

(3) The meter may be installed otherwise than within the outside wall of the building if it is installed either

(a) in accommodation of a type and construction approved by the public gas supplier by an approval given in relation to buildings generally, or to any class or description of buildings; or

(b) in a separate meter house or other accommodation outside the building approved by the supplier in the case of that particular building.

(4) If the requirements of this paragraph are not complied with, the public gas supplier may refuse to supply gas to the premises until those requirements have been complied with.

Recovery of gas charges etc

7(1) A public gas supplier may recover from a tariff customer any charges due to him in respect of the supply of gas, or in respect of the supplying and fixing of any meter or fittings.

(2)   If a tariff customer quits any premises at which gas has been supplied to him through a meter by a public gas supplier without giving notice thereof to the supplier so that it is received by the supplier at least twenty-four hours before he quits the premises, he shall be liable to pay the supplier all charges in respect of the supply of gas to the premises accruing due up to whichever of the following first occurs, namely
   (a)   the twenty-eighth day after he gives such notice to the supplier;
   (b)   the next day on which the register of the meter falls to be ascertained; and
   (c)   the day from which any subsequent occupier of the premises requires the supplier to supply gas to the premises.

(3)   Sub-paragraph (2) above, or a statement of the effect thereof, shall be endorsed upon every demand note for gas charges payable to a public gas supplier by a tariff customer.

(4)   If a tariff customer quits any premises at which gas has been supplied to him by a public gas supplier without paying any amount due from him by way of charges in respect of the supply, the supplier
   (a)   may refuse to furnish him with a supply of gas at any other premises until he pays the amount so due; but
   (b)   shall not be entitled to require payment of that amount from the next occupier of the premises.

(5)   If a tariff customer has not, after the expiry of twenty-eight days from the making of a demand in writing by a public gas supplier for payment thereof, paid the charges due from him in respect of the supply of gas by the supplier to any premises, the supplier, after the expiration of not less than seven days' notice of his intention, may
   (a)   cut off the supply to the premises by disconnecting the service pipe at the meter (whether the pipe belongs to the supplier or not) or by such other means as he thinks fit; and
   (b)   recover any expenses incurred in so doing from the customer.

(5A) The powers conferred by sub-paragraph (5) above shall not be exercisable as respects any amount which is genuinely in dispute.

(6)   Where a public gas supplier has cut off the supply of gas to any premises in consequence of any default on the part of a tariff customer, the supplier shall not be under any obligation to resume the supply of gas to the customer so in default until he has made good the default and paid the reasonable expenses of re-connecting the supply.

Improper use of gas

9   If any person supplied with gas by a public gas supplier improperly uses or deals with the gas so as to interfere with the efficient supply of gas by the supplier (whether to that person or to any other person), the supplier may, if he thinks fit, discontinue the supply of gas to that person.

Injury to gas fittings and interference with meters

10(1) If any person intentionally or by culpable negligence
   (a)   injures or allows to be injured any gas fitting belonging to a public gas supplier;
   (b)   alters the index to any meter used for measuring the quantity of gas supplied by such a supplier; or

(c) prevents any such meter from duly registering the quantity of gas supplied, he shall be guilty of an offence and liable on summary conviction to a fine not exceeding level 3 on the standard scale.

(2) If an offence under sub-paragraph (1) above involves any injury to or interference with any gas fitting belonging to the public gas supplier, the supplier may also, until the matter has been remedied, but no longer, discontinue the supply of gas to the person so offending (notwithstanding any contract previously existing).

(3) Where any person is prosecuted for an offence under sub-paragraph (1)(b) or (c) above, the possession by him of artificial means for causing an alteration of the index of the meter or, as the case may be, the prevention of the meter from duly registering shall, if the meter was in his custody or under his control, be prima facie evidence that the alteration or prevention was intentionally caused by him.

Restoration of supply without consent

11(1) Where a supply of gas to any premises has been cut off by a public gas supplier otherwise than in the exercise of a power conferred by regulations under section 18(2) of this Act, no person shall, without the consent of the supplier, restore the supply.

(2) If any person acts in contravention of sub-paragraph (1) above, he shall be guilty of an offence and liable on summary conviction to a fine not exceeding level 3 on the standard scale and the supplier may again cut off the supply.

Failure to notify connection or disconnection of service pipe

12(1) No person shall connect any meter with a service pipe through which gas is supplied by a public gas supplier, or disconnect any meter from any such pipe, unless he has given to the supplier, so that it is received by the supplier at least twenty-four hours before he does so, notice of his intention to do so, specifying the time and place of the proposed connection or disconnection.

(2) If any person acts in contravention of sub-paragraph (1) above, he shall be guile of an offence and liable on summary conviction to a fine not exceeding level 2 on the standard scale.

Prevention of escapes of gas

13(1) Where any gas escapes from any pipe of a public gas supplier, or from any pipe or other gas fitting used by a person supplied with gas by a public gas supplier, the supplier shall, immediately after being informed of the escape, prevent the gas from escaping (whether by cutting off the supply of gas to any premises or otherwise).

(2) If a public gas supplier fails within twelve hours from being so informed effectually to prevent the gas from escaping, he shall be guilty of an offence and liable on summary conviction to a fine not exceeding level 3 on the standard scale.

(3) In any proceedings for an offence under sub-paragraph (2) above it shall be a defence for the public gas supplier to prove that it was not reasonably practicable for him effectually to prevent the gas from escaping within the said period of twelve hours, and that he did effectually prevent the escape as soon as it was reasonably practicable for him to do so.

(4) Where a public gas supplier has reasonable cause to suspect that gas supplied by him is escaping, or may escape, in any premises, any officer authorised by

the supplier may, on production of some duly authenticated document showing his authority, enter the premises, inspect the gas fittings, carry out any work necessary to prevent the escape and take any other steps necessary to avert danger to life or property.

(5) Where a public gas supplier has reasonable cause to suspect that gas supplied or conveyed by him which has escaped has entered, or may enter any premises, any officer authorised by the supplier may on production of some duly authenticated document showing his authority, enter the premises and take any steps necessary to avert danger to life or property

Information as to escapes of gas

14 It shall be the duty of a public gas supplier to take such steps as are necessary to ensure that, if he is informed of an escape of gas that he is not required by paragraph 13 above to prevent, he passes the information on, as soon as reasonably practicable

(a) to the person who appears to the public gas supplier to be responsible (whether under that paragraph or otherwise) for preventing the escape; or

(b) in the case of an escape occurring in the authorised area of another public gas supplier, to that other public gas supplier.

Entry during continuance of supply

15(1) Any officer authorised by a public gas supplier may at all reasonable times, on the production of some duly authenticated document showing his authority, enter any premises in which there is a service pipe connected with a gas main of the supplier for the purpose of

(a) inspecting gas fittings;

(b) ascertaining the quantity of gas supplied;

(c) performing the duty imposed on the supplier by paragraph 1 or 2 above;

(d) exercising the power conferred on the supplier by paragraph 4(3) or 8(7) above; or

(e) in the case of premises where the supplier has reason to believe that a compressor or compressed air or extraneous gas is being used, inspecting the premises and ascertaining whether the provisions of paragraph 8 above are being complied with.

(2) Paragraphs (a) and (b) of sub-paragraph (1) above do not apply where the consumer has applied in writing to the supplier for the supplier to disconnect the service pipe and cease to supply gas to the premises and the supplier has failed to do so within a reasonable time.

(3) In this paragraph 'compressor', 'compressed air' and 'extraneous gas' have the same meanings as in paragraph 8 above.

Entry on discontinuance of supply

16(1) Where

(a) a public gas supplier is authorised by any provision of this Act (including any such provision as applied by such an agreement as is mentioned in section 14(4) of this Act) to cut off or discontinue the supply of gas to any premises;

(b) a person occupying premises supplied with gas by a public gas supplier ceases to require such a supply;

(c) a person entering into occupation of any premises previously supplied with gas by a public gas supplier does not take a supply of gas from the supplier; or

(d) a person entering into occupation of any premises previously supplied with gas through a meter belonging to a public gas supplier does not hire or borrow that meter, any officer authorised by the supplier, after twenty-four hours' notice to the occupier, or to the owner or lessee of the premises if they are unoccupied, may at all reasonable times, on production of some duly authenticated document showing his authority, enter the premises for the purpose of removing any gas fitting.

(2) The notice required to be given by sub-paragraph (1) above may, in the case of unoccupied premises the owner or lessee of which is unknown to the supplier and cannot be ascertained after diligent inquiry, be given by affixing it upon a conspicuous part of the premises not less than forty-eight hours before the premises are entered.

Entry for replacing, repairing or altering pipes

17(1) Any officer authorised by a public gas supplier, after seven clear days' notice to the occupier of any premises, or to the owner or lessee of any premises which are unoccupied, may at all reasonable times, on production of some duly authenticated document showing his authority, enter the premises for the purpose of

(a) placing a new pipe in the place of any existing pipe which has already been lawfully placed; or

(b) repairing or altering any such existing pipe.

(2) The notice required to be given by sub-paragraph (1) above may, in the case of unoccupied premises the owner or lessee of which is unknown to the supplier and cannot be ascertained after diligent inquiry, be given by affixing it upon a conspicuous part of the premises.

(3) In cases of emergency arising from defects in any pipes entry may be made under sub-paragraph (1) above without the notice required to be given by that sub-paragraph, but the notice shall then be given as soon as possible after the occurrence of the emergency.

Provisions as to powers of entry

18(1) Where in pursuance of any powers of entry conferred by this Part of this Schedule, entry is made on any premises by an officer authorised by a public gas supplier

(a) the officer shall ensure that the premises are left no less secure by reason of the entry; and

(b) the supplier shall make good, or pay compensation for, any damage caused by the officer, or by any person accompanying him in entering the premises, in taking any action therein authorised by this Schedule, or in making the premises secure.

(2) Any officer exercising powers of entry conferred by this Part of this Schedule may be accompanied by such persons as may be necessary or expedient for the purpose for which the entry is made, or for the purposes of sub-paragraph (1) above.

(3)   If any person intentionally obstructs any officer exercising powers of entry conferred by this Part of this Schedule, he shall be guilty of an offence and liable on summary conviction to a fine not exceeding level 3 on the standard scale.

(4)   The Rights of Entry (Gas and Electricity Boards) Act 1954 (entry under a justice's warrant) shall apply in relation to any powers of entry conferred by this Part of this Schedule.

Gas fittings not to be subject to distress

19(1)   Any gas fittings let for hire or lent to a consumer by a public gas supplier and marked or impressed with a sufficient mark or brand indicating the supplier as the owner thereof

(a)   shall not be subject to distress or be liable to be taken in execution under process of any court or any proceedings in bankruptcy against the person in whose possession they may be; and

(b)   shall not be deemed to be landlord's fixtures, notwithstanding that they may be fixed or fastened to any part of the premises in which they may be situated.

(2)   In the application of sub-paragraph (1)(a) above to Scotland, for the word 'distress' and the words 'in bankruptcy against' there shall be substituted respectively the word 'poinding' and the words 'for the sequestration of the estate of'.

GAS SAFETY (RIGHTS OF ENTRY) REGULATIONS 1983

Right of entry for inspection, testing and disconnection if appliance found to be dangerous

2   Any officer authorised by the relevant authority may, on the production of some duly authenticated document showing his authority, with such other persons (if any) as may be necessary:

(a)   enter any premises in which there is a service pipe connected with gas mains, for the purpose of inspecting any gas fitting on the premises, any flue or means of ventilation used in connection with any such gas fitting or any service pipe or other apparatus (not being a gas fitting) which is on the premises and is used for the supply of gas or is connected with gas mains.

(b)   where he so enters any such premises, examine or apply any test to any object as is mentioned in paragraph (a) above and (where the object is a gas fitting) verify what supply of air is available for it, with a view to ascertaining whether the provisions of any regulations made under section 31 of the Gas Act 1972 have been complied with or whether the object is in such a condition, or (in the case of a gas fitting) the supply of air available for it is so inadequate, that it (or, in the case of a flue or means of ventilation, the gas fitting in connection with which it is used) is likely to constitute a danger to any person or property, and

(c)   where in his opinion it is necessary to do so for the purpose of averting danger to life or property, and notwithstanding any contract previously existing, disconnect and seal off any gas fitting or any part of the gas supply system on the premises, or cut off the supply of gas to the premises or, if no such supply is being given, signify the refusal of the relevant authority to give or, as the case may be, allow such a supply.

Notice – Right of Appeal
Notification to consumer

3(1) Where an officer authorised by the relevant authority takes any action in relation to any premises in the exercise of a power conferred by Regulation 2(c) above, the relevant authority shall, within five clear working days after the action is taken, serve on the consumer a notice in writing:
  (a) specifying:
     (i) the nature of the defect or other circumstances in consequence of which the power has been exercised; and
     (ii) the nature of the danger in question and the action taken in the exercise of the power; and
  (b) stating:
     (i)   that the consumer has a right to appeal under these Regulations to the Secretary of State against the action taken in the exercise of the power within the period of 21 days beginning with the date of service of the notice, or such longer period as the Secretary of State may at any time in any particular case allow:
     (ii) the grounds on which and the manner in which he can appeal;
     (iii) the effect of Regulation 7 and 8 below.
  (2) In this Regulation 'working day' does not include a Saturday, Sunday or a bank or other public holiday.

Appeals

5 The consumer on whom is served such notice as is mentioned in Regulation 3 above may, within the period of 21 days beginning with the date of service of the notice, or such longer period as the Secretary of State may at any time in any particular case allow, appeal to the Secretary of State against the action taken in the exercise of a power conferred by Regulation 2(c) above on any of the following grounds, that is to say:
  (a) that the defect or other circumstances specified in the notice did not constitute a danger such as to justify the action taken specified in the notice;
  (b) that the defect or other circumstances so specified did not exist at the time the action was taken; or
  (c) that the defect or other circumstances so specified have ceased to exist.

Procedure for appeals

6(1) An appeal under Regulation 5 above shall be of no effect unless it is made by notice in writing given to the Secretary of State for the time being discharging the functions conferred by paragraphs (2) and (3) below at his principal office and indicates the grounds of the appeal.
  (2) On any such appeal the Secretary of State may, if either the consumer or the relevant authority so desire, afford to each of them an opportunity of appearing before, and being heard by, a person appointed by the Secretary of State for the purpose.
  (3) On the determination of the appeal, the Secretary of State may direct that, subject to any right of the supplier to withhold supply:

(a) any gas fitting or part of the gas supply system on the premises which has been disconnected under these Regulations either shall remain disconnected or shall or may be reconnected;

(b) any supply of gas to the premises which has been cut off under these Regulations either shall remain cut off or shall or may be restored; or

(c) where the refusal of the relevant authority to give or, as the case may be, allow such a supply has been signified under these Regulations, the supplier either shall not give a supply of gas or shall or may cause gas to be supplied to the premises, and may give such supplementary directions as he considers to be appropriate in consequence of the appeal.

No reconnection of supply without consent

7   No person shall, except with the consent of the relevant authority or in pursuance of any directions given by the Secretary of State under Regulation 6(3) above:

(a) reconnect any gas fitting or part of a gas supply system which has been disconnected by or on behalf of the relevant authority in the exercise of a power conferred by these Regulations where he knows or has reason to believe that it has been so disconnected; or

(b) restore the supply of gas to any premises where it has been cut off by or on behalf of the relevant authority in the exercise of any such power and he knows or has reason to believe that it has been so cut off; or

(c) cause gas from gas mains to be supplied to any premises where in pursuance of these Regulations the refusal of the relevant authority to give or, as the case may be, allow a supply to those premises has been signified and that refusal has not been withdrawn and he knows or has reason to believe that such refusal has been signified and has not been withdrawn.

Penalties for contravention or failure to comply

8   Any person contravening or failing to comply with any provision of these Regulations of Gas Safety Regulations 1972(a) shall be guilty of an offence and liable on summary conviction to a fine not exceeding £1,000.

GAS (CONNECTION CHARGES) REGULATIONS 1986

Power to charge for gas main

2   A public gas supplier may require a person requiring a supply of gas under section 10(1) of the Gas Act 1986 to pay to the supplier an amount in respect of the expenses of the laying of the main used for the purpose of giving that supply if:

(a) the supply is required within five years after the laying of the main;

(b) a person for the purpose of supplying whom the main was laid has made a payment to the supplier in respect of those expenses;

(c) the amount required does not exceed any amount paid in respect of those expenses by such a person or by any person previously required to make a payment under these Regulations;
(d) the supplier has not recovered those expenses in full; and
(e) the supplier has made available to the person requiring the supply such information as may have been reasonably requested by that person for the purpose of ascertaining:
    (i)   the expenses of the laying of the main;
    (ii) the date of the laying of the main: and
    (iii) the amounts paid in respect of those expenses by the persons for the purpose of supplying whom the main was laid, or by persons previously required to make a payment under those Regulations.

ELECTRICITY ACT 1989

General duties of Secretary of State and Director

3(1) The Secretary of State and the Director shall each have a duty to exercise the functions assigned or transferred to him by this Part in the manner which he considers is best calculated
    (a) to secure that all reasonable demands for electricity are satisfied;
    (b) to secure that licence holders are able to finance the carrying on of the activities which they are authorised by their licences to carry on; and
    (c) subject to subsection (2) below, to promote competition in the generation and supply of electricity.
(2) The Secretary of State and the Director shall each have a duty to exercise the functions assigned or transferred to him by this Part in the manner which he considers is best calculated to secure
    (a) that the prices charged to tariff customers by public electricity suppliers for electricity supplied in pursuance of section 16(1) below to premises in any area of Scotland specified in an order made by the Secretary of State are in accordance with tariffs which do not distinguish (whether directly or indirectly) between different parts of that area; and
    (b) that public electricity suppliers are not thereby disadvantaged in competing with persons authorised by a licence or exemption to supply electricity to such premises.
(3) Subject to subsections (1) and (2) above, the Secretary of State and the Director shall each have a duty to exercise the functions assigned or transferred to him by this Part in the manner which he considers is best calculated
    (a) to protect the interests of consumers of electricity supplied by persons authorised by licences to supply electricity in respect of
        (i)   the prices charged and the other terms of supply;
        (ii) the continuity of supply; and
        (iii) the quality of the electricity supply services provided;
    (b) to promote efficiency and economy on the part of persons authorised by licences to supply or transmit electricity and the efficient use of electricity supplied to consumers;
    (c) to promote research into, and the development and use of, new techniques by or on behalf of persons authorised by a licence to generate, transmit or supply electricity;

(d) to protect the public from dangers arising from the generation, transmission or supply of electricity; and

(e) to secure the establishment and maintenance of machinery for promoting the health and safety of persons employed in the generation, transmission or supply of electricity; and a duty to take into account, in exercising those functions, the effect on the physical environment of activities connected with the generation, transmission or supply of electricity.

(4) In performing his duty under subsection (3)(a)(i) above, the Secretary of State or the Director shall take into account, in particular, the protection of the interests of consumers of electricity in rural areas.

(5) In performing his duty under subsection (3)(a)(iii) above, the Secretary of State or the Director shall take into account, in particular, the interests of those who are disabled or of pensionable age.

(6) In this section references to the functions assigned to the Secretary of State by this Part do not include references to functions under section 36 or 37 below and references to the functions so assigned to the Director do not include references to functions relating to the determination of disputes.

(7) In this Part, unless the context otherwise requires 'exemption' means an exemption under section 5 below; 'licence' means a licence under section 6 below and 'licence holder' shall be construed accordingly.

Duty to supply on request

16(1) Subject to the following provisions of this Part and any regulations made under those provisions, a public electricity supplier shall, upon being required to do so by the owner or occupier of any premises

(a) give a supply of electricity to those premises; and

(b) so far as may be necessary for that purpose, provide electric lines or electrical plant or both.

(2) Where any person requires a supply of electricity in pursuance of subsection (1) above, he shall give to the public electricity supplier a notice specifying

(a) the premises in respect of which the supply is required;

(b) the day on which the supply is required to commence;

(c) the maximum power which may be required at any time; and

(d) the minimum period for which the supply is required to be given.

(3) Where a public electricity supplier receives from any person a notice under subsection (2) above requiring him to give a supply of electricity to any premises and

(a) he has not previously given a supply of electricity to those premises; or

(b) the giving of the supply requires the provision of electric lines or electrical plant or both; or

(c) other circumstances exist which make it necessary or expedient for him to do so, the supplier shall, as soon as practicable after receiving that notice, give to that person a notice under subsection (4) below.

(4) A notice under this subsection shall

(a) state the extent to which the proposals specified in the other person's notice under subsection (2) above are acceptable to the supplier and specify any counter proposals made by the supplier;

(b) state whether the prices to be charged by the supplier will be determined by a tariff under section 18(1) below, or a special

agreement under section 22(1) below, and specify the tariff or the proposed terms of the agreement;
(c) specify any payment which that person will be required to make under subsection (1) of section 19 below, or under regulations made under subsection (2) of that section;
(d) specify any security which that person will be required to give under section 20 below;
(e) specify any other terms which that person will be required to accept under section 21 below; and
(f) state the effect of section 23 below.
(5) In this section and sections 17 to 23 below
(a) any reference to giving a supply of electricity includes a reference to continuing to give such a supply;
(b) any reference to requiring a supply of electricity includes a reference to requiring such a supply to continue to be given; and
(c) any reference to the provision of an electric line or an item of electrical plant is a reference to the provision of such a line or item either by the installation of a new one or by the modification of an existing one.

Exceptions from duty to supply

17(1) Nothing in section 16(1) above shall be taken as requiring a public electricity supplier to give a supply of electricity to any premises if
(a) such a supply is being given to the premises by a private electricity supplier; and
(b) that supply is given (wholly or partly) through the public electricity supplier's electric lines and electrical plant; and in this Part 'private electricity supplier' means a person, other than a public electricity supplier, who is authorised by a licence or exemption to supply electricity.
(2) Nothing in section 16(1) above shall be taken as requiring a public electricity supplier to give a supply of electricity to any premises if and to the extent that
(a) he is prevented from doing so by circumstances not within his control; or
(b) circumstances exist by reason of which his doing so would or might involve his being in breach of regulations under section 29 below, and he has taken all such steps as it was reasonable to take both to prevent the circumstances from occurring and to prevent them from having that effect; or
(c) it is not reasonable in all the circumstances for him to be required to do so.
(3) Paragraph (c) of subsection (2) above shall not apply in relation to a supply of electricity which is being given to any premises unless the public electricity supplier gives to the occupier, or to the owner if the premises are not occupied, not less than seven working days' notice of his intention to discontinue the supply in pursuance of that paragraph.

Power to recover charges

18(1) Subject to the following provisions of this section, the prices to be charged by a public electricity supplier for the supply of electricity by him in pursuance of section 16(1) above shall be in accordance with such tariffs (which, subject to any condition included in his licence, may relate to the supply of electricity in different areas, cases and circumstances) as may be fixed from time to time by him.

(2)   A tariff fixed by a public electricity supplier under subsection (1) above
   (a)   shall be so framed as to show the methods by which and the principles on which the charges are to be made as well as the prices which are to be charged; and
   (b)   shall be published in such manner as in the opinion of the supplier will secure adequate publicity for it.

(3)   A tariff fixed by a public electricity supplier under subsection (1) above may include
   (a)   a standing charge in addition to the charge for the actual electricity supplied;
   (b)   a charge in respect of the availability of a supply of electricity; and
   (c)   a rent or other charge in respect of any electricity meter or electrical plant provided by the supplier; and such a charge as is mentioned in paragraph (b) above may vary according to the extent to which the supply is taken up.

(4)   In fixing tariffs under subsection (1) above, a public electricity supplier shall not show undue preference to any person or class of persons, and shall not exercise any undue discrimination against any person or class of persons.

Power to recover expenditure

19(1)   Where any electric line or electrical plant is provided by a public electricity supplier in pursuance of section 16(1) above, the supplier may require any expenses reasonably incurred in providing it to be defrayed by the person requiring the supply of electricity to such extent as is reasonable in all the circumstances.

(2)   The Secretary of State may, after consultation with the Director, make provision by regulations for entitling a public electricity supplier to require a person requiring a supply of electricity in pursuance of section 16(1) above to pay to the supplier, in respect of any expenses reasonably incurred in providing any electric line or electrical plant used for the purpose of giving that supply, such amount as may be reasonable in all the circumstances if
   (a)   the supply is required within the prescribed period after the provision of the line or plant; and
   (b)   a person for the purpose of supplying whom the line or plant was provided ('the initial contributor') has made a payment to the supplier in respect of those expenses.

(3)   Regulations under subsection (2) above may require a public electricity supplier who, in pursuance of this section or the regulations, has recovered any amount in respect of expenses reasonably incurred in providing any electric line or electrical plant
   (a)   to exercise his rights under the regulations in respect of those expenses; and
   (b)   to apply any payments received by him in the exercise of those rights in making such payments as may be appropriate towards reimbursing the initial contributor and any persons previously required to make payments under the regulations.

(4)   Any reference in this section to any expenses reasonably incurred in providing an electric line or electrical plant includes a reference to the capitalised value of any expenses likely to be so incurred in maintaining it,

insofar as they will not be recoverable by the supplier as part of the charges made by him for the supply.

Power to require security

20(1) Subject to the following provisions of this section, a public electricity supplier may require any person who requires a supply of electricity in pursuance of subsection (1) of section 16 above to give him reasonable security for the payment to him of all money which may become due to him
(a) in respect of the supply; or
(b) where any electric line or electrical plant falls to be provided in pursuance of that subsection, in respect of the provision of the line or plant; and if that person fails to give such security, the supplier may if he thinks fit refuse to give the supply, or to provide the line or plant, for so long as the failure continues.

(2) Where any person has not given such security as is mentioned in subsection (1) above, or the security given by any person has become invalid or insufficient
(a) the public electricity supplier may by notice require that person, within seven days after the service of the notice, to give him reasonable security for the payment of all money which may become due to him in respect of the supply; and
(b) if that person fails to give such security, the supplier may if he thinks fit discontinue the supply for so long as the failure continues; and any notice under paragraph (a) above shall state the effect of section 23 below.

(3) Where any money is deposited with a public electricity supplier by way of security in pursuance of this section, the supplier shall pay interest, at such rate as may from time to time be fixed by the supplier with the approval of the Director, on every sum of 50p so deposited for every three months during which it remains in the hands of the supplier.

(4) A public electricity supplier shall not be entitled to require security in pursuance of subsection (1)(a) above if
(a) the person requiring the supply is prepared to take the supply through a pre-payment meter; and
(b) it is reasonably practicable in all the circumstances (including in particular the risk of loss or damage) for the supplier to provide such a meter.

Additional terms of supply

21 A public electricity supplier may require any person who requires a supply of electricity in pursuance of section 16(1) above to accept in respect of the supply
(a) any restrictions which must be imposed for the purpose of enabling the supplier to comply with regulations under section 29 below; and
(b) any terms restricting any liability of the supplier for economic loss resulting from negligence which it is reasonable in all the circumstances for that person to be required to accept.

Special agreements with respect to supply

22(1) Notwithstanding anything in sections 16 to 21 above, a person who requires a supply of electricity in pursuance of section 16(1) above

(a) may enter into a special agreement with the public electricity supplier for the supply on such terms as may be specified in the agreement; and

(b) shall enter into such an agreement in any case where
  (i) the maximum power to be made available at any time exceeds 10 megawatts; or
  (ii) it is otherwise reasonable in all the circumstances for such an agreement to be entered into.

(2) The Secretary of State may by order provide that subsection (1) above shall have effect as if for the wattage mentioned in paragraph (b) there were substituted such other wattage as may be specified in the order; but before making such an order, he shall consult with public electricity suppliers and with persons or bodies appearing to him to be representative of persons likely to be affected.

(3) So long as any such agreement as is mentioned in subsection (1) above is effective, the rights and liabilities of the parties to the agreement shall be those arising under the agreement and not those provided for by sections 16 to 21 above; but nothing in this subsection shall prejudice the giving of a notice under section 16(2) above specifying as the day on which the supply is required to commence the day on which such an agreement ceases to be effective.

(4) In this Part 'tariff customer' means a person who requires a supply of electricity in pursuance of section 16(1) above and is supplied by the public electricity supplier otherwise than on the terms specified in such an agreement as is mentioned in subsection (1) above.

Determination of disputes

23(1) Any dispute arising under sections 16 to 22 above between a public electricity supplier and a person requiring a supply of electricity
  (a) may be referred to the Director by either party; and
  (b) on such a reference, shall be determined by order made either by the Director or, if he thinks fit, by an arbitrator, or in Scotland arbiter, appointed by him; and the practice and procedure to be followed in connection with any such determination shall be such as the Director may consider appropriate.

(1A) Any person making an order under subsection (1) above shall include in the order the reasons for reaching his decision with respect to the dispute.

(2) Where any dispute arising under sections 16 to 22 above between a public electricity supplier and a person requiring a supply of electricity to be given falls to be determined under this section, the Director may give directions as to the circumstances in which, and the terms on which, the supplier is to give the supply pending the determination of the dispute.

(3) Where any dispute arising under section 20(1) above falls to be determined under this section, the Director may give directions as to the security (if any) to be given pending the determination of the dispute.

(4) Directions under subsection (2) or (3) above may apply either in cases of particular descriptions or in particular cases.

(5) An order under this section
  (a) may include such incidental, supplemental and consequential provision (including provision requiring either party to pay a sum in respect of the costs or expenses incurred by the person making the order) as that person considers appropriate; and

(b) shall be final and
  (i) in England and Wales, shall be enforceable, in so far as it includes such provision as to costs or expenses, as if it were a judgment of the county court;
  (ii) in Scotland, shall be enforceable as if it were an extract registered decree arbitral bearing a warrant for execution issued by the sheriff.

(6) In including in an order under this section any such provision as to costs or expenses as is mentioned in subsection (5) above, the person making the order shall have regard to the conduct and means of the parties and any other relevant circumstances.

Orders for securing compliance

25(1) Subject to subsections (2) and (5) and section 26 below, where the Director is satisfied that a licence holder is contravening, or is likely to contravene, any relevant condition or requirement, he shall by a final order make such provision as is requisite for the purpose of securing compliance with that condition or requirement.

(2) Subject to subsection (5) below, where it appears to the Director
  (a) that a licence holder is contravening, or is likely to contravene, any relevant condition or requirement; and
  (b) that it is requisite that a provisional order be made, he shall (instead of taking steps towards the making of a final order) by a provisional order make such provision as appears to him requisite for the purpose of securing compliance with that condition or requirement.

(3) In determining for the purposes of subsection (2)(b) above whether it is requisite that a provisional order be made, the Director shall have regard, in particular
  (a) to the extent to which any person is likely to sustain loss or damage in consequence of anything which, in contravention of the relevant condition or requirement, is likely to be done, or omitted to be done, before a final order may be made; and
  (b) to the fact that the effect of the provisions of this section and section 27 below is to exclude the availability of any remedy (apart from under those provisions or for negligence) in respect of any contravention of a relevant condition or requirement.

(4) Subject to subsection (5) and section 26 below, the Director shall confirm a provisional order, with or without modifications, if
  (a) he is satisfied that the licence holder to whom the order relates is contravening, or is likely to contravene, any relevant condition or requirement; and
  (b) the provision made by the order (with any modifications) is requisite for the purpose of securing compliance with that condition or requirement.

(5) The Director shall not make a final order or make or confirm a provisional order in relation to a licence holder if he is satisfied
  (a) that the duties imposed on him by section 3 above preclude the making or, as the case may be, the confirmation of the order;
  (b) that the licence holder has agreed to take and is taking all such steps as it appears to the Director for the time being to be appropriate for the licence holder to take for the purpose of securing or facilitating compliance with the condition or requirement in question; or

(c) that the contraventions were, or the apprehended contraventions are, of a trivial nature.

(6) Where the Director is satisfied as mentioned in subsection (5) above, he shall
    (a) serve notice that he is so satisfied on the licence holder; and
    (b) publish the notice in such manner as he considers appropriate for the purpose of bringing the matters to which the notice relates to the attention of persons likely to be affected by them.

(7) A final or provisional order
    (a) shall require the licence holder to whom it relates (according to the circumstances of the case) to do, or not to do, such things as are specified in the order or are of a description so specified;
    (b) shall take effect at such time, being the earliest practicable time, as is determined by or under the order; and
    (c) may be revoked at any time by the Director.

(8) In this Part

'final order' means an order under this section other than a provisional order;

'provisional order' means an order under this section which, if not previously confirmed in accordance with subsection (4) above, will cease to have effect at the end of such period (not exceeding three months) as is determined by or under the order;

'relevant condition', in relation to a licence holder, means any condition of his licence;

'relevant requirement', in relation to a licence holder, means any duty or other requirement imposed on him by or under section 9 or sections 16 to 23 above or sections 40(3), 41(3), 42A or 42B below.

Procedural requirements

26(1) Before he makes a final order or confirms a provisional order, the Director shall give notice
    (a) stating that he proposes to make or confirm the order and setting out its effect;
    (b) setting out
        (i) the relevant condition or requirement for the purpose of securing compliance with which the order is to be made or confirmed;
        (ii) the acts or omissions which, in his opinion, constitute or would constitute contraventions of that condition or requirement; and
        (iii) the other facts which, in his opinion, justify the making or confirmation of the order; and
    (c) specifying the period (not being less than 28 days from the date of publication of the notice) within which representations or objections with respect to the proposed order or proposed confirmation may be made, and shall consider any representations or objections which are duly made and not withdrawn.

(2) A notice under subsection (1) above shall be given
    (a) by publishing the notice in such manner as the Director considers appropriate for the purpose of bringing the matters to which the notice relates to the attention of persons likely to be affected by them; and

(b) by serving a copy of the notice, and a copy of the proposed order or of the order proposed to be confirmed, on the licence holder to whom the order relates.

(3) The Director shall not make a final order with modifications, or confirm a provisional order with modifications, except
    (a) with the consent to the modifications of the licence holder to whom the order relates; or
    (b) after complying with the requirements of subsection (4) below.

(4) The requirements mentioned in subsection (3) above are that the Director shall
    (a) serve on the licence holder to whom the order relates such notice as appears to him requisite of his proposal to make or confirm the order with modifications;
    (b) in that notice specify the period (not being less than 28 days from the date of the service of the notice) within which representations or objections with respect to the proposed modifications may be made; and
    (c) consider any representations or objections which are duly made and not withdrawn.

(5) As soon as practicable after making a final order or making or confirming a provisional order, the Director shall
    (a) serve a copy of the order on the licence holder to whom the order relates; and
    (b) publish the order in such manner as he considers appropriate for the purpose of bringing it to the attention of persons likely to be affected by it.

(6) Before revoking a final order or a provisional order which has been confirmed, the Director shall give notice
    (a) stating that he proposes to revoke the order and setting out its effect; and
    (b) specifying the period (not being less than 28 days from the date of publication of the notice) within which representations or objections with respect to the proposed revocation may be made, and shall consider any representations or objections which are duly made and not withdrawn.

(7) If, after giving a notice under subsection (6) above, the Director decides not to revoke the order to which the notice relates, he shall give notice of his decision.

(8) A notice under subsection (6) or (7) above shall be given
    (a) by publishing the notice in such manner as the Director considers appropriate for the purpose of bringing the matters to which the notice relates to the attention of persons likely to be affected by them; and
    (b) by serving a copy of the notice on the licence holder to whom the order relates.

Validity and effect of orders

27(1) If the licence holder to whom a final or provisional order relates is aggrieved by the order and desires to question its validity on the ground
    (a) that its making or confirmation was not within the powers of section 25 above; or
    (b) that any of the requirements of section 26 above have not been complied with in relation to it, he may, within 42 days from the date of

service on him of a copy of the order, make an application to the court under this section.

(2) On any such application the court may, if satisfied that the making or confirmation of the order was not within those powers or that the interests of the licence holder have been substantially prejudiced by a failure to comply with those requirements, quash the order or any provision of the order.

(3) Except as provided by this section, the validity of a final or provisional order shall not be questioned by any legal proceedings whatever.

(4) The obligation to comply with a final or provisional order shall be a duty owed to any person who may be affected by a contravention of the order.

(5) Where a duty is owed by virtue of subsection (4) above to any person, any breach of the duty which causes that person to sustain loss or damage shall be actionable at the suit or instance of that person.

(6) In any proceedings brought against a licence holder in pursuance of subsection (5) above, it shall be a defence for him to prove that he took all reasonable steps and exercised all due diligence to avoid contravening the order.

(7) Without prejudice to any right which any person may have by virtue of subsection (5) above to bring civil proceedings in respect of any contravention or apprehended contravention of a final or provisional order, compliance with any such order shall be enforceable by civil proceedings by the Director for an injunction or for interdict or for any other appropriate relief.

(8) In this section and section 28 below 'the court' means the High Court in relation to England and Wales and the Court of Session in relation to Scotland.

Power to require information etc

28(1) Where it appears to the Director that a licence holder may be contravening, or may have contravened, any relevant condition or requirement, the Director may, for any purpose connected with such of his functions under section 25 above or 42B below as are exercisable in relation to that matter, serve a notice under subsection (2) below on any person.

(2) A notice under this subsection is a notice signed by the Director and
   (a) requiring the person on whom it is served to produce, at a time and place specified in the notice, to the Director or to any person appointed by the Director for the purpose, any documents which are specified or described in the notice and are in that person's custody or under his control; or
   (b) requiring that person, if he is carrying on a business, to furnish, at a time and place and in the form and manner specified in the notice, to the Director such information as may be specified or described in the notice.

(3) No person shall be required under this section to produce any documents which he could not be compelled to produce in civil proceedings in the court or, in complying with any requirement for the furnishing of information, to give any information which he could not be compelled to give in evidence in any such proceedings.

(4) A person who without reasonable excuse fails to do anything required of him by notice under subsection (2) above shall be liable on summary conviction to a fine not exceeding level 5 on the standard scale.

(5) A person who intentionally alters, suppresses or destroys any document which he has been required by any notice under subsection (2) above to produce shall be liable
   (a) on summary conviction, to a fine not exceeding the statutory maximum;
   (b) on conviction on indictment, to a fine.
(6) If a person makes default in complying with a notice under subsection (2) above, the court may, on the application of the Director, make such order as the court thinks fit for requiring the default to be made good; and any such order may provide that all the costs or expenses of and incidental to the application shall be borne by the person in default or by any officers of a company or other association who are responsible for its default.

Procedures for dealing with complaints

42B(1) Each public electricity supplier shall establish a procedure for dealing with complaints made by his customers or potential customers in connection with the provision of electricity supply services.
(2) No such procedure shall be established, and no modification of such a procedure shall be made, unless
   (a) the supplier has consulted the consumers' committee to which he has been allocated; and
   (b) the proposed procedure or modification has been approved by the Director.
(3) The supplier shall
   (a) publicise the procedure in such manner as may be approved by the Director; and
   (b) send a description of the procedure, free of charge, to any person who asks for one.
(4) The Director may give a direction to any public electricity supplier requiring the supplier to review his procedure or the manner in which it operates.
(5) A direction under subsection (4) above
   (a) may specify the manner in which the review is to be conducted; and
   (b) shall require a written report of the review to be made to the Director.
(6) Where the Director receives a report under subsection (5)(b) above, he may, after consulting the supplier, direct him to make such modifications of
   (a) the procedure; or
   (b) the manner in which the procedure operates,
as may be specified in the direction.
(7) Subsection (2) above does not apply to any modification made in compliance with a direction under subsection (6) above.

Fixing maximum charges for reselling electricity

44(1) This section applies to electricity supplied to a consumer's premises by an authorised electricity supplier, that is to say, a person who is authorised by a licence or exemption to supply electricity.
(2) The Director may from time to time fix maximum prices at which electricity to which this section applies may be resold, and shall publish any prices so fixed in such manner as in his opinion will secure adequate publicity for them.
(3) Different prices may be fixed under this section in different classes of cases, which may be defined by reference to areas, tariffs applicable to electricity

supplied by the authorised electricity suppliers or any other relevant circumstances.

(4) If any person resells electricity to which this section applies at a price exceeding the maximum price fixed under this section and applicable thereto, the amount of the excess shall be recoverable by the person to whom the electricity was resold.

Billing disputes

44A(1) The Secretary of State may by regulations make provision for billing disputes to be referred to the Director for determination in accordance with the regulations.

(2) In this section 'billing dispute' means a dispute between a public electricity supplier and a tariff customer concerning the amount of the charge which the supplier is entitled to recover from the customer in connection with the provision of electricity supply services.

(3) Regulations under this section may only be made after consulting
   (a) the Director; and
   (b) persons or bodies appearing to the Secretary of State to be representative of persons likely to be affected by the regulations.

(4) Regulations under this section may provide that, where a billing dispute is referred to the Director, he may either
   (a) determine the dispute, or
   (b) appoint an arbitrator (or in Scotland an arbiter) to determine it.

(5) Any person determining any billing dispute in accordance with regulations under this section shall, in such manner as may be specified in the regulations, give his reasons for reaching his decision with respect to the dispute.

(6) Regulations under this section may provide
   (a) that disputes may be referred to the Director under this section only by prescribed persons; and
   (b) for any determination to be final and enforceable
      (i) in England and Wales, as if it were a judgment of a county court; and
      (ii) in Scotland, as if it were an extract registered decree arbitral bearing a warrant for execution issued by the sheriff.

(7) Except in such circumstances (if any) as may be prescribed
   (a) the Director or an arbitrator (or in Scotland an arbiter) appointed by him shall not determine any billing dispute which is the subject of proceedings before, or with respect to which judgment has been given by, any court; and
   (b) neither party to any billing dispute which has been referred to the Director for determination in accordance with regulations under this section shall commence proceedings before any court in respect of that dispute pending its determination in accordance with the regulations.

(8) No public electricity supplier may commence proceedings before any court in respect of any charge in connection with the provision by him of electricity supply services unless, not less than 28 days before doing so, the tariff customer concerned was informed by him, in such form and manner as may be prescribed, of
   (a) his intention to commence proceedings;
   (b) the customer's rights by virtue of this section; and
   (c) such other matters (if any) as may be prescribed.

(9) The powers of the Director under section 28 above shall also be exercisable for any purpose connected with the determination of any dispute referred to him in accordance with regulations made under this section.

Investigation of enforcement matters

45(1) Subject to subsection (2) below, it shall be the duty of the Director to investigate any matter which appears to him to be an enforcement matter and which
  (a) is the subject of a representation (other than one appearing to the Director to be frivolous) made to the Director by or on behalf of a person appearing to the Director to have an interest in that matter; or
  (b) is referred to him by a consumers' committee under subsection (3) below.

(2) The Director may, if he thinks fit, require a consumers' committee to investigate and report to him on any matter falling within subsection (1) above which relates to a person authorised by a licence to supply electricity in the committee's area.

(3) It shall be the duty of each consumers' committee to refer to the Director any matter which
  (a) appears to the committee to be an enforcement matter; and
  (b) is the subject of a representation (other than one appearing to the committee to be frivolous) made to the committee by or on behalf of a person appearing to the committee to have an interest in that matter.

(4) In this section and section 46 below 'enforcement matter' means any matter in respect of which any functions of the Director under section 25 above are or may be exercisable.

Investigation of certain other matters

46(1) It shall be the duty of each consumers' committee to investigate any matter which appears to the committee to be a relevant matter and which
  (a) is the subject of a representation (other than one appearing to the committee to be frivolous) made to the committee by or on behalf of a person appearing to the committee to have an interest in that matter; or
  (b) is referred to the committee by the Director under subsection (2) below.

(2) Subject to subsection (3) below, it shall be the duty of the Director to refer to a consumers' committee any matter which
  (a) appears to the Director to be a relevant matter; and
  (b) is the subject of a representation (other than one appearing to the Director to be frivolous) made to the Director by or on behalf of a person appearing to the Director to have an interest in that matter.

(3) Nothing in subsection (2) above shall require the Director to refer to a consumers' committee any matter in respect of which he is already considering exercising functions under this Part.

(4) Where on an investigation under subsection (1) above any matter appears to a consumers' committee to be a matter in respect of which it would be appropriate for the Director to exercise any functions under this Part, the committee shall refer that matter to the Director with a view to his exercising those functions with respect to that matter.

(5) In this section 'relevant matter', in relation to a consumers' committee, means any matter (other than an enforcement matter)

(a) in respect of which any functions of the Director under this Part are or may be exercisable; and

(b) which relates to a public electricity supplier allocated to the committee or to any other person authorised by a licence to supply electricity in that committee's area.

General duty of consumers' committees to advise Director etc.

51 It shall be the duty of each consumers' committee

(a) to make representations to and consult with each public electricity supplier allocated to the committee about all such matters as appear to the committee to affect the interests of customers or potential customers of that supplier;

(b) to keep under review matters affecting the interests of consumers of electricity supplied to premises in the committee's area; and (c) to advise the Director on any matter relating to the supply of electricity in that area on which they consider they should offer advice or which is referred to them by the Director.

Service of documents

109(1) Any document required or authorised by virtue of this Act to be served on any person may be served

(a) by delivering it to him or by leaving it at his proper address or by sending it by post to him at that address; or

(b) if the person is a body corporate, by serving it in accordance with paragraph (a) above on the secretary of that body; or

(c) if the person is a partnership, by serving it in accordance with paragraph (a) above on a partner or a person having the control or management of the partnership business.

(2) For the purposes of this section and section 7 of the Interpretation Act 1978 (which relates to the service of documents by post) in its application to this section, the proper address of any person on whom a document is to be served shall be his last known address, except that

(a) in the case of service on a body corporate or its secretary, it shall be the address of the registered or principal office of the body;

(b) in the case of service on a partnership or a partner or a person having the control or management of a partnership business, it shall be the address of the principal office of the partnership; and for the purposes of this subsection the principal office of a company registered outside the United Kingdom or of a partnership carrying on business outside the United Kingdom is its principal office within the United Kingdom.

(3) If a person to be served by virtue of this Act with any document by another has specified to that other an address within the United Kingdom other than his proper address (as determined in pursuance of subsection (2) above) as the one at which he or someone on his behalf will accept documents of the same description as that document, that address shall also be treated as his proper address for the purposes of this section and for the purposes of the said section 7 in its application to this section.

(4) If the name or address of any owner or occupier of land on whom by virtue of this Act any document is to be served cannot after reasonable inquiry be ascertained, the document may be served by

(a) addressing it to him by the description of 'owner' or 'occupier' of the land (describing it); and
(b) either leaving it in the hands of a person who is or appears to be resident or employed on the land or leaving it conspicuously affixed to some building or object on or near the land.

(5) This section shall not apply to any document in relation to the service of which provision is made by rules of court.

(6) In this section 'secretary', in relation to a local authority within the meaning of the Local Government Act 1972 or the Local Government (Scotland) Act 1973, means the proper officer within the meaning of that Act.

SCHEDULE 6
The Public Electricity Supply Code

Recovery of electricity charges etc.

1(1) Subject to sub-paragraph (2) below, a public electricity supplier may recover from a tariff customer any charges due to him in respect of the supply of electricity, or in respect of the provision of any electricity meter, electric line or electrical plant.

(2) A public electricity supplier who, for the purpose of meeting the needs of a disabled person
(a) alters the position of any electricity meter which has been provided by him; or
(b) replaces such a meter with one which has been specially adapted, shall not make any charge for the alteration or replacement; and section 23 of this Act shall apply in relation to any dispute arising under this sub-paragraph as if it were a dispute arising under sections 16 to 22 of this Act.

(3) If a tariff customer quits any premises at which electricity has been supplied to him by a public electricity supplier without giving notice thereof to the supplier so that it is received by the supplier at least two working days before he quits the premises, he shall be liable to pay the supplier all charges in respect of the supply of electricity to the premises accruing due up to whichever of the following first occurs, namely
(a) the second working day after he gives such notice to the supplier;
(b) the next day on which the register of any meter falls to be ascertained; and
(c) the day from which any subsequent occupier of the premises requires the supplier to supply electricity to the premises.

(4) Sub-paragraph (3) above, or a statement of the effect thereof, shall be endorsed upon every demand note for electricity charges payable to a public electricity supplier by a tariff customer.

(5) If a tariff customer quits any premises at which electricity has been supplied to him by a public electricity supplier without paying all charges due from him in respect of the supply, or the provision of any electricity meter, electric line or electrical plant for the purposes of the supply, the supplier
(a) may refuse to furnish him with a supply of electricity at any other premises until he pays the amount due; but

(b) shall not be entitled to require payment of that amount from the next occupier of the premises.

(6) If a tariff customer has not, within the requisite period, paid all charges due from him to a public electricity supplier in respect of the supply of electricity to any premises, or the provision of any electricity meter, electric line or electrical plant for the purposes of that supply, the supplier, after the expiration of not less than two working days' notice of his intention, may
(a) cut off the supply to the premises, or to any other premises occupied by the customer, by such means as he thinks fit; and
(b) recover any expenses incurred in so doing from the customer.

(7) In sub-paragraph (6) above 'the requisite period' means
(a) in the case of premises which are used wholly or mainly for domestic purposes, the period of 20 working days after the making by the supplier of a demand in writing for payment of the charges due; and
(b) in the case of any other premises, the period of 15 working days after the making of such a demand.

(8) The powers conferred by sub-paragraph (6) above shall also be exercisable at any time which, in relation to a tariff customer, is after
(a) the effective date for the purposes of section 233 of the Insolvency Act 1986 (supplies of gas, water, electricity etc. to insolvent companies); or
(b) the relevant day for the purposes of section 372 of that Act or section 70 of the Bankruptcy (Scotland) Act 1985 (supplies of gas, water, electricity etc. to insolvent individuals).

(9) The powers conferred by sub-paragraph (6) above shall not be exercisable as respects any amount which is genuinely in dispute; but there shall be disregarded for this purpose any dispute arising under section 39 of this Act or regulations made under it.

(10) In this paragraph a reference to the provision of any electric line or item of electrical plant is a reference to the provision of such a line or item by the installation of a new one or by the modification of an existing one.

Restoration of supply by supplier

2(1) Where a public electricity supplier has cut off the supply of electricity to any premises in consequence of any default on the part of a tariff customer, the supplier shall be under an obligation to resume the supply of electricity before the end of the period of two working days beginning with the time when the requirements of sub-paragraph (2) below are satisfied.

(2) The requirements of this sub-paragraph are that the customer in default
(a) has made good the default;
(b) has paid the reasonable expenses of disconnecting and re-connecting the supply; and
(c) has given such security as is mentioned in section 20(1) of this Act.

(3) The obligation imposed by sub-paragraph (1) above shall be a duty owed to any person who may be affected by a failure to comply with the obligation.

(4) Where a duty is owed by virtue of sub-paragraph (3) above to any person any breach of the duty which causes that person to sustain loss or damage shall be actionable at the suit or instance of that person.

(5) In any proceedings brought against a public electricity supplier in pursuance of sub-paragraph (4) above, it shall be a defence for the supplier to prove that he took all reasonable steps and exercised all due diligence to avoid failing to comply with the obligation imposed by sub-paragraph (1) above.

(6) Without prejudice to any right which any person may have by virtue of sub-paragraph (4) above to bring civil proceedings in respect of any failure to comply with the obligation imposed by sub-paragraph (1) above, compliance with that obligation shall be enforceable by civil proceedings by the Director for an injunction or for interdict or for any other appropriate relief.

Restoration of supply without consent

3(1) Where a supply of electricity to any premises has been cut off by a public electricity supplier otherwise than in the exercise of a power conferred by regulations under section 29 of this Act, no person shall, without the consent of the supplier, restore the supply.

(2) If any person acts in contravention of sub-paragraph (1) above, he shall be liable on summary conviction to a fine not exceeding level 3 on the standard scale and the supplier may again cut off the supply.

Damage to electrical plant etc

4(1) If any person intentionally or by culpable negligence damages or allows to be damaged
   (a) any electrical plant or electric line belonging to a public electricity supplier; or
   (b) any electricity meter so belonging, he shall be liable on summary conviction to a fine not exceeding level 3 on the standard scale.

(2) Where an offence has been committed under sub-paragraph (1)(a) above, the supplier may discontinue the supply of electricity to the person so offending until the matter has been remedied.

(3) Where an offence has been committed under sub-paragraph (1)(b) above, the supplier
   (a) may discontinue the supply of electricity to the person so offending until the matter has been remedied; and
   (b) remove the meter as respects which the offence was committed.

(4) Where a public electricity supplier removes a meter under sub-paragraph (3) above, he shall keep it safely until the Director authorises him to destroy or otherwise dispose of it.

Entry during continuance of supply

5(1) Any officer authorised by a public electricity supplier may at all reasonable times, on the production of some duly authenticated document showing his authority, enter any premises to which a supply of electricity is being given by the public electricity supplier, or by a private electricity supplier (wholly or partly) through the public electricity supplier's electric lines and electrical plant, for any of the following purposes, namely
   (a) inspecting any electric line or electrical plant belonging to the supplier;
   (b) ascertaining the register of any electricity meter and, in the case of a prepayment meter, removing any money or tokens belonging to the supplier;
   (c) removing, inspecting or re-installing any electricity meter or installing any substitute meter.

(2) Except where a supply of electricity is being given to the premises by a private electricity supplier (wholly or partly) through the public electricity supplier's

electric lines and electrical plant, sub-paragraph (1)(a) and (b) above does not apply if
  (a) the consumer has applied in writing to the supplier for the supplier to cease to supply electricity to the premises; and
  (b) the supplier has failed to do so within a reasonable time.
(3) Sub-paragraph (1)(c) above does not apply in relation to the removal of a meter unless two working days' notice is given to the occupier, or the owner of the premises if they are unoccupied.

Entry on discontinuance of supply

6(1) Where a public electricity supplier is authorised by sub-paragraph (3) of paragraph 4 above or sub-paragraph (3) of paragraph 11 of Schedule 7 to this Act
  (a) to discontinue the supply of electricity to any premises; and
  (b) to remove the electricity meter as respects which the offence under that paragraph was committed, any officer authorised by the supplier may at all reasonable times, on production of some duly authenticated document showing his authority, enter the premises for the purpose of disconnecting the supply and removing the meter.

(2) Where
  (a) a public electricity supplier is authorised by any other provision of this Act or of regulations made under it (including any such provision as applied by such an agreement as is mentioned in section 22(1) of this Act) to cut off or discontinue the supply of electricity to any premises;
  (b) a person occupying premises supplied with electricity by a public electricity supplier, or by a private electricity supplier (wholly or partly) through a public electricity supplier's electric lines and electrical plant, ceases to require such a supply;
  (c) a person entering into occupation of any premises previously supplied with electricity by a public electricity supplier, or by a private electricity supplier (wholly or partly) through a public electricity supplier's electric lines and electrical plant, does not require such a supply; or
  (d) a person entering into occupation of any premises previously supplied with electricity through a meter belonging to a public electricity supplier does not hire or borrow that meter, any officer authorised by the supplier, after one working day's notice to the occupier, or to the owner of the premises if they are unoccupied, may at all reasonable times, on production of some duly authenticated document showing his authority, enter the premises for the purpose of disconnecting the supply or removing any electrical plant, electric line or electricity meter.

Entry for replacing, repairing or altering lines or plant

7(1) Any officer authorised by a public electricity supplier, after five working days' notice to the occupier of any premises, or to the owner of any premises which are unoccupied, may at all reasonable times, on production of some duly authenticated document showing his authority, enter the premises for the purpose of

    (a) placing a new electric line or new electrical plant in the place of or in addition to any existing line or plant which has already been lawfully placed; or

    (b) repairing or altering any such existing line or plant.

(2) In the case of emergency arising from faults in any electric line or electrical plant entry may be made under sub-paragraph (1) above without the notice required to be given by that sub-paragraph, but the notice shall then be given as soon as possible after the occurrence of the emergency.

Provisions as to powers of entry

8(1) Where in pursuance of any powers of entry conferred by this Schedule, entry is made on any premises by an officer authorised by a public electricity supplier

    (a) the officer shall ensure that the premises are left no less secure by reason of the entry; and

    (b) the supplier shall make good, or pay compensation for, any damage caused by the officer, or by any person accompanying him in entering the premises, in taking any action authorised by this Schedule, or in making premises secure.

(2) Any officer exercising powers of entry conferred by this Schedule may be accompanied by such persons as may be necessary or expedient for the purpose for which the entry is made, or for the purposes of sub-paragraph (1) above.

(3) If any person intentionally obstructs any officer exercising powers of entry conferred by this Schedule, he shall be liable on summary conviction to a fine not exceeding level 3 on the standard scale.

(4) The Rights of Entry (Gas and Electricity Boards) Act 1954 (entry under a justice's warrant) shall apply in relation to any powers of entry conferred by this Schedule.

Electrical plant etc. not to be subject to distress

9 Any electrical plant, electric line or electricity meter owned by or let for hire or lent to a customer by a public electricity supplier and marked or impressed with a sufficient mark or brand indicating the supplier as the owner thereof

    (a) shall be deemed not to be landlord's fixtures, notwithstanding that they may be fixed or fastened to any part of the premises in which they may be situated; and

    (b) shall not in England and Wales be subject to distress or be liable to be taken in execution under process of any court or any proceedings in bankruptcy against the person in whose possession they may be.

SCHEDULE 7
Use etc. of Electricity Meters

Consumption to be ascertained by appropriate meter

1(1) Where a customer of an electricity supplier is to be charged for his supply wholly or partly by reference to the quantity of electricity supplied, the supply shall be given through, and the quantity of electricity shall be ascertained by, an appropriate meter.

(2)   If the electricity supplier agrees, the meter may be provided by the electricity supplier (whether by way of sale, hire or loan).

(2A)   A public electricity supplier may refuse to allow one of his customers to provide a meter only if there are reasonable grounds for his refusal.

(3)   The meter shall be installed on the customer's premises in a position determined by the electricity supplier, unless in all the circumstances it is more reasonable to place it outside those premises or in some other position.

(4)   The electricity supplier may require the replacement of any meter provided and installed in accordance with sub-paragraphs (2) and (3) above where its replacement
   (a)   is necessary to secure compliance with this Schedule or any regulations made under it; or
   (b)   is otherwise reasonable in all the circumstances; and any replacement meter shall be provided and installed in accordance with those sub-paragraphs.

(5)   If the customer refuses or fails to take his supply through an appropriate meter provided and installed in accordance with sub-paragraphs (2) and (3) above, the supplier may refuse to give or may discontinue the supply.

(6)   For the purposes of this paragraph a meter is an appropriate meter for use in connection with any particular supply if it is of a pattern or construction which, having regard to the terms on which the supply is to be charged for, is particularly suitable for such use.

(7)   Section 23 of this Act shall apply in relation to any dispute arising under this paragraph between a public electricity supplier and a customer as if it were a dispute arising under sections 16 to 22 of this Act.

(8)   Pending the determination under section 23 of this Act of any dispute arising under this paragraph, the meter and its provision and installation shall be such as the Director may direct; and directions under this sub-paragraph may apply either in cases of particular descriptions or in particular cases.

(9)   Part I of this Act shall apply as if any duty or other requirement imposed on a public electricity supplier by directions under sub-paragraph (8) above were imposed by directions under section 23 of this Act.

(10)   In this Schedule 'exempt supply' means a supply of electricity to any premises where
   (a)   the premises are not premises used wholly or mainly for domestic purposes; or
   (b)   the electricity supplier or the customer is a person authorised by an exemption to supply electricity to those premises.

Restrictions on use of meters

2(1)   No meter shall be used for ascertaining the quantity of electricity supplied by an electricity supplier to a customer unless the meter
   (a)   is of an approved pattern or construction and is installed in an approved manner; and
   (b)   subject to sub-paragraph (2) below, is certified under paragraph 5 below; and in this Schedule 'approved' means approved by or under regulations made under this paragraph.

(2)   Paragraph (b) of sub-paragraph (1) above shall not apply to a meter used in connection with an exempt supply if the electricity supplier and the customer have agreed in writing to dispense with the requirements of that paragraph.

(3)   Regulations under this paragraph may provide

(a) for determining the fees to be paid for approvals given by or under the regulations;

(b) for revoking an approval so given to any particular pattern or construction of meter and requiring meters of that pattern or construction which have been installed to be replaced with meters of an approved pattern or construction within a prescribed period;

(c) for revoking an approval so given to any particular manner of installation and requiring meters which have been installed in that manner to be installed in an approved manner within such a period;

and may make different provision for meters of different descriptions or for meters used or intended to be used for different purposes.

3(1) If an electricity supplier supplies electricity through a meter which is used for ascertaining the quantity of electricity supplied and

(a) is not of an approved pattern or construction or is not installed in an approved manner; or

(b) in the case of a meter to which paragraph 2(1)(b) above applies, is not certified under paragraph 5 below, he shall be liable on summary conviction to a fine not exceeding level 3 on the standard scale.

(2) Where the commission by any person of an offence under this paragraph is due to the act or default of some other person, that other person shall be guilty of the offence; and a person may be charged with and convicted of the offence by virtue of this sub-paragraph whether or not proceedings are taken against the first-mentioned person.

(3) In any proceedings in respect of an offence under this paragraph it shall be a defence for the person charged to prove that he took all reasonable steps and exercised all due diligence to avoid committing the offence.

(4) No proceedings shall be instituted in England and Wales in respect of an offence under this paragraph except by or on behalf of the Director.

Testing etc. of meters

7(1) It shall be the duty of a meter examiner, on being required to do so by any person and after giving notice to such persons as may be prescribed

(a) to examine and test any meter used or intended to be used for ascertaining the quantity of electricity supplied to any premises;

(b) to determine whether it is of an approved pattern or construction and, if it is installed for use, whether it is installed in an approved manner;

(c) to determine whether it is in proper order for ascertaining the quantity of electricity supplied within the prescribed margins of error and, if it has been in use and there is a dispute as to whether it registered correctly at any time, to determine if possible whether it registered within those margins at that time; and

(d) to make a written report of his conclusions as to the matters mentioned in paragraphs (b) and (c) above.

(2) If a meter examiner determines that a meter is, or was at any time, operating outside the prescribed margins of error, he shall if possible give an opinion as to

(a) any period for which the meter has or may have been so operating; and

(b) the accuracy (if any) with which it was or may have been operating for any such period.

(3) Regulations under this paragraph may make provision for determining the fees to be paid for examining and testing meters, and the persons by whom and the circumstances in which they are to be paid.

(4)   In relation to a meter used or intended to be used in connection with an exempt supply, this paragraph shall have effect as if any reference to the prescribed margins of error included a reference to any margins of error agreed between the electricity supplier and the customer (in this Schedule referred to as 'agreed margins of error').

8(1)   This paragraph applies where there is a genuine dispute as to the accuracy of a meter used for ascertaining the quantity of electricity supplied to any premises and notice of the dispute
   (a)   is given to the electricity supplier by the customer, or to the customer by the electricity supplier; or
   (b)   is given to the electricity supplier and to the customer by any other person interested.

(2)   Except with the approval of a meter examiner and, if he so requires, under his supervision, the meter shall not be removed or altered by the supplier or the customer until after the dispute is resolved by agreement or the meter is examined and tested under paragraph 7 above, whichever first occurs.

(3)   If the supplier or the customer removes or alters the meter in contravention of sub-paragraph (2) above, he shall be liable on summary conviction to a fine not exceeding level 2 on the standard scale.

Presumptions and evidence

9(1)   This paragraph applies to meters used for ascertaining the quantity of electricity supplied to any premises.

(2)   The register of a meter to which this paragraph applies shall be admissible in any proceedings as evidence of the quantity of electricity supplied through it.

(3)   Where electricity has been supplied for any period through such a meter which is of an approved pattern or construction and is installed in an approved manner, the register of the meter shall be presumed to have been registering for that period
   (a)   within the prescribed margins of error; and
   (b)   in the case of a meter used in connection with an exempt supply, within any agreed margins of error, unless the contrary is proved.

(4)   Where a meter to which this paragraph applies has been operating for any period
   (a)   within the prescribed margins of error; and
   (b)   in the case of a meter used in connection with an exempt supply, within any agreed margins of error, the meter shall be conclusively presumed to have been correctly registering for that period the quantity of electricity supplied through it.

(5)   The report of a meter examiner on any question relating to such a meter shall be admissible in evidence in any proceedings in which that question is raised; and any conclusions in the report as to the accuracy of the meter when it was tested shall be presumed to be correct unless the contrary is proved.

Meters to be kept in proper order

10(1) A customer of an electricity supplier shall at all times, at his own expense, keep any meter belonging to him in proper order for correctly registering the quantity of electricity supplied to him; and in default of his doing so the supplier may discontinue the supply of electricity through that meter.

(2) An electricity supplier shall at all times, at his own expense, keep any meter let for hire or lent by him to any customer in proper order for correctly registering the quantity of electricity supplied and, in the case of pre-payment meters, for operating properly on receipt of the necessary payment.

(3) An electricity supplier shall have power to remove, inspect and re-install any meter by which the quantity of electricity supplied by him to a customer is registered, and shall, while any such meter is removed, fix a substituted meter on the premises; and the cost of removing, inspecting and re-installing a meter and of fixing a substituted meter shall be defrayed by the supplier.

(4) Sub-paragraphs (2) and (3) above are without prejudice to any remedy the supplier may have against the customer for failure to take proper care of the meter.

Interference with meters

11(1) If any person intentionally or by culpable negligence
  (a) alters the register of any meter used for measuring the quantity of electricity supplied to any premises by an electricity supplier; or
  (b) prevents any such meter from duly registering the quantity of electricity supplied, he shall be liable on summary conviction to a fine not exceeding level 3 on the standard scale.

(2) Where any person is prosecuted for an offence under sub-paragraph (1) above, the possession by him of artificial means for causing an alteration of the register of the meter or, as the case may be, the prevention of the meter from duly registering shall, if the meter was in his custody or under his control, be prima facie evidence (or in Scotland sufficient evidence) that the alteration or prevention was intentionally caused by him.

(3) Where an offence under sub-paragraph (1) above has been committed, the supplier may discontinue the supply of electricity to the premises until the matter has been remedied and remove the meter in respect of which the offence was committed.

(4) Where an electricity supplier removes a meter under sub-paragraph (3) above, he shall keep it safely until the Director authorises him to destroy or otherwise dispose of it.

Special provisions for prepayment meters

12(1) A customer of an electricity supplier who takes his supply through a pre-payment meter shall be under a duty to take all reasonable precautions for the safekeeping of any money or tokens which are inserted into that meter.

(2) A pre-payment meter shall not be used to recover any sum owing to an electricity supplier otherwise than in respect of the supply of electricity, the provision of an electric line or electrical plant or the provision of the meter.

Interpretation

13 In this Schedule
  'agreed margins of error' has the meaning given by paragraph 7(4) above;
  'approved' means approved by or under regulations made under paragraph 2 above;
  'electricity supplier' means a person authorised by a licence or exemption to supply electricity;
  'exempt supply' has the meaning given in paragraph 1(10) above;
  'prescribed' means prescribed by regulations;

'prescribed margins of error' has the meaning given by paragraph 5(2) above; 'regulations' means regulations made by the Director with the consent of the Secretary of State.

ELECTRICITY SUPPLY REGULATIONS 1988

Supply and safety

General conditions as to customers

27(1)   No supplier shall be compelled to commence or, subject to regulation 28, to continue to give a supply to any consumer unless he is reasonably satisfied that each part of the consumer's installation is so constructed, installed, protected and used, so far as is reasonably practicable, as to prevent danger and not to cause undue interference with the supplier's system or with the supply to others.

(2)   Any consumer's installation which complies with the provisions of the Institution of Electrical Engineers Regulations shall be deemed to comply with the requirements of this regulation as to safety.

Safety and disconnection

Discontinuance of supply in certain circumstances

28(1)   Where a supplier, after making such examination as the circumstances permit, has reasonable grounds for supposing that a consumer's installation or any part of it, including any supplier's works situated on the consumer's side of the supply terminals, fails to fulfil any relevant requirement of regulation 27, paragraphs (2) to (7) shall apply.

(2)   Where, in an emergency, the supplier is satisfied that immediate action is justified in the interests of safety, he may without prior notice discontinue the supply to the consumer's installation and notice in writing of the disconnection and the reasons for it shall be given to the consumer as soon as is reasonably practicable.

(3)   Subject to paragraph (2), the supplier may, by notice in writing specifying the grounds, require the consumer within such reasonable time as the notice shall specify to comply with one or both of the following:

(a)   to permit a person duly authorised by the supplier in writing to inspect and test the consumer's installation or any part of it at a reasonable time;

(b)   to take, or desist from, such action as may be necessary to correct or avoid undue interference with the supplier's supply or apparatus or with the supply to, or the apparatus of, other consumers.

(4)   In any of the circumstances specified in paragraph (5) the supplier may, on the expiry of the period specified in the notice referred to in paragraph (3), discontinue the supply to the consumer's installation and shall give immediate notice in writing to the consumer of the discontinuance.

(5)   The circumstances referred to in paragraph (4) are:

(a)   that, after service of a notice under paragraph (3)(a), the consumer does not give facilities for inspection or testing; or

    (b) in any other case:
        (i) after any such test or inspection the person authorised makes a report confirming that the consumer's installation (or any part of it) fails to fulfil any relevant requirement of regulation 27; or
       (ii) The consumer fails to show to the reasonable satisfaction of the supplier within the period so required that the matter complained of has been remedied or is the responsibility of the supplier.

(6) Any difference between the consumer and the supplier in relation to the grounds or the period specified in any notice of the kind mentioned in paragraph (3)(b) shall be determined in the manner provided by regulation 29.

(7) The supplier shall not discontinue the supply in pursuance of paragraph (4) pending the determination of any difference of the kind mentioned in paragraph (6), and shall not discontinue the supply to the whole of the consumer's installation where it is reasonable to disconnect only a portion of that installation in respect of which complaint is made.

(8) Where in pursuance of this regulation a supplier has disconnected the supply to a consumer's installation (or any part of it) the supplier shall not recommence the supply unless:
    (a) he is satisfied in respect of the consumer's installation that the relevant requirements of regulation 27 have been fulfilled; or
    (b) It has been determined in the manner provided by regulation 29 that the supplier is not entitled under regulation 27 to decline to recommence the supply; and if he is so satisfied or it is so determined, the supplier shall forthwith recommence the supply.

Disputes

Notices and determination of differences

29(1) In any case where in pursuance of these Regulations a supplier refuses to commence or to continue a supply to a consumer's installation or to a part thereof or to connect or reconnect a consumer's installation with his electric lines
    (a) the supplier shall as soon as practicable give to the consumer notice in writing of such refusal and the reasons therefore;
    (b) any difference which may arise between the consumer and the supplier with regard to the consumer's installation, the refusal or the notice shall be determined by a person appointed by the Secretary of State on the application of the consumer or the supplier and such person may make a direction as to whether any or all of the costs of such determination (including any fees or expenses payable to him) shall be borne by the supplier or the consumer.

(2) A person appointed under paragraph (1) shall not determine that the supplier was or is entitled under regulations 27 and 28 to refuse a supply to that installation if the appointed person is satisfied that:
    (a) the installation has continued to function satisfactorily and without risk of danger up to the material time; and
    (b) the installation is to be, or is being, continued in use only within the limits of the maximum power for which it was intended; and
    (c) there are no grounds for supposing that the installation will fail to function satisfactorily for a further reasonable period without risk of

danger or of undue interference with the supplier's system or with the supply to others.

(3) A copy of this regulation and regulation 28 shall be endorsed upon or accompany every notice given by the supplier to a consumer pursuant to this Part of these regulations.

GREATER LONDON COUNCIL (GENERAL POWERS) ACT 1972

Council's power to pay reconnection charges where owner has not paid bill and supply has been disconnected further power to pay all future bills (as amended by the Local Government Planning and Land Act 1980, Schedule 6, paragraph 14, Schedule 34, Part VI)

19. Restoration of gas and electricity services

(1) Where any building used for human habitation has ceased to be supplied with gas or electricity sufficient for the domestic purposes of any occupier thereof (hereinafter in this section referred to as 'the occupier') by reasons of the failure of the owner to pay to the statutory undertakers such charges as are properly due from him for the supply of gas or electricity, the borough council may, without prejudice to any action or proceedings which may be taken under any other enactment, pay to the statutory undertakers their reasonable expenses of reconnecting the supply of gas or electricity to the building to secure that such a supply is restored and shall thereafter, for so long as they consider necessary, pay the statutory undertakers' charges in respect of the subsequent supply of gas or electricity to the building.

(2) A borough council shall give not less than twenty-four hours' notice to the statutory undertakers of their intention to terminate payments in respect of the subsequent supply of gas or electricity.

(3) The borough council may, without prejudice to any action or proceedings which may be taken under any other enactment, recover from the owner or from the occupier of the building as a simple contract debt in any court of competent jurisdiction:

   (a) any expenses reasonably incurred by the borough council (including their establishment charges) in exercising their powers under this section in relation to the building; and

   (b) the amount of charges properly due to the statutory undertakers in respect of the building at the time the supply of gas or electricity was restored thereto in consequence of the exercise by the borough council of their powers under the foregoing subsection: Provided that:

      (i) proceedings shall not be commenced under this subsection against the owner or the occupier until notice in writing has been served on him by the borough council requiring him to pay to them any such expenses or other amount due and he has failed to comply with that notice;

      (ii) no greater sum shall be recovered at any one time from the occupier than the amount of any rent which is for the time being owed by him to the owner, or which has accrued due since such notice as aforesaid was served on him; and(i)

      (iii) if the occupier, as between himself and the owner, is not liable to pay to the statutory undertakers their charges in respect of the supply of gas or electricity to the building, he shall be entitled to deduct from the rent payable by him to the owner any sum paid by him in compliance with such a notice as aforesaid, or so recovered from him, and every sum so paid shall be a valid discharge of the rent to the extent of that sum.

(4) Any amount received by the borough council by virtue of paragraph (b) of the last foregoing subsection shall be forwarded by them to the statutory undertakers in reduction of the amount of charges properly due to them.

(5) In any proceedings under subsection (3) of this section for the recovery of any expenses or other amount due, the court may enquire whether the whole or any part thereof should, instead of being borne by the person from whom they are sought to be recovered, be borne by any other person (being the owner or the occupier) and the court may make such order as appears to it to be just in the circumstances of the case with respect to the person (being either the owner or the occupier) by whom the said expenses or other amount due are to be borne or as to the apportionment between any such persons of their liability to bear them; Provided that the court shall not under this subsection order the said expenses or other amount due or any part thereof to be borne by such other person as aforesaid unless it is satisfied that he has, at the instance of the person from whom they are sought to be recovered, had due notice of the proceedings and an opportunity of being heard.

(6) (a) Any expenses incurred by a borough council in respect of any building and recoverable from the owner under this section, together with interest thereon (at such reasonable rate as borough council may determine) from the date of service on the owner of the building of the notice referred to in paragraph (i) of the proviso to subsection (3) of this section shall, from the date when such expenses were incurred until recovered, be a charge on the building and on the appropriate estates and interests therein or, if the building is part of larger premises having the same owner, on those premises and on the appropriate estates and interests therein.

     (b) The borough council shall, for the purpose of enforcing a charge under this subsection, have all the same powers and remedies under the Law of Property Act 1925 and otherwise as if they were mortgagees by deed having powers of sale and lease, of accepting surrenders of leases and of appointing a receiver.

(7) The borough council may, if they think fit, themselves bear the whole or any part of any expenses recoverable under paragraph (a) of subsection (3) of this section.

(8) In this section:
    'appropriate estates and interests' means all estates and interests of the owner and of all persons deriving title under him;
    'building' means a building in a borough and includes any part of a building;
    'owner' means any person for the time being receiving or entitled to receive the rack-rent of the building in connection with which the word is used, whether on his own account or as agent or trustee for any other person, or who would so receive or be entitled to receive the same if the building were let at a rack-rent;
    'premises' includes messuages, buildings, lands, easements and hereditaments;

'statutory undertakers' means the persons authorised by any enactment to carry on any undertaking for the supply of gas or electricity, as the case may be, to the building in connection with which the words are used.

(9) This section shall extend and apply to the Common Council and to the city as it applies to a borough council and a borough respectively.

LOCAL GOVERNMENT (MISCELLANEOUS PROVISIONS) ACT 1976

Local authorities to keep separate account of expenditure on heating (as amended by the Building Act 1984, Schedule 6)

12. Provisions supplementary to s.11

(1) A local authority which supplies or proposes to supply heat, hot air, hot water or steam in pursuance of the preceding section may make byelaws:

    (a) with respect to the works and apparatus to be provided or used by persons other than the authority in connection with the supply;

    (b) for preventing waste and unauthorised use of the supply and unauthorised interference with works and apparatus used by the authority or any other person in connection with the supply;

    (c) providing for any specified contravention of the byelaws to be an offence punishable on summary conviction with a fine of such an amount, not exceeding level 3 on the standard scale as is specified in the byelaws.

(2) Subsections (1) to (5) of section 82 of Schedule 3 to the Water Act 1945 (which relates to the entry of premises by authorised officers of water undertakers) shall have effect for the purpose of authorising the entry of premises by authorised officers of an authority which provides or proposes to provide such a supply as is mentioned in the preceding subsection as if for any reference to undertakers there were substituted a reference to the authority and as if in subsection (1) of that section:

    (a) for paragraph (a) there were substituted the following paragraph:(a) for the purpose of installing, examining, adjusting, removing or reading any meter used or to be used by the authority for measuring the heat, hot air, hot water or steam supplied or to be supplied by the authority;

    (b) for the words from 'the special Act' onwards in paragraph (b) there were substituted the words 'byelaws in force by virtue of section 12 of the Local Government (Miscellaneous Provisions) Act 1976'; and

    (c) for the words 'the special Act' in paragraphs (c) and (d) there were substituted the words 'section II of that Act'.

(3) Subsections (1) and (2) above have effect subject to paragraph 11(2) of Schedule I to the Building Act 1984; and section 80 of the Health and Safety at Work etc. Act 1974 (which among other things provides that regulations under subsection (1) of that section may repeal or modify any provision to which that subsection applies if it appears to the authority making the regulations that it is expedient to do so in consequence of any provision made by or under Part I of that Act) shall have effect as if the provisions to which subsection (1) of that section applies included subsection (1) of this section and byelaws in force by virtue of subsection (1) of this section.

(4) The accounts of a local authority by which expenditure is incurred under any of the provisions of the preceding section and this section shall include a separate account of that expenditure and of any income connected with functions conferred on the authority by those provisions.

Power of council to pay any necessary charge for reconnection where disconnection has happened or is threatened because of owner's failure to pay

33. Restoration or continuation of supply of water, gas or electricity
    (1) If any premises in the area of a district council, a London borough council or the Common Council are occupied as a dwelling and the supply of water, gas or electricity to the premises:
        (a) is cut off in consequence of the failure of the owner or former owner of the premises to pay a sum payable by him in connection with the supply; or
        (b) is in the opinion of the council likely to be cut off in consequence of such a failure, the council may, at the request in writing of the occupier of the premises, make such arrangements as it thinks fit with the undertakers who provided the supply for it to be restored to the premises or, as the case may be, for it to be continued to the premises.

LONDON COUNTY COUNCIL (GENERAL POWERS) ACT 1949

Definitions
    4. Interpretations of expressions in Part II of this Act:
        'heating authority' means the Greater London Council or the council of a London borough;
        'heating charges' means charges authorised by this Part of this Act to be made by a heating authority for heat supplied by them;
        'heating undertaking' means an undertaking for the supply of heat by a heating authority under and in accordance with the provisions of this Part of this Act.

Power to make heating charges; the duty to keep separate account and the duty to break even

22. Heating charges
    (1) A heating authority may make and recover charges for heat supplied by them under the powers of this Part of this Act and may from time to time prescribe scales of heating charges in respect of any heating undertaking established by them and may prescribe different scales in respect of different heating undertakings: Provided that the prescription of a scale of charges under this subsection:
        (a) shall not affect any agreement then in force under subsection (1) of section 20 (Conditions of supply) of this Act unless and except to the extent that the agreement otherwise provides; and

    (b) subject to the provisions of subsection (3) of the said section 20 shall not affect the power of the heating authority under the said subsection (1) to make an agreement providing for the payment of charges differing from those prescribed by the scale.

(2) (a) Where a heating authority supply heat to any premises let by them, the heating charges shall, unless otherwise agreed between them and the tenant, be payable by the tenant in accordance with any scale which may be so prescribed as aforesaid and may be applicable.

    (b) The heating charges payable, pursuant to this subsection, shall be shown separately by the heating authority in rent books or on demand notes and receipts issued by them.

(3) The heating charges in respect of a heating undertaking shall be so fixed from time to time by the heating authority that as far as is reasonably practicable the total of the income in respect of that undertaking shown in the revenue accounts of the undertaking required by section 24 (Separate accounts) of this Act to be kept by the authority shall be not less than the total of the expenditure in respect of the undertaking shown in those accounts.

(4) Where a heating authority are themselves the occupiers of any premises which are included within the scope of a heating undertaking established by them, they shall in respect of any heat supplied to those premises under the powers of this Part of this Act carry to the credit of the revenue accounts of the undertaking and to the debit of the revenue accounts of the service for the purposes of which they occupy the premises, the like sums as would have been recoverable by them as heating charges if they had not been the occupiers and the occupier had agreed to pay heating charges in accordance with scales from time to time prescribed by them under this section.

RIGHTS OF ENTRY (GAS AND ELECTRICITY BOARDS) ACT 1954

Entry without warrant or permission in emergency only

1. Restriction on exercise of rights of entry

(1) No right of entry to which this Act applies shall be exercisable in respect of any premises except:

    (a) with consent given by or on behalf of the occupier of the premises, or

    (b) under the authority of a warrant granted under the next following section: Provided that this subsection shall not apply where entry is required in a case of emergency.

(2) This Act applies to all rights of entry conferred by

    (a) the Gas Act 1986, regulations made under it, or any other enactment relating to gas,

    (b) Schedule 6 to the Electricity Act 1989, and

    (c) any local enactment relating to gas or electricity, in so far as those rights are exercisable for the purposes of a public gas supplier or a public electricity supplier.

(3) No person shall be liable to a penalty, under any enactment relating to obstruction of the exercise of a right to which this Act applies, by reason

only of his refusing admission to a person who seeks to exercise the right of entry without a warrant granted under the next following section.

Issue of warrant

2. Warrant to authorise entry

(1) Where it is shown to the satisfaction of a justice of the peace, on sworn information in writing:

    (a) that admission to premises specified in the information is reasonably required by a public gas supplier, a public electricity supplier or by an employee of such a supplier:

    (b) that the supplier or his employee, as the case may be, would, apart from the preceding section, be entitled for that purpose to exercise in respect of the premises a right of entry to which this Act applies; and

    (c) that the requirements (if any) of the relevant enactment have been complied with, then subject to the provisions of this section, the justice may by warrant under his hand authorise the supplier or his employee, as the case may be, to enter the premises, if need be by force.

(2) If, in a case to which the preceding subsection applies, the relevant enactment does not require notice of an intended entry to be given to the occupier of the premises, the justice shall not grant a warrant under the section in respect of the right of entry in question unless he is satisfied:

    (a) that admission to the premises for the purpose specified in the information was sought by a person lawfully requiring entry in the exercise of that right, and was so sought after not less than twenty-four hours' notice of the intended entry had been given to the occupier; or

    (b) that admission to the premises for that purpose was sought in a case of emergency and was refused by or on behalf of the occupier; or

    (c) that the premises are unoccupied; or

    (d) that an application for admission to the premises would defeat the object of the entry.

(3) Where paragraph (a) of subsection (2) above applies

    (a) section 46 of the Gas Act 1986 (if entry is required for the purposes of a public gas supplier); or

    (b) section 109 of the Electricity Act 1989 (if entry is required for the purposes of a public electricity supplier), shall apply to the service of the notice required by that paragraph.

(4) Every warrant granted under this section shall continue in force until the purpose for which the entry is required has been satisfied.

(5) Any person who, in the exercise of a right of entry under the authority of a warrant granted under this section, enters any premises which are unoccupied, or premises of which the occupier is temporarily absent, shall leave the premises as effectually secured against trespassers as he found them.

(6) Where a warrant is granted under this section in respect of a right of entry, then for the purposes of any enactment whereby:

    (a) an obligation is imposed to make good damage, or to pay compensation, or to take any other step, in consequence of the exercise of the right of entry, or

    (b) a penalty is imposed for obstructing the exercise of that right, any entry effected, or sought to be effected, under the authority of the warrant shall be treated as an entry effected, or sought to be effected, in the exercise of that right of entry.

(7)   This section shall, in its application to Scotland, have effect as if for any reference to a justice of the peace there were substituted a reference to the sheriff and to a magistrate or justice of the peace having jurisdiction in the place where the premises entry to which is sought are situated.

COUNTY COURTS ACT 1984

Section 13(5) of the Court and Legal Services Act 1990 provides that from a 'date to be appointed' Section 112A of the County Courts Act 1984 will say:

112A Further Powers of the Court

(1)   Where the court is satisfied that it has the power to make an administration order with respect to the debtor concerned; but that an order restricting enforcement would be a more satisfactory way of dealing with the case, it may make such an order instead of making an administration order.

(2)   Where an order restricting enforcement is made, no creditor specified in the order shall have any remedy against he person or property of the debtor in respect of any debt so specified, without leave of the court.

(3)   Subsection (4) applies to any creditor who is named in the schedule to an administration order or in an order restricting enforcement; and who provides the debtor with mains gas, electricity or water for the debtors own domestic purposes.

(4)   While the order has effect, the creditor may not stop supplying the debtor with mains gas, electricity or (as the case may be) water for the debtor's own domestic purposes; or any associated service which it provides for its customers, without leave of the court unless the reason for doing so is unconnected with non-payment by the debtor.

(5)   In this section 'mains gas' means a supply of gas by the British Gas Corporation or a public gas supplier within the meaning of Part 1 of the Gas Act 1986.

(6)   Rules of the court may make provision with respect to the period for which any order restricting enforcement is to have effect and for the circumstances in which any such order may be revoked.

BIRMINGHAM AND STAFFORDSHIRE GAS CO. v RADCLIFFE (1871) LR 6EXCH 224

Where a consumer has used gas fraudulently at the same time as using gas in the normal way, the board may sue in contract as if it had all been lawfully consumed.

EDMUNDSON v LONGTON CORPORATION (1902) 19 TLR 15 D.C.

E. had a gas coin meter which was burgled. There was no suggestion that he was to blame. The corporation, which supplied the gas, tried to recover the sum due from E. The court decided that E. had paid for the gas by putting money in the meter and could not be made to pay again.

JOSEPH v EAST HAM CORPORATION (1936) I K.B. 367

The court in this case decided that: in order to be conclusive evidence of electricity supplied, a meter must be properly certified;* cutting off electricity under the 1882 Act (see A.2) is a form of refusal to supply under the 1909 Act (see A.4); and that consequently* the board is not entitled to cut off a consumer's supply during the course of a bona fide dispute about the amount of electricity consumed.

MARTIN v MARSH (1955) CRIM. L.R. 781 D.C.

M. broke into his meter and was charged with larceny by the board. He argued that the money in the meter was not the property of the board and that provided he eventually paid for the electricity consumed, he had done no wrong. The magistrates found him not guilty, saying that he had used the meter as a moneybox. The board appealed to the Divisional Court, which decided that the money became the property of the board as soon as it was put into the meter and that, therefore, an offence had been committed.

WOODCOCK v SOUTH WESTERN ELECTRICITY BOARD (1975) 2 ALL E.R. 545

It was decided in this case that for the purpose of an electricity supply a person whose original entry onto premises was unlawful and forcible (a 'squatter') is not an occupier for the purpose of the supply legislation and thus does not have the right to be supplied with electricity.

HAYWARD v EAST LONDON WATERWORKS CO. (1884) 28 CH.D 138

The Act in question provided that disputes about water rate calculations were to be resolved by two magistrates. Before this was done, the company threatened to cut off the supply. The court said that it could prevent the disconnection by issuing an injunction, if the consumer brought the dispute to the magistrates as soon as possible.

WILLMORE AND WILLMORE v SOUTH EASTERN ELECTRICITY BOARD (1957) 2 LLOYDS REPORTS 375

On applying for a supply, the consumers told the Board that they wanted the electricity to power infra-red lamps under which they wished to raise chicks. The voltage was too irregular to keep the lamps going and many chicks died. The consumers sued for breach of contract. The court decided that there was no contract, as the Board was supplying under a statutory duty.

SCOTTISH GAS BOARD v FISHER (1960) SLT 51

Money was stolen from the consumer's prepayment meter, and the meter damaged. The supply agreement made the consumer liable for such loss and damage. The court decided that the conditions in the agreement were ultra vires; the Board has no power to impose conditions other than those authorised by the Gas Act.

STEVENS v ALDERSHOT GAS, WATER AND DISTRICT LIGHTING CO. (1932)102 LJKB 12

The consumer claimed that fluctuating voltage had damaged machines used in her business and sued for damages. The court decided that she was supplied with electricity under a statutory duty, not under a contract, and that, therefore, only the penalty provided by the Electricity Acts could be recovered by her, not damages for breach of contract or for negligence.

HUSEY v LONDON ELECTRIC SUPPLY CORPORATION (1902) 1 CH 411

A company which owned a hotel went bankrupt, owing a large amount for electricity. A receiver took over the hotel and wanted to carry on using the electricity. The Court of Appeal decided that until the receiver entered into a new contract with the board, the board was entitled to withhold the supply (NB. this case was decided under an Act of 1882 which provided for 'contracts' for supply. This provision has been repealed and replaced by the statutory duty to supply).

R v DIRECTOR-GENERAL FOR GAS SUPPLY AND BRITISH GAS, EX PARTE SMITH 31/7/89 UNREPORTED (PILL J.)

(1)   A conviction is not a pre-condition to being disconnected for tampering with a meter;

(2)   to exercise the power to disconnect, a supplier need only show on a balance of probabilities that tampering took place;

(3)   for the purposes of re-connecting supply, the matters to be remedied include payment for gas wrongly obtained;

(4)   the supplier may exercise the power to disconnect because of tampering even if there are innocent persons also receiving supply in the same house;

(5)   the decision of OFGAS that British Gas had acted correctly was quashed because they had not given the customer the opportunity to respond to new evidence put forward by British Gas.

Non-statutory Authorisations and Conditions

BRITISH GAS AUTHORISATION TO SUPPLY

Condition 12: Codes of Practice for tariff gas supplies and payment of bills

(1) The Supplier shall prepare within three months after the date on which this Authorisation comes into force

 (a) a Code of Practice describing the nature of service available to tariff customers in relation to gas supplied by the Supplier; and

 (b) a Code of Practice concerning the payment of gas bills including guidance to domestic customers if they have difficulty in paying.

(2) In preparing each such Code and in making any substantive revision of either of them the Supplier shall consult the Gas Consumers' Council and the Director and shall consider any representations made by the Director or the Council about the operation of the Codes.

(3) The Supplier shall -

 (a) send a copy of each Code and each revision of either of them to the Director and the Gas Consumers' Council;

 (b) make available for inspection a copy of each such Code in its latest form to members of the public at each of the relevant premises during its normal opening hours; and

 (c) give or send a copy of each such Code in its latest form to any person requesting it.

Condition 12a: Methods for Dealing with Tariff Customers in Default

(1) The Supplier shall adopt methods for dealing with tariff customers who, through misfortune or inability to cope with gas supplied on credit terms, incur obligations to pay for gas so supplied which they find difficulty in discharging, including, in particular, methods for -

 (a) distinguishing such tariff customers from others in default;

 (b) detecting failures by such tariff customers to comply with arrangements entered into for paying by instalments charges for gas supplied;

 (c) making such arrangements so as to take into account the tariff customers ability to comply with them;

 (d) ascertaining, with the assistance of other persons or organisations, the ability of tariff customers to comply with such arrangements;

    (e)   providing for such a tariff customer who has failed to comply with such arrangements a prepayment meter where safe and practical to do so; and

    (f)   calibrating any prepayment meter so provided so as to take into account the tariff customer's ability to pay any of the charges due from the customer under such arrangements in addition to the other charges lawfully being recovered through the prepayment meter;

(2)   The Supplier shall not make any substantial change in the methods adopted under this condition without the consent of the Director.

(3)   The Supplier shall furnish the Director with such information as to such methods as he may from time to time direct.

BRITISH GAS: PRINCIPLES FOR THE COLLECTION OF DOMESTIC GAS DEBT

(1)   British Gas continues to recognise that it needs to operate in accordance with the Gas Act 1986 and to have due regard to the needs of customers experiencing hardship. The Company's objective is to operate a balanced, practical and caring policy for debt collection on a national basis.

(2)   Revised procedures have been introduced to improve the Company's ability to deal with the problem of domestic gas debts. All British Gas staff are required to act in accordance with these principles and procedures.

(3)   The procedures aim to recover charges for gas already used, to prevent the build up of debt and to safeguard payment for future supplies.

(4)   Disconnection of a gas supply will only take place as a last resort, when every other alternative has been exhausted.

(5)   The majority of customers pay on time, either by prompt payment of each quarterly bill or by participation on one of the companies' payment plans. The procedures therefore concentrate on people who 'can't pay' ie those who due to illness, unemployment or other misfortune do not have the means to meet their commitments in full and may well have a number of other debts. For these customers, where contact with them is established and payment in full is not received, debt collection staff will counsel the customers on the range of payment alternatives available, and try to establish which is most likely to suit the particular circumstances. Staff will also advise customers, where appropriate, to contact the Department of Social Security, the Social Services Departments of Local Authorities and/or Citizen's Advice Bureaux or other advice agencies which provide a recognised counselling service.

(6)   The Company's policy is to encourage customers in difficulty to get in touch as early as possible so that advice and assistance can be given. Customers who make contact and indicate that they have a debt problem will be routed to the appropriate staff. British Gas will ensure that customers with payment difficulties who make contact with appropriate staff will receive sympathetic treatment at all times.

(7)   In cases where the customer fails to make contact with debt collection staff, the latter will deliver a helpline Pack including a copy of the Code of Practice and a Customer Helpline card. This card encourages the customer to contact the company with a specific payment offer and/or to contact the DSS or an

appropriate advice agency. It also gives the customer the opportunity of seeing a prepayment meter.

(8) The Company remains committed to the Code of Practice, which provides definitions of potential hardship categories and of the measures available to help customers in those categories. The Gas Consumers Council monitors these principles and the operation of the Code of Practice and represents the interests of any customers who feel they have an unresolved problem with the company.

(9) The Company will continue to attempt to resolve all disputes without giving the customer the need to refer the matter to the Gas Consumers Council or the Director General of Gas Supply.

(10) The Department of Social Security (DSS) and, where appropriate, Local Authority Social Services Departments will be notified of potential disconnection cases and given time to investigate and assist if they are able to do so. In cases where the customer has been advised to contact the DSS and/or Social Services, further debt collection action will be delayed for 21 days, an increase of 7 days over the period previously allowed. This delay could be even longer where there is a positive response.

(11) The aim is to establish long-term sensible and lasting solutions to customers' debt problems. A payment arrangement agreed with a customer will, therefore, take full account of whatever information is available about the customer's ability to pay. The key factors to take into consideration when determining the length of the repayment period are:

- the level of repayment which the customer can be expected to sustain (depending on the customer's circumstances, this may be more or less than the standard fuel direct weekly deduction in respect of arrears plus current consumption);

- any history of previous (broken) payment plans which would suggest that the customer cannot manage this type of payment arrangement.

(12) Customers who leave the DSS Fuel Direct scheme should join a Gas Payment Plan on payments which correspond to the previous DSS deduction for current consumption plus at least the standard weekly Fuel Direct amount towards any arrears.

(13) The alternative of a token-operated prepayment meter will be offered before disconnection, but only where it is safe and practicable and where a customer cannot manage a Gas Payment Plan arrangement, which continues to be the preferred option in all cases. Where it is not feasible to fit a token-operated meter, the alternative of a coin operated meter will be offered where it is safe and practical. Where arrears need to be recovered through a prepayment meter, the customer will need to agree to the recovery of the outstanding arrears by setting the meter at a rate which will take into account the customer's ability to pay.

(14) No prepayment meter will be installed where:
  (i) there are any secondary (subsidiary meters) supplied with gas through that meter;
  (ii) the position of the meter physically prevents installation, eg a prepayment meter cannot physically be fitted into a semi-concealed meter box. However, the possibility of relocation will be considered to avoid this situation;
  (iii) the location of the meter prevents safe operation of the token mechanism by the customer, taking account of the customer's circumstances, eg a disabled person could not cope with a meter

located above a door. Again the possibility of relocation will be considered to avoid this situation.

(iv) no contact with the customer, including non return of the helpline card;

(v) refused by customer.

The cost of re-positioning the meter to enable a prepayment meter to be fitted, where the customer has demonstrated to the satisfaction of the Company an inability to handle credit payment alternatives, will not be charged to the customer.

(15) Where token meters are installed, regions will make tokens available from their showroom and selected main and sub-post offices and other authorised agents.

(16) A domestic customer's gas supply will only be disconnected for non-payment of a debtor security deposit, without the customer's consent, where:

• the customer has been notified in advance of the proposed disconnection;

• the DSS (and Social Services where appropriate) has been informed of the proposed disconnection;

• there has been no offer of help from the DSS or any other agency which might help the customer either financially or with counselling; *and*

• a prepayment meter cannot be installed or has been refused by the customer or where there is no contact with the customer at the disconnection visit.

(17) In addition to the special procedures designed to help those customers who 'can't pay' procedures have also been introduced in respect of those customers who 'won't pay', ie those who continually delay payment to the last possible moment and for whom special action will be taken, which may consist of a request for a security deposit.

(18) The Company will always endeavour to treat each case of debt sympathetically and with due regard to the known circumstances.

Revised June 1990

A LETTER FROM OFGAS

The contents of this *letter to a welfare rights worker give British Gas the authority to recover arrears for gas on a pro rata basis with other creditors in situations of multiple debt.*

Thank you for your letter of 7 November, concerning rates of debt recovery under Condition 12A. I am sorry for the delay in replying, but as you know, I wanted to consider fully the implications of your letter and to have the opportunity of discussing these issues with British Gas, with whom we have continued in discussion throughout this year on the implementation of the new arrangements.

Let me say firstly, without qualification, that British Gas has confirmed that where satisfactory evidence can be provided of a customer's circumstances, in the form of an income and expenditure statement submitted by an acknowledged money advice agency, the rate of debt repayment which the company will accept will be on a pro-rata basis with the other creditors. There should, therefore, be no question of British Gas seeking a more advantageous rate of repayment than, say, a bank, in a multiple debt situation.

It may be useful, before going on to consider the position in more detail, to go back to first principles. British Gas has the power, by virtue of statute, to disconnect a customer's supply if following twenty-eight days from the making of a demand, plus seven days' notice, a bill remains unpaid (para 7(5) to Schedule 5, Gas Act 1986). This provision is intended to safeguard British Gas who, like any other creditor, will wish to be relieved from making further supplies on credit to a customer who is in default.

OFGAS' concern has been to ensure that British Gas' powers of disconnection are not exercised without the customer first being given every opportunity to reach a settlement for repayment of debt which can be sustained, in order to allow the supply of gas to continue. Hence, Condition 12A provides for the making of payment arrangements which take into account the customer's ability to comply, whether the debt is paid by weekly or monthly amounts, or through the calibration of a prepayment meter.

I should perhaps emphasise that OFGAS' interests are primarily directed towards ensuring that tariff customers who wish to pay for gas have continued access to a supply, on reasonable terms, on credit if they are able, or through a prepayment meter if they are not. The treatment of other creditors in a multiple debt situation is strictly not a consideration for OFGAS, although clearly the successful rehabilitation of multiple debt customers will depend upon an amicable solution being reached all round.

The procedures now operated by British Gas provide that any payment arrangement agreed with a customer must take full account of whatever information is available about the customer's ability to pay, and for the counselling of customers who have multiple debts or who are unable to manage their own affairs, using the services of care organisations such as CABx.

As is vital in such circumstances, British Gas has agreed to allow time for a client's affairs to be examined by CABx, etc, in order that a suitable level of repayment can be agreed. Equally important, where a payment arrangement fails or proves unsuitable, British Gas has agreed to offer a further arrangement or a prepayment meter, before considering disconnection.

On the question of levels of repayment you refer to the Fuel Direct rate. This is indeed used by British Gas as a reference point for customers on low incomes, but the company has confirmed that where the customer's circumstances are such as to merit it, less than the standard fuel direct weekly deduction in respect of arrears will be accepted.

A number of enhancements are being introduced by British Gas into the operation of the methods under Condition 12A, which should ensure customers' circumstances are fully considered:

(a) a new training package for customer accounting staff emphasises the needs of customers requiring specialist help;

(b) a new Helpline Pack shortly to become available in all British Gas regions includes a Factsheet on Benefits and Money Advice;

(c) All regions are being instructed to compile comprehensive reference lists of welfare organisations within their areas, and are being encouraged to maintain regular contact and liaison with them.

I trust you will see that we are in a continually developing situation, and that attitudes of even only a couple of months ago are changing. If British Gas does all it has promised, I believe the company will come to be regarded as one of the most enlightened of creditors. I shall be keeping in close touch over the coming months to learn whether or not your members agree.

D W Barnes   19 December 1989
Consumer Affairs Section
Office of Gas Supply

PUBLIC ELECTRICITY SUPPLY LICENCE

Condition 18: Code of Practice on Payment of Bills

(1) The licensee shall within three months after this licence has come into force prepare and submit to the Director for his approval a Code of Practice concerning the payment of electricity bills by customers occupying domestic premises, and including appropriate guidance for the assistance of such customers who may have difficulty in paying such bills.

(2) The licensee shall, whenever requested to do so by the Director, review the Code prepared in accordance with paragraph 1, and the manner in which it has been operated, with a view to determining whether any modification should be made to it or to the manner of its operation.

(3) In preparing the Code, and in carrying out any review (including in accordance with paragraph 2), the licensee shall consult the relevant consumers' committee and shall have regard to any representations made by it about the Code or the manner in which it is likely to be or (as the case may be) has been operated.

(4) The licensee shall submit any revision of the Code which, after consulting the relevant consumers' committee in accordance with paragraph 3, it wishes to make to the Director for his approval.

(5) The licensee shall:

   (a) send a copy of the Code and of any revision of it (in each case, in the form approved by the Director) to the Director and the relevant consumers' committee;

   (b) draw to the attention of customers occupying domestic premises the existence of the Code and each substantive revision of it and how they may inspect or obtain a copy of the Code in its latest form;

   (c) make a copy of the Code (as from time to time revised) available for inspection by members of the public at each of the relevant premises during normal working hours; and

   (d) give or send free of charge a copy of the Code (as from time to time revised) to any person who requests it.

Condition 19: Methods for Dealing With Tariff Customers in Default

(1) The licensee shall within three months after this licence has come into force, after consultation with the relevant consumers' committee, prepare and submit to the Director for his approval methods for dealing with tariff customers who, through misfortune or inability to cope with electricity supplied for domestic use on credit terms, incur obligations to pay for electricity so supplied which they find difficulty in discharging including, in particular, methods for:

   (a) distinguishing such customers from others in default;

   (b) detecting failures by such tariff customers to comply with arrangements entered into for paying by instalments charges for electricity supplied;

   (c) making such arrangements so as to take into account the tariff customers' ability to comply with them.;

   (d) ascertaining, with the assistance of other persons or organisations, the ability of tariff customers to comply with such arrangements;

(e) providing for such a tariff customer who has failed to comply with such arrangements a prepayment meter where safe and practical to do so; and

(f) calibrating any prepayment meter so provided so as to take into account the tariff customer's ability to pay any of the charges due from the customer under such arrangements in addition to the other charges lawfully being recovered through the prepayment meter.

(2) The licensee shall not make any substantial change in the methods adopted under this condition without the consent of the Director.

(3) The licensee shall furnish the Director with such information as to such methods as he may from time to time direct.

OFGAS Position Paper

OFGAS Position Paper about matters arising from British Gas Plc's duty under section 10(1) of The Gas Act 1986 to continue to give a gas supply to tariff customers

A. Disconnection of supply on grounds of injury to or interference with gas meters

(1) The only grounds on which the supply of gas to any premises may be discontinued by reason of injury to a meter (as in the case of theft from a prepayment meter) or interference with a meter (as in the case of the bypassing of a meter to obtain gas without payment) are provided by paragraph 10(2) of Schedule 5 to the Gas Act 1986.

(2) Paragraph 10(2) of that Schedule provides that 'if an offence under sub-paragraph (1) of the paragraph involves any injury to or interference with any gas fitting belonging to a public gas supplier, the supplier may also, until the matter has been remedied, but no longer, discontinue the supply of gas to the person so offending (notwithstanding any contract previously existing)'. The words in parentheses have no application in the case of supply to a tariff customer.

(3) Paragraph (10)1 of the Schedule provides that 'if any person intentionally or by culpable negligence:
    (a) injures or allowed to be injured any gas fitting belonging to a public gas supplier;
    (b) alters the index to any meter used for measuring the quantity of gas supplied by such a supplier; or
    (c) prevents any such meter from duly registering the quantity of gas supplied, he shall be guilty of an offence and liable on summary conviction to a fine not exceeding level 3 on the standard scale (presently £400).

(4) It should be noted that a person commits an offence if he does the prohibited acts either intentionally or by culpable negligence. It is considered that culpable negligence must involve some reprehensible conduct deserving of punishment by the criminal law. It should also be noted that, while there is an offence of allowing a gas fitting to be injured, it would not be an offence under paragraph 10(1) of the Schedule merely to allow the index of a meter to be altered or to allow a meter to be prevented from duly registering the quantity of gas supplied. That is not to say that, in an appropriate case, a person could not be convicted under the general criminal law as an accessory to the theft of gas (in Scotland, art and part of the theft) where he was a party to acts of that nature.

(5) The power to discontinue the supply of gas in consequence of an offence under paragraph 10(a) of the Schedule is only exercisable where the offender (who might have committed the offence of allowing a gas fitting to be injured by some other person) is the person to whom the gas is supplied. As to such persons, see the discussion under section C below.

(6) It is considered that the power of discontinuance arises in any case where the commission of an appropriate offence by the person supplied with gas can be established. It is not necessary that there should be a conviction for an offence under the paragraph nor a finding by a court of the facts constituting such an offence in other proceedings as, for example, a prosecution for theft of gas. On the other hand, if the Director General of Gas Supply was satisfied (or, as the case might be, it appeared to him) that no appropriate offence by the person supplied with gas was established and that, in consequence, there was no justification for the discontinuation as a result of the alleged offence, his enforcement duties under section 28 of the Gas Act 1986 would become exercisable. In coming to a conclusion as to whether an appropriate offence was established it seems likely that the proper standard of proof should be that in civil actions, being based on a balance of probabilities, rather than that in criminal proceedings where proof is required beyond reasonable doubt (*Hornal v Neuberger Products Ltd* [1957] 1 QB 247). In that case it was pointed out that even in civil actions the appropriate standard of proof would give due weight to the seriousness of the alleged offence.

(7) The power of discontinuance conferred by paragraph 10(2) of the Schedule subsists 'until the matter has been remedied, but no longer'. The question arises as to whether these words should be restricted to the repair of the injury, the correction of the alteration or the removal of the prevention, as the case may be, or should be construed more widely so as to cover the remedying of the consequences of the injury or negligence as, for example, the refunding of the money stolen from a prepayment meter or payment being made for gas abstracted without registration.

(8) It is considered that the first interpretation gives the phrase its ordinary meaning. Paragraph 10(2) is only triggered when a gas fitting belonging to the supplier is injured or interfered with; 'the matter', therefore, must refer back to the injury or interference. Confirmation is provided by the existence of the powers under paragraph 7 of the Schedule to recover sums due in respect of gas supplied and the history of the paragraph. The equivalent provision in the Gas Act 1948 and the Gas Act 1972 expressly referred to the Board and Corporation respectively being able to recover from their customer the amount of any damage caused to them by the offence, and then went on to set out the right to disconnect where a gas fitting had been damaged or interfered with. This way of framing the provision strongly suggested that 'the matter' was the injury to or interference with the gas fittings. The position was even clearer under the Gas Work Clauses Act 1871, which stated that disconnection could be made if the customer had damaged or interfered with gas fittings 'until the matter *complained of*' had been remedied. In the context this could only have referred to the damage or interference.

Note: The reasons for preferring the first interpretation set out in paragraph 8, are not accepted by British Gas who regard the second interpretation as correct.

B. Liability of Tariff Customer for Money Stolen from Prepayment Meter

(1)   Money may be stolen from a prepayment meter in circumstances where the person supplied with gas commits an offence under paragraph 10(1) of Schedule 5 to the Gas Act. As to that, see discussion in section A above.

(2)   Where the tariff customer commits no such offence, he may have a liability to account for the stolen moneys but failure to account for them cannot be grounds for a discontinuation of supply. The public gas supplier's power to cut off the supply for failing to pay the charges due from him in respect of the supply of gas conferred by paragraph 7(5) of the Schedule does not apply because the property in the moneys stolen has already passed to the supplier and the customer has already discharged his obligation to pay the charges due from him (Edmundson v Mayor etc of Longton (1902) 19 T.L.R. 15 and see also Martin v March (1955 Crim L.R. 781)). It should be noted that in sub-paragraph (1) of the paragraph a distinction is drawn between charges in respect of the supply of gas and charges in respect of the supplying and fixing of any meter fittings. The power of cut off in sub-paragraph (5) cannot therefore be exercised in respect of charges of the latter sort.

(3)   Notwithstanding the absence of a power of disconnection in the circumstances referred to, the tariff customer as borrower of the meter has a liability to the supplier who lends the meter to take proper care of it and of anything accessory to it such as the moneys deposited in it.

(4)   At common law the proper duty of care in the case of gratuitous bailee for use, as the borrower is, is to take all reasonable care in the circumstances. Consequently the borrower would be liable at common law to reimburse the amount of any moneys stolen from the meter unless he could prove (Port Swettenham Authority v T.W. Wu & Co [1978] 3 AllER 337) that he had taken all reasonable steps to prevent the theft. One circumstance which may affect the degree of care to be taken by the borrower is the requirement in paragraph 6(2) of the Schedule that, subject to sub-paragraph (3) of that paragraph (which allows a meter to be placed outside a building in certain cases), a meter should be installed as near as practicable to the main but within the outside wall of the building.

(5)   The common law obligations of a borrower or bailee may be enlarged by agreement between the parties but it is understood that British Gas do not seek the agreement of the borrower to any modification of his common law obligation to take care of the bailed chattel. This is reflected in paragraphs 2(iii) and 4 of the announcements made under the heading 'Meters and other equipment' in the tariff notices published by British Gas on 18 March 1988.

(6)   For completeness, it should be added that a public gas supplier is entitled under paragraph 4(3) of the Schedule to remove a damaged prepayment meter but he must, while the meter is removed, fix a substituted meter at his own expense.

C. Liability for Payment of Charges for the Supply of Gas

(1) Paragraph 7(1) of Schedule 5 to the Gas Act 1986 provides that a public gas supplier may recover from a tariff customer any charges due to him in respect of the supply of gas or in respect of the supplying and fixing of any meter or fittings. A tariff customer is defined by section 14(5) of the Act for the purposes of Part I of the Act as a person who is supplied with gas by a public gas supplier otherwise than in pursuance of a special agreement under section 14(4).

(2) The question arises who is the person supplied with gas and who therefore is liable to pay for the gas supplied in cases where two or more persons are resident in any premises during the period in which the gas was supplied.

(3) The obligation of a public gas supplier under section 10(1) of the Act, upon being required to do so by the owner or occupier, to give and continue to give a supply of gas to any premises which:
    (a) are situated within 25 yards from a relevant main of the supplier; or
    (b) are connected by a service pipe to any such main, is expressed to be subject to the following provisions of Part I of the Act and any regulations made under those provisions.

(4) One of the following provisions referred to is sub-section (2) of section 10 which provides that where any person requires a supply of gas in pursuance of sub-section (1), he should serve on the gas supplier a notice in writing (see definition of 'notice' in section 48(1) of the Act) specifying:
    (a) the premises in respect of which the supply is required;
    (b) the day… upon which the supply is required to commence.
It is considered that this obligation to give written notice only applies to the original connection of the premises because the matters to be specified in the notice are only relevant in such a case. Consequently the obligation of the public gas supplier to continue to give a supply of gas to premises which have already been given a supply is not dependent on a written notice but on any sufficient indication that a continued supply is required. It follows that the provisions of section 10(1) and (2) do not help to decide the question as to who is the person who may be supplied with gas at the premises in question.

(5) It is considered that the answer to the question must depend on the circumstances attending the occupancy of the premises except in those cases where the owner of the premises, as distinct from its occupiers, has made it clear to the supplier that the supply is made at his request and is to be regarded as made to him.

(6) There are many cases where two or more persons are together legally entitled to occupy premises and in such cases it may be that each of them can properly be regarded as being supplied with gas. It is thought that the proper criterion is the nature of the control exercised by any person over the activities at the premises and in particular the use of the gas supplied to them. This could, for example, justify regarding each of two spouses or a number of sharing students as persons to whom gas is supplied but not regarding young adults resident in premises with their parents as such persons.

This paper should be read together with the court decision in *R v Director-General of Gas Supply ex parte Smith* (see Appendix 1, p248).

Tampering

Reproduced below is the standard handout British Gas has prepared for advice agencies on its theft and tampering policy.

NOTES FOR THE ASSISTANCE OF CARING AGENCIES

The following notes have been prepared to provide assistance in dealing with clients who have been found tampering with the gas supply.

British Gas' Policy

The policy of British Gas is to operate a uniform Company policy on tampering, in accordance with its statutory obligations.

Injury to and interference with gas fittings and meters are offences under schedule 5, paragraph 10, of the Gas Act 1986 (usually referred to as 'Tampering'). Where a customer commits a tampering offence under schedule 5 paragraph 10(1), British Gas may disconnect the supply under paragraph 10(2) of the same schedule. Disconnection is carried out to ensure the safety of the supply, to prevent the continuance of the tampering and to retain control of the situation until the matter is remedied. In this respect, remedying the matter will include payment of, or arrangement to pay, the assessed charges. When the matter has been remedied the gas supply will be promptly reconnected.

British Gas recognises that this right to disconnect must be exercised properly in accordance with the Gas Act 1986 and Company procedures. British Gas is not responsible for requiring that any social penalty be applied to the offender by the legal system but is obliged to report any offence to the Police. British Gas views it as the responsibility of the Police and Crown Prosecution Service, or the Procurator Fiscal in Scotland, to assess any offence and bring any prosecution. The Company's aim, therefore, is to adopt measures to deter and detect tampering, occasioned by injury to gas fittings and interference with meters. In so doing we consider that security and safety of the gas supply are of overriding importance .

British Gas personnel must be satisfied that any tampering has been intentionally committed. If they consider this to be the case and the evidence supports this, then they have the grounds for disconnection and to withhold the supply until the matter is remedied.

When a case of tampering is established, the Company aims recover those costs (including the cost of stolen gas) incurred by the Company as a result of the offence. Such costs will be levied as a condition of reconnection. Outlined below are the actions which will be taken by British Gas when the illegal use of gas is discovered, plus information about our conditions for reconnection. We hope these notes will assist you in advising any person who may come to you for help in situations of alleged tampering with the gas supply.

The problem

Interfering with a gas meter or associated pipework is an offence. It is also extremely dangerous, putting both people and property at risk and may also lead to prosecution by the authorities for the tampering offence, or for theft of gas, or both. British Gas will take appropriate action to detect and deter Theft of Gas and Tampering and this may include, for example, mounting special exercises in areas where we believe it may be of benefit.

Action taken by British Gas when illegal use of gas is discovered

Where it is evident that the customer has obtained gas illegally, the Gas Act 1986 gives us the power to withhold a supply of gas to the premises concerned. We disconnect in such cases because of the safety and other implications. We also always refer such cases to the Police who may proceed under the Gas Act as outlined above and/or under the Theft Act.

We would like to emphasise that only specially trained staff undertake calls to investigate possible illegal use of gas and this training is regularly reviewed. The procedures followed by these staff are standard throughout the Company and have been drawn up in consultation with the Gas Consumers Council and OFGAS. Any meters or other gas fittings removed as evidence of interference are held in a secure area for possible presentation and examination.

Conditions for reconnection

At the time of disconnection, customers are given a standard letter. This letter gives them a contact name and a local number to call to discuss our conditions for reconnection. We are always willing to give our terms and conditions for reconnection over the telephone. We also ensure that these are notified to the customer in writing within one working day of discovery of the offence, wherever possible.

Our terms and conditions for reconnection are:
1. Payment for the amount of gas which we assess has been obtained illegally.
2. Payment for the cost of reconnection and for any damage to our gas fixtures and fittings.
3. Provision of appropriate security to safeguard payment of future gas accounts, e.g. agreement to join our Gas Payment Plan or to make payments via the Department of Social Security's Direct Payments Scheme.

The assessment of the amount of gas used illegally will depend on the circumstances of individual cases. For example, obvious irregularities in gas usage or plastic token purchases will often indicate the period over which it is reasonable to assess. We are also always willing to consider information provided by the individuals concerned.

As soon as arrangements have been made to meet our terms and conditions for reconnection, the gas supply will be promptly restored. We are always willing to discuss different methods of meeting our terms for reconnection. Particularly in cases of hardship, we may spread payments over a period of time. Options available to customers for doing this include weekly, fortnightly or monthly payments via direct debit, standing order or payment booklet; payments via the Department of Social Security's Direct Payment Scheme or via the installation of a prepayment meter, if it is safe and practical to do so.

Meter testing

Sometimes, when there are grounds for suspecting that gas has been used illegally but an Investigator finds no illegal connection at the time of his/her call, meters are exchanged for testing. Again these exchanges are only carried out by specially trained staff, following standard Company procedures. The tests are conducted by British Gas Scientific Services staff and can identify meter reversal and other forms of tampering. Customers are always asked if they would like to see the tests being carried out or find out more about them (a standard letter with a contact name and local number is left at the time of the meter exchange). Customers are always notified of the outcome of the meter test. Where tampering is identified, a British Gas representative will visit the customer(s) to inform them of the result and seek their comments. The next step is to assess charges and negotiate payment of these with the customer. Again arrangements can be made to pay these charges over a period of time as above. Before charges are assessed, full consideration will be given to any relevant information with which the customer is able to provide us.

Assistance in theft of gas cases

If you have a client whose gas supply has been disconnected for illegal use, find out whether or not he/she has been notified of our conditions for reconnection. If not, please telephone ....

If the client does not dispute the charges but is unable to pay them at once, call us on the above number to discuss different payment options. If the client is in receipt of Income Support, suggest that he/she contacts their local Department of Social Security office to find out if he/she is eligible to join their Direct Payments Scheme.

If the client disputes any of our charges or the disconnection, please ask them to contact us (or you contact us on their behalf). We are always willing to listen to what the customer has to say.

If we are provided with information which indicates that our assessment is inappropriate we will reconsider and may revise our charges.

If any members of the disconnected household are especially vulnerable, please let us know. We will then ensure that conditions for reconnection are met as quickly as possible. It may even be possible in certain cases to effect immediate restoration of the gas supply.

British Gas contact point for the agency

All tampering enquiries should be addressed to ....

If your client has not already spoken to us, please ask them to make contact so that we may resolve the matter as quickly as possible. We are equally willing to talk to you on their behalf. If necessary, we can also arrange to meet with the customer and/or their representative to help to resolve the matter.

Further advice

If your client has contacted us but is still dissatisfied with the way in which their case is being handled, you could advise them to contact their local Regional Gas Consumers Council Office, an independent body representing the interest of gas customers. Their address is .... phone ....

If they are still not satisfied with the way their case is being handled, representation may be made to the Office of Gas Supply (OFGAS). The Director General of Gas Supply has legal powers to resolve complaints and disputes. OFGAS' address is Stockley House, 130 Wilton Road, London, SW1V 1LQ.

Note: You can find out the address and telephone number for your area from your local British Gas regional office (see Appendix 10).

Joint Statement of Intent on Direct Payment for Fuel

Introduction

This statement has been agreed by the Department of Social Security ('the DSS') on the one hand, and British Gas plc and the Regional Electricity Companies ('the industries') on the other hand. It describes the circumstances and the manner in which a person in receipt of income support (the 'beneficiary') may be protected from having his fuel supply disconnected by the electricity or gas supplier ('the supplier') with whom he is a registered consumer because of his failure to pay an account from that supplier within the normal time allowed by the supplier.

Direct Payments

(2) The method by which this is achieved is that the adjudication officer ('the AO') may make a determination under the Social Security (Claims and Payments) Regulations 1987 ('the regulations') to institute direct payments from benefit to the third party where there is a debt and, in his opinion, it would be in the interests of the beneficiary and his family for such payments to be made. Where such a determination is made, an amount shall be deducted from the beneficiary's benefit each week and paid direct to the supplier promptly at regular intervals, provided that direct payments are acceptable to the supplier. The size of the debt shall not, of itself, be a bar to such acceptance. Every reasonable endeavour will be made to make a determination within 14 calendar days (21 days for British Gas) of learning that the beneficiary has a debt which he is unable to pay.

(3) 'Debt' is defined in the regulations and the Adjudication Officers Guide. It includes debt initially brought to the AO's attention for decision, additional debt between that and a date as close as possible to when deductions start, and any reconnection charges.

The Aims

(4) The aims of this Statement of Intent are, therefore, to ensure:
   (a) for the beneficiary, a continuation, or restoration, of his fuel supply so as to prevent the hardship which its disconnection would be likely to cause him or members of his family;
   (b) for the industries, regular payment to cover that continued supply, together with reduction of the original debt.

Persons Affected

(5)   The AO can consider making a determination for direct payment in respect of any recipient of weekly income support who is in debt, with the following exceptions laid down by the regulations:

    (a)   where the debt is for less than the income support personal allowance for a single beneficiary aged not less than 25;

    (b)   where the beneficiary's income support, and any benefit from which direct payment deductions can be made under the regulations, is less than the amount which would otherwise be deducted under paragraph 8 below.

(6)   Where the debt is the responsibility of a person who has deserted his partner, direct payment arrangements will not be made for the deserted partner unless the AO has made a fresh determination as in paragraph 2.

(7)   Where a prepayment meter, calibrated to pay towards a debt as well as for current consumption, has been installed, direct payment will not normally be made for that fuel.

Amounts of Deductions for Direct Payment

(8)   The amount to be deducted by the DSS each week from the beneficiary's benefit is laid down in the regulations and shall consist of:

    (a)   An amount to reduce the debt owed to the supplier by the beneficiary. For beneficiaries who have only one fuel debt, the amount shall be 5% of the income support personal allowance for a single beneficiary aged not less than 25. For beneficiaries who have two fuel debts, the amount deducted for each debt shall be 5% of the income support personal allowance for a single beneficiary aged not less than 25.

    (b)   An amount equal to the estimated average weekly cost (including standing charges) of the beneficiary's fuel consumption.

In any individual case the supplier shall provide the AO on request with details of how the estimate was arrived at. In making his estimate under (b), the AO will take into account the suppliers' estimate of current consumption. The formula that the supplier will use for calculating his estimate is given below. In practice, the supplier will calculate the beneficiary's average weekly consumption for electricity or gas, including fixed or standing charges, and will take into consideration any proposed price increases. This is the basis of the estimate for current consumption.

At the end of each assessment period (normally six months but see paragraph 11) the supplier will compare the actual expenditure with the estimated expenditure in the last twelve months, and will adjust the new deduction upwards or downwards according to whether the beneficiary is in debit or credit.

The formula ensures that the debit or credit is cleared by the end of the next assessment period by spreading it over 26 weeks;

$$DX = \left(\frac{Q1 + Q2 + Q3 + Q4}{S2} \right) - Y - Z + \frac{SC}{26}$$

where

    DX = rate of future weekly deductions

    Q = quarterly consumption of units (previous 12 months where known)

    Y = charge per unit in last assessment period

    Z = new price per unit as percentage of old*

    S = the difference between the actual and estimated billed charges since the last assessment, to be recovered or repaid over 26 weeks.

    SC = quarterly, weekly, daily (or other period) standing or fixed charges converted to weekly figure.

*   The proposed price increase should be expressed as a percentage of the current charges – an increase of 8% would be shown as 108%, and a decrease of 3% would be shown as 97%.

The basis of the estimate for current consumption shall generally be the beneficiary's billed charges during the previous 52 weeks. It will, however, be necessary for the supplier to

- base the estimate on previous consumption over a part year where the beneficiary has been a consumer for less than a year; or

- fix the estimate taking account of the appliances in use where there is insufficient history of fuel consumption at the address.

In such cases the supplier will arrange for a further estimate based on the beneficiary's actual consumption as soon as possible.

Minor variations agreed between the DSS and the fuel industries may be necessary to take account of particular circumstances, for example in areas where the fuel industry operates a bi-monthly billing system. The following paragraphs give details of other situations where it may not be appropriate to apply the formula precisely.

(9)   Where a prepayment meter is installed just for current consumption an amount under paragraph 8(a) only may be deducted to reduce the outstanding debt.

(10)   Where a beneficiary is also in debt in respect of his housing costs or service charges, as defined in the regulations, deductions for these items shall take precedence over those for fuel debt. Where a beneficiary also has more than one fuel debt (eg gas and electricity) the AO shall decide which of the debts should take priority taking account of the circumstances, the views of the industries, and any requests of the beneficiary. Deductions for fuel shall take precedence over debts for water and sewerage.

Frequency of Reassessments

(11)   The amounts to be deducted in an individual case will be decided by the AO. This will normally be at intervals of 26 weeks, though more frequent reviews will be made where they are essential. In particular where the supplier or the beneficiary exceptionally represents within that period that the amount deducted under paragraph 8(b) is no longer a realistic estimate of the beneficiary's average weekly fuel costs, the AO will make every reasonable endeavour to review his determination within 14 days of being advised and may revise the amount of the deduction.

Variations of the Amount Deducted

(12)   No variations in the weekly amount of deductions will be made on account of seasonal variations in consumption. Any credits occurring during the summer will not, for example, cause the beneficiary to be treated as having cleared his debt and be removed from the scheme.

Clearance of Debts and Termination of Direct Payments

(13)   Direct payments shall continue, in an individual case, for as long as the AO considers it necessary to discharge the beneficiary's obligations and the level of deductions remains acceptable to the supplier. Normally, direct payments

shall continue as long as the original debt to the supplier remains uncleared. They may be continued for current consumption where the AO determines it would be in the interests of the beneficiary and his family for such payments to be made. In making his decision the AO will consider the circumstances of the case, including the beneficiary's ability and opportunity to budget for the next bill, and any representations from the supplier. Where direct payments are no longer appropriate, the Department will tell the beneficiary of the date on which deductions for direct payment will cease, and advise him to contact the supplier to make his own arrangements. The DSS will notify the supplier promptly of the date on which deductions ceased.

Refund of Incorrect Payments

(14)   The DSS will notify the supplier and the beneficiary in writing as soon as it is discovered that an incorrect payment, outside an AO's determination, has been made to the supplier. On receipt of such a notification the supplier shall count back 8 weeks from the date of notification and refund to the DSS an amount equal to any incorrect payments in respect of weeks occurring within that 8-week period. The supplier will not refund any incorrect payments where the beneficiary has ceased to take a supply of the relevant fuel or has moved to any address unknown to the supplier or in an area dealt with any other supplier.

Reconnection Charges and Cost of Installing a Prepayment Meter

(15)   Reconnection charges are normally included in the definition of the debt for which an arrears deduction is being made. Where deductions are not, or cannot, be made, the Social Fund Officer may consider the award of a grant or loan from the Social Fund to meet reconnection charges. The Social Fund Officer may also consider an award of a discretionary grant or loan from the Social Fund to meet the cost of installing a prepayment meter to assist the beneficiary with budgeting for fuel.

The Code of Practice

(16)   The Electricity and Gas industries act in accordance with their published Code(s) of Practice covering the payment of domestic electricity and gas bills. This statement of intent does not in any way modify the terms or spirit of the Code(s) of Practice.

(17)   These arrangements shall come into operation with effect from 1 November 1991.

Standards of Performance

GAS

The electricity provisions below are set out in legislation. Similar provisions can be introduced for gas but this has not yet been done and there are no plans to do so. In the meantime, there are some provisions for gas which are the result of negotiation between OFGAS and British Gas. A new Condition 13A has been inserted in British Gas's Authorisation to Supply so that if British Gas fails to meet the agreed standards of performance, OFGAS can take enforcement action.

Condition 13A is set out below. The standards of performance, and the amounts of compensation payable for failure to comply with them, are set out in two leaflets available from your local showroom or British Gas regional office: 'Standards of Service' and 'Complaints Handling Procedure and Compensation Scheme'. New revised standards of performance will be introduced in January 1994.

Condition 13A: Service Standards

1. The supplier shall establish, and shall diligently take all reasonable steps to achieve, standards of performance in relation to the provision by the Supplier of gas supply services to tariff customers and potential tariff customers including services relating to:
   (a) the giving of, and the continuation of the giving of, supplies of gas;
   (b) the ascertainment of quantities of gas supplied;
   (c) the recovery of gas charges; and
   (d) the prevention of escapes of gas.
2. The standards of performance so established (in this Condition referred to as 'the established standards') shall, in particular, govern the making of visits to customers' premises and the response to complaints and enquiries made in person, by telephone, in writing or otherwise in respect of gas supply services.
3. The Supplier shall keep records of the levels of performance achieved by the Supplier (which in circumstances where the Director so directs shall extend to individual cases) in relation to the established standards and the costs incurred by the Supplier in such performance.
4. The Supplier shall not make any change in the established standards without the consent of the Director.
5. The Supplier shall establish and shall operate a scheme for compensating persons affected by failures to meet the established standards.
6. The Supplier shall:
   (a) furnish to the Director; and
   (b) publish, in such a manner as will secure adequate publicity for them, the established standards and particulars of the scheme established under paragraph 5 above (in this Condition referred to as 'the

compensation scheme') including an explanation of the principles on which compensation will be made.

7(1)   The Supplier shall furnish to the Director and publish, in such manner as will secure adequate publicity for it, a statement of the levels of performance proposed to be achieved by the Supplier in the period beginning on 1st April 1992 and ending on 31st December 1992 in relation to the established standards.

(2)   The Supplier shall, as soon as practicable after the end of the financial year ending on 31st December 1992 and of each subsequent financial year, furnish to the Director and publish, in such manner as will secure adequate publicity for each of them,:

(a)   a report on
   (i)   the levels of performance achieved by the supplier in that year in relation to the establishment standards; and
   (ii)   the operation of the compensation scheme during that year; and
(b)   a statement of the levels of performance proposed to be achieved by the Supplier in the ensuing financial year in relation to the established standards.

(3)   In respect of the report for the financial year ending on 31st December 1992 the references in sub-paragraph (2)(a)(i) and (ii) above to 'that year' shall be construed as references to the period beginning on 1st April 1992 and ending on 31st December 1992.

8(1)   Any statement to be furnished and published under paragraph 7(2)(b) above shall include any proposals for modifying the established standards.

(2)   In formulating any such proposals the Supplier shall take account of any representations with regard to standards of performance in relation to the provision by the Supplier of gas supply services made by the Director to the Supplier in the preceding financial year.

9.   The Supplier shall furnish the Director with such information as to:
(a)   the achievement by the Supplier of levels of performance in relation to the established standards;
(b)   the records kept under paragraph 3 above; and
(c)   the operation of the compensation scheme, as he may from time to time direct.

ELECTRICITY

Below is a summary of the provisions of the Electricity (Standards of Performance) Regulations 1993 (SI No. 1193). The regulations give time limits within which electricity suppliers must respond to consumers on 10 subjects. Failure to meet one of the time limits means the consumer is entitled to a fixed payment. The time limits and payments are set out in the regulations for each supply company but are virtually identical for all. Only one table is set out here (overleaf), but you should be able to get a leaflet from your local showroom which will set this out in detail, including any extended time limits or increased payments.

Reg	Subject	Time limit working days/hours	Payment £
3	To visit after failure of supplier's fuse	4 hours *a*	20
4	Re-connection after interruption of supply	24 hours, and for each additional 12 hours	40 20
5 (2) (3)	Providing a supply – failure to make an appointment – failure to keep an appointment	3 days *b*	20 40
6 (2) (3)	Providing estimates of charges – no significant work required – significant work required	10 days *c* 20 days *d*	40 40
7	Giving notice of interruption of supply	2 days *e*	20
8 (2) (4)a (4)b	Response to complaint about voltage – failure to make appointment – failure to keep appointment – failure to send explanation	10 days *f* 10 days *g*	20 20 20
9 (2) (4)a (4)b	Meter not working properly – failure to make appointment – failure to keep appointment – failure to send explanation	10 days *f* 10 days *g*	20 20 20
10	Queries on charges/payments	10 days *h*	20
11(2) 11(3)	Failure to make appointment Failure to keep appointment		20 20
14	Giving notice of right to payment	10 days *j*	20

Some variances between companies on the above time scales are set out below.

Ref.	Time Limits	Supplier(s)
a	3 hours	Eastern Electricity, Midlands Electricity
b	2 days	Eastern Electricity, Midlands Electricity
b	5 days	Scottish Power
b	6 days	Scottish Hydro-Electric
c	5 days	Eastern Electricity, Midlands Electricity
d	15 days	Eastern Electricity, Midlands Electricity
d	30 days	Scottish Hydro-Electric
e	3 days	MANWEB
e	5 days	Midlands Electricity, SEEBOARD, Southern Electric
f	7 days	Southern Electric
g	5 days	Eastern Electricity, East Midlands Electricity
g	7 days	Southern Electric
h	5 days	Eastern Electricity, East Midlands Electricity, Midlands Electricity
j	5 days	Midlands Electricity
j	20 days	Scottish Hydro-Electric

Draft Court Claim

This appendix gives a precedent for a court claim in England and Wales against a supplier for breach of their duty to supply. Hopefully, this will be useful for legal advisers who are not familiar with this area of the law. This draft claim is put in the county court which is where most claims will be heard.

IN THE _____ COUNTY COURT   Case No:_____

BETWEEN: A.N. OTHER   Plaintiff

and

-X- ELECTRICITY PLC
-Y- GAS PLC   Defendants

PARTICULARS OF CLAIM

1. The Defendants are public [*electricity/gas*] suppliers and are [*licensed/authorised*] to supply [*electricity/gas*] to an authorised area, within the meaning of the [*Electricity Act 1989/Gas Act 1986*]. The said authorised area includes the premises known as and situate at [*your address*] ('the premises') which are [*owned/occupied*] by the Plaintiff.

2. The Plaintiff has been a tariff customer of the Defendants at the premises within the meaning of the [*Electricity Act 1989 section 22(4)/Gas Act 1986 section 14(5)*] since [*insert date when you started paying the bill at present address*].

3. By notice dated [—/—/—] the Plaintiff required the Defendants to [*give/continue to*] supply to the premises in accordance with the [*Electricity Act 1989 section 16/Gas Act 1986 section 10*].

4. In breach of the provisions of the [*Electricity Act 1989/Gas Act 1986*] set out in paragraph 3 above, the Defendants have failed to [*give/continue supply to the premises*].

PARTICULARS OF BREACH

[Set out here concisely the facts of the situation on which you would rely as supporting your case in a trial – below is an example].

On 30th October 1991, representatives of the Defendants came to the premises and found a hole in the side of the [*electricity/gas*] meter. The meter was removed by the said representatives on the same day. The Plaintiff has been without a supply since then.

The Defendants demanded the sum of £00.00 for the damage to the meter and for disconnection and reconnection charges and this was paid on 10th November 1991.

The Defendants claim, by letter dated 14th November 1991, that the Plaintiff owes the further sum of £00.00 in respect of [*electricity/gas*] supplied but not registered on the damaged meter and refuse to reconnect supply until this sum is paid. The Plaintiff does not know how this sum is calculated and genuinely disputes that any part of it is owed.

5. Further, the Defendants are in breach of [*Schedule 6 paragraph 1(9) of the Electricity Act 1989/Schedule 5 paragraph 7(5A) of the Gas Act 1986 – can't disconnect when sum genuinely in dispute*].

PARTICULARS OF BREACH

The Plaintiff relies on the particulars set out in paragraph 4 above.

6. By reason of the matters aforesaid, the Plaintiff has suffered loss, damage, inconvenience, anxiety and distress.

PARTICULARS OF DAMAGE

[*Again, what follows below is an example*]
The Plaintiff lives at the premises with her husband, John, and two daughters: Helen (5 years old) and Joanna (3 years old). John and Joanna both suffer from asthma which is made worse by cold conditions.

The Plaintiff has been unable to use the central heating system at the premises and has had to buy coal and paraffin to heat the premises – this costs an average of £00.00 a [*day/week*].

Because there is no working cooker or fridge/freezer, the Plaintiff and her family have had to eat meals at restaurants. On average, £00.00 more is spent on each meal than if it had been made at home.

7. Further, the Plaintiff claims interest pursuant to section 69 of the County Courts Act 1984 on such sums as may be found due to the Plaintiff, at such rate and for such period as the court shall think fit.

AND THE PLAINTIFF CLAIMS:

1. A declaration that the Plaintiff does not owe the Defendants the sum of £00.00 or any other amount in respect of the supply of [*electricity/gas*];

2. An injunction requiring the Defendants to install a new meter at the premises and to restore supply forthwith;

3. Damages; and

4. Interest pursuant to the County Courts Act 1984 section 69 as aforesaid.

Dated this_____day of_____199__

Signed _____
         Solicitor for the Plaintiff

Reading Meters

ELECTRICITY

There are two types of electricity meter, the digital meter and the dial meter.

The Digital Meter

The number of units consumed is shown by a simple row of figures. The figure shown is cumulative, so to get the amount of consumption since the last reading, subtract the figure given for the total number of units consumed on the previous reading from the current reading. Economy Seven and White Meters show two sets of figures: one for electricity consumed at the day rate, marked 'Normal', and one for electricity consumed at the night rate, marked 'Low'.

The Dial Meter

Dial meters can appear difficult to read because each type of unit (tens, hundreds, etc.) is shown on a different dial and adjacent dials revolve in the opposite directions. However, do not be put off. Read the dials in the following order:

- dial on far left: tens of thousands, revolves clockwise

- second from left: thousands, revolves anti-clockwise

- centre dial: hundreds, revolves clockwise

- second from right: tens, revolves anti-clockwise

- dial on far right: single units, revolves clockwise.

If the reading on each dial was 5, then the meter would be recording 55,555 units consumed to date. As with the digital meter, the reading is cumulative and the previous reading must be subtracted from the current reading to find out consumption since the last reading.

You should note the following points about reading dial meters:

- ignore the dial marked 1/10

- write down the number that the pointer has passed, not the number that the pointer is nearest to – eg, if the pointer is between 6 and 7, write down 6, because the pointer has passed it.

- if the pointer is directly over a number (eg, 5), look at the dial immediately on the right (unless it is the single unit dial, in which case write down '5'); if the pointer on this right-hand dial is between 9 and 0, write down 4; if it is between 0 and 1, write down 5, and so on.

GAS

There are two types of gas meter, digital meters and dial meters. They both measure consumption of gas in the old imperial measurement of cubic feet. On your gas bill, this used to be converted into 'therms' which was the unit of charge for payment for gas. However, British Gas is now going metric: on your bill, you will find the cubic feet measured by your meter are converted into cubic metres so that you can be charged by the 'Kilowatt/hour' (kWh) instead of by the therm. To get from the reading on your meter to the number of Kilowatt/hours for which you will be charged, use the following formula:

- current meter reading – previous meter reading = amount of gas consumed

- cubic feet x 2.83 = reading in cubic metres

- $\dfrac{\text{reading in cubic metres} \times \text{calorific value}}{3.6} = kWh$

(*Note*: the calorific value for your region is normally shown on your bill; otherwise, you can ask your British Gas regional office what it is.)

For example: if the current meter reading is 4800, the previous meter reading was 4600 and the calorific value is 38.2, then the formula works out as follows:

- $4800 - 4600 = 200$

- $200 \times 2.83 = 566$

- $\dfrac{566 \times 38.2}{3.6} = 6,006 \; kWh$

The British Gas leaflet 'Understanding your metric gas bill' explains this calculation as it is set out in your gas bill.

The Digital Meter

Hundreds of units upwards appear as white figures, units of less than a hundred as red figures. Only read the white figures.

The Dial Meter

Only read the dial with black hands, which should be read in the following order:

- dial on far left: hundreds of thousands

- second from left: tens of thousands

- second from right: thousands

- dial on far right: hundreds

If the reading on each dial was 1, then 111,100 cubic feet of gas would have been consumed since the meter was first set. Where a hand is between two figures, write down the low figure, unless the hand is between 9 and 0, in which case write down 9.

Useful Books and Leaflets

From British Gas

Commitment to customers
Payment of gas bills
How to get help if you can't pay your gas bill
Your gas supply – a guide to gas supply services for tariff customers
Complaints handling procedure and compensation scheme
Standards of service
Understanding your metric gas bill
Our commitment to older or disabled customers
Advice for disabled people
Advice for older people

From the electricity suppliers

Codes of Practice from each supply company on:

- payment of bills

- services for disabled people

- energy efficiency

- complaints procedures

From OFGAS

OFGAS – protecting the rights of the consumer
Maximum price for the resale of gas – a guide for landlords and tenants, industrial suppliers and their customers

From OFFER

Consumer matters
Metering issues
Landlords, Tenants & Electricity Charges
'Electricity Services: The Customer Perspective', report prepared by MORI for the Office of Electricity Regulation, 1993
Annual Reports

From Right to Warmth (in Scotland)

Paying for Fuel – A guide to policies and practices of fuel companies in Scotland with advice on repaying fuel debt and avoiding disconnection.
Warm Homes: The Law

From CPAG

Debt Advice Handbook
A Guide to Money Advice in Scotland
Disability Rights Handbook
National Welfare Benefits Handbook
Rights Guide to Non-means-tested Benefits
Welfare Rights Bulletin

From other sources

On electricity
The Electricity Supply Handbook (1991 edn - available from *The Electrical Times*)

On legal action
Small claims in the Sheriff's court (available from Scottish Courts Administration)

On general news and campaigning on fuel and fuel-related issues

Fuel News - quarterly newsletter of the National Right to Fuel Campaign

On fuel poverty

Fuel Poverty: From Cold Homes to Affordable Warmth by Brenda Boardman (Belhaven Press, 1991)
Fuel Poverty and the Greenhouse Effect (FoE, NEA, NRFC, Heatwise)
Ten Years Cold (NEA)
Fuel Poverty is Different (Policy Studies Institute)
Poverty and Power - the Efficient Use of Electricity in Low Income Households (Trevor Houghton, Bristol Energy Centre)

On debt issues

Dealing with Your Debts - advice on debt problems for people with mortgages (available from National Debtline)
Dealing with Your Debts - advice on debt problems for people who pay rent (available from National Debtline)
There's No Money in my Meter
Contains No Cash - the experiences and options of fifty users of gas key meters
Plastic Power - a survey of fifty users of electric token meters in North Braunstone, Leicester (available from Family Service Unit)
Fuel Savers: a feasibility study (available from the Birmingham Settlement)

On warm homes and energy efficiency

Taking Action on Cold Homes (available from TRIS)

Useful Addresses

GAS
Office of Gas Supply (OFGAS)
Stockley House
130 Wilton Road
London SW1V 1LQ
071-828 0898

Gas Consumers Council
Head Office
Abford House
15 Wilton Road
London SW1V 1LT
071-931 0977

Regional Offices
Scotland
86 George Street
Edinburgh EH2 3BU
031-226 6523

Wales
Caradog House
St Andrews Place
Cardiff CF1 3BE
0222 226547

Northern
Plummer House
Market Street East
Newcastle upon Tyne NE1 6NF
091-261 9561

North East
3rd floor
National Deposit House
1 Eastgate
Leeds LS2 7RL
0532 439961

North West
Boulton House
Chorlton Street
Manchester M1 3HY
061-236 1926

East Midlands
Pennine House
31-33 Millstone Lane
Leicester LE1 5JN
0533 536633

West Midlands
Broadway House
60 Calthorpe Road
Birmingham B15 1TH
021-454 5510

Eastern
51 Station Road
Letchworth
Herts SG6 3BQ
0462 685399

North Thames
6th floor
Abford House
15 Wilton Road
London SW1V 1LT
071-931 9151

Southern
3rd floor
Roddis House
4-12 Old Christchurch Road
Bournemouth BH1 1LG
0202 556654

South East
6th floor
Abford House
15 Wilton Road
London SW1V 1LT
071-931 9155

South West
3rd floor
Prudential Building
115 Armada Way
Plymouth PL1 1HP
0752 667707

British Gas Regions
Scotland
Granton House
4 Marine Drive
Edinburgh EH5 1YB
031-559 5000

Wales
Helmont House
Churchill Way
Cardiff
CF1 4NB
0222 239290

Northern
Norgas House
PO Box 1GB
Killingworth
Newcastle upon Tyne NE99 1GB
091-216 3000

North Western
Welman House
Altrincham
Cheshire WA15 8AE
061-928 6311

Eastern
New York Road
Leeds LS2 7PE
0532 436291

East Midlands
PO Box 145
De Montfort Street
Leicester LE1 9DB
0533 551111

West Midlands
7 Wharf Lane
Solihull
West Midlands B91 2JP
021-705 6811

Eastern
Star House
Potters Bar
Herts EN6 2PD
0707 51151

North Thames
North Thames House
London Road
Staines
Middx TW18 4AE

South Eastern
Katharine Street
Croydon CR9 1JU
081-688 4466

Southern
80 St Mary's Road,
Southampton SO9 7GJ
0703 824100

South Western
Riverside
Temple Street
Keynsham
Bristol BS18 1EQ

ELECTRICITY
**Office of Electricity Supply
(OFFER) and Electricity
Consumers' Committees** can be
contacted at these addresses:

Scotland
Scottish Headquarters
48 St Vincent Street
Glasgow G2 5TS
041-248 5917

South Scotland Consumers'
    Committee
48 St Vincent Street
Glasgow G2 5TS
041-248 5588

North Scotland Consumers'
    Committee
24 Marshall Place
Perth PH2 8AG
0738 36669

England and Wales
Head Office
Hagley House
Hagley Road
Birmingham B16 8QG
021-456 2100

London
2nd floor
11 Belgrave Road
London SW1V 1RB
071-233 6366

Eastern
4th floor
Waveney House
Handford Road
Ipswich
Suffolk IP1 2BJ

East Midlands
Suite 3c
Langford House
Friar Lane
Nottingham NG1 6DQ
0602 508738

Merseyside and North Wales
4th floor
Hamilton House
Hamilton Road
Chester CH1 2BH
0244 320849

Midlands
11th floor
Hagley House
Hagley Road
Birmingham B16 8QG
021-456 4424

North Eastern
1st floor
St Cuthbert's Chambers
35 Nelson Street
Newcastle upon Tyne NE1 5AN
091-221-2071

North Western
1st floor
Boulton House
17/21 Chorlton Street
Manchester M1 3HY
061-236 3484

Southern
30/31 Friar Street
Reading RG1 1DX
0734 560211

South Eastern
1/4 Lamberts Yard
Tonbridge
Kent TN9 1ER
0732 351356

South Wales
St David's House (West Wing)
Wood Street
Cardiff CF1 1ES
0222 2238388

South Western
Unit 1
Hide Market
West Street
St Philips
Bristol BS2 0BH
0272 540934

Yorkshire
4th floor
Fairfax House
Merrion Street
Leeds LS2 8JU
0532-341866

Regional Electricity Companies
Eastern Electricity plc
Wherstead Park
PO Box 40
Wherstead
Ipswich
Suffolk IP9 2AQ
0473 688688

East Midlands Electricity plc
PO Box 4
North PDO
398 Coppice Road
Arnold
Nottingham NG5 7HX
0602 269711

London Electricity plc
Templar House
81-87 High Holborn
London WC1V 6NU
071-242 9050

MANWEB plc
Sealand Road
Chester CH1 4LR
0244 377111

Midlands Electricity plc (MEB)
Mucklow Hill
Halesowen
West Midlands B62 8BP
021-423 2345

Northern Electric plc
Carliol House
Newcastle upon Tyne NE99 1SE
091-221 2000

NORWEB plc
Talbot Road
Manchester M16 0HQ
061-873 8000

Scottish Hydro-Electric plc
16 Rothesay Terrace
Edinburgh EH3 7SE
031-225 1361

Scottish Power plc
Cathcart House
Spean Street
Glasgow G44 4BE
041-637 7177

SEEBOARD plc
Grand Avenue
Hove
East Sussex BN3 2LS
0273 724522

Southern Electric plc
Littlewick Green
Maidenhead
Berkshire SL6 3QB
0628 822166

South Wales Electricity plc
   (Trydan De Cymru)
St Mellons
Cardiff CF3 9XW
0222 792111

South Western Electricity plc
   (SWEB)
800 Park Avenue
Aztec West
Almondsbury
Bristol BS12 4SE
0454 201101

Yorkshire Electricity plc
Wetherby Road
Scarcroft
Leeds LS14 3HS
0532 892123

Energy Surveys
National Home Energy Rating
   Scheme
The National Energy Foundation
Rockingham Drive
Lindford Wood
Milton Keynes MK14 6EG
0908 672787

Starpoint Home Energy Label
   Scheme
MVM Starpoint Ltd
16 Park Place
Clifton
Bristol BS8 1JP
0272 253769

Other Useful Addresses
Age Concern
1268 London Road,
London SW16 4ER
081-679 8000

Campaign for Cold Weather
   Credits
PO Box 211
Glasgow
041-226 3061

Child Poverty Action Group
4th floor
1-5 Bath Street
London EC1V 9PY
071-253 3406

Combined Heat and Power
  Association
District Heating Association
Grosvenor Gardens House
35-37 Grosvenor Gardens
London SW1W 0BS
071-828 4077

Confederation for the
  Registration of Gas Installers
  (CORGI)
4 Elmwood
Chineham Business Park
Crockford Lane
Basingstoke RG24 0WG
0256 707060

Consumers Association
2 Marylebone Road
London NW1 4DF
071-486 5544

Department of Trade and Industry
1-19 Victoria Street
London SW1H 0ET
071-215 5000

Draughtproofing Advisory
  Association Ltd
National Association of Loft
  Insulation Contractors
PO Box 12
Haslemere
Surrey GU27 3AH
0428 654011

The Electrical Times
Quadrant House
The Quadrant
Sutton
Surrey SM2 5AS
081-661 8742

Energy Action Grants Agency
PO Box 1NG
Newcastle-upon-Tyne NE99 1NG
0800 181667 (freephone)

Energy Efficiency Office
c/o Department of the
  Environment
1 Palace Street
London SW1E 5HE
0345 247347

Energy Inform
9-10 Charlotte Square
Newcastle upon Tyne NE1 4XF
091-232 8284

Energy Savings Trust
11-12 Buckingham Gate,
London SW1E 6LB
071-828 1346

Family Service Units
207 Marylebone Road
London NW1 5QP
071-402 5175

Heating and Ventilating
  Contractors' Association
Esca House
34 Palace Court
London W2 4JG
0345 581158

Heatwise
9 Elliott Place
Glasgow G3 8EP
041-248 3993

Help the Aged
St James Walk
London EC1 0BE
Advice Line: 0800 289404

Institution of Electrical Engineers
Savoy Place
London WC2R 0BL
071-240 1871

Low Frequency Noise Sufferers
    Association
c/o Mrs E Griggs (Secretary)
6 Hyatt Place
Shepton Mallet
Somerset BA4 5XY

National Consumers Council
20 Grosvenor Gardens,
London SW1W 0BD
071-730 3469

National Debtline
c/o The Birmingham Settlement
318 Summer Lane
Birmingham B19 3RL
021-359 8501

National Right to Fuel Campaign
c/o The Birmingham Settlement
318 Summer Lane
Birmingham B19 3RL
021-359 3562

Neighbourhood Energy Action
2-4 Bigg Market
Newcastle upon Tyne NE1 1UW
091-261 5677

Office of Data Protection
    Registrar
Wycliffe House
Water Lane
Wilmslow
Cheshire SK9 5AF
0625 535777

Public Utilities Access Forum
c/o Agenda Services,
8 Ridgemount Road,
London SW18
081-870 3259

Right to Warmth
21 West Nile Street,
Glasgow G1 2NF
041-221 7781

Solid Fuel Advisory Service
Hobart House
Grosvenor Place
London SW1X 7AE
071-235 2020

Tenants Energy Advice Service
Energy Conservation and Solar
    Centre
PO Box 1802
London NW1 1UW
071-833 5597

Tenants' Resource & Information
    Service (TRIS)
First Floor,
1 Pink Lane,
Newcastle NE1 5DW

Winter Warmth Line (operates
   22 Oct – 31 March)
0800 289404 (freephone)

**Travellers, Gypsies and
Caravan-Dwellers**
East Anglian Gypsy Council
Plot 3
Travellers' Site
Oxney Road
Peterborough PE1 5NX

Essex Romany Association
10 Main Road
Hart Road Caravan Site
Thundersley
Benfleet
Essex SS7 3HQ

North County Travellers
   Association
c/o Old School House
High Bentham
Nr Lancaster LA2 7JX

Northern Gypsy Council
1 Shore Road
Gypsy Common Side
Lynemouth
Northumberland N61 S52

Northern Ireland Council for
   Travelling People
Eia House
224 Antrim Road
Belfast
0232 351561

National Gypsy Council
Greenacres Caravan Park
Hapsford
Helsby
Warrington WA6 OJS

Mary Hinde
Leeds Citizens' Advice Bureau
31 New York Street
Leeds
West Yorkshire LS2 7DT
0532 326035

Notes

Abbreviations used in these notes

AllER   All England Reports
LG(MP)A 1976   The Local Government (Miscellaneous Provisions) Act 1976
R(S)A 1984   The Rent (Scotland) Act 1974
LTA 1985   The Landlord and Tenant Act 1985
GA 1986   The Gas Act 1986
H(S)A 1987   The Housing (Scotland) Act 1987
EA 1989   The Electricity Act 1989
RA 1977   The Rent Act 1977
CS(U)A 1992   The Competition and Services (Utilities) Act 1992
GM   Housing Benefit Guidance Manual
GS(RE)Regs   Gas Safety (Rights of Entry) Regulations 1983 SI No. 1575
SS(C&P)Regs   Social Security (Claims and Payments) Regulations 1987 SI No. 1968
SFCWP Regs   The Social Fund Cold Weather Payments Regulations 1988 SI No. 1724
HB Regs   The Housing Benefit (General) Regulations 1987 SI No. 1971
PCDGD   Principles for the Collection of Domestic Gas Debt
ibid   In the same place
op. cit.   In the work quoted

Chapter 2: The Right to a Supply

(pp6-24)

1. ss16 and 64 EA 1989; s10 GA 1986
2. *Woodcock v South Western Electricity Board*, Weekly Law Reports, 27 June 1975.
3. s16 EA 1989
4. s10 GA 1989
5. See Appendix to Joint Circular from the Department of the Environment and the Welsh Office, 25 March 1977: Circular 28/77(DoE); Circular 51/77 (Welsh Office)
6. See Joint Circular from the Department of the Environment and the Welsh Office, 17 April 1989: Circular 14/89 (DoE); Circular 23/89, Welsh Office; and Caravan Sites and Control of Development Act 1960, Section 5, Model Standards 1989: Permanent Residential Mobile Home Sites
7. para 17, Model Standards 1989: Permanent Residential Mobile Home Sites, op. cit.
8. Sch 6 para 1(6) EA 1989
9. Sch 6 para 6 EA 1989
10. *See also* Appendix 2
11. Sch 6 para 6 EA 1989
12. Sch 6 para 6 EA 1989
13. Sch 6 para 6 EA 1989
14. s20 EA 1989
15. s22 EA 1989
16. s17 EA 1989
17. ss17 and 19 EA 1989: Electricity Supply Regs 1988 SI No. 1057 and 1990
18. Sch 7 para 1(5) EA 1989
19. Sch 6 paras 4 and 7(11) EA 1989
20. s17 EA 1989
21. s17(2)(c) EA 1989
22. s17(3) EA 1989
23. s22(4) EA 1989

24. ss16 and 64 EA 1989
25. s 16 EA 1989
26. s16(3) EA 1989
27. OFFER Determination S23/C/015/(B). Advisers may wish to obtain a copy of this important decision from the Library at OFFER Headquarters, Birmingham.
28. ibid.
29. s64 EA 1989
30. S16(4) EA 1989
31. s16 EA 1989
32. ss39 and 40 EA 1989; Electricity Standards of Performance Regs 1993. See Appendix 6.
33. ss39 and 40 EA 1989; Electricity Standards of Performance Regs 1993. See Appendix 6.
34. s16 EA 1989
35. Case History 7, OFFER Annual Report 1991, p68
36. s22(4) EA 1989
37. ss22 and 16 EA 1989
38. s22 EA 1989
39. s22 EA 1989 provides that ss 16-21 would not apply
40. s22(1)(a) EA 1989
41. s22(1)(b) EA 1989
42. OFFER Determination s23/C/001/B
43. s23 EA 1989
44. OFFER Determination S23/C/001/B
45. s19(1) EA 1989, Condition 8 of Supplier's Licence.
46. A Statement by the Director General of Electricity Supply on Domestic Connection Charges, 25 February 1992. Available from OFFER Library.
47. See OFFER Determinations:
    - S23/R/011(B) Dispute concerning connection of a farm over 1km from nearest point on distribution system. Costs of £25,059 reduced to £18,995.S23/R/014/(B) Dispute over connection charge to bungalow under construction. Costs of £2,831 reduced to £1,283.
    - S23/R/017/(B) Dispute concerning connection charge to block of 14 new flats under construction.

Costs of £284.80 per flat reduced to £245.
- S23/R/019/B Dispute concerning the level of charges quoted for a new supply to three adjacent plots of land. Land was subject to a planning dispute. Supplier delayed providing customer with an initial quotation and subsequently delayed providing an itemisation of costs. Costs of connection were substantially reduced by OFFER.
- S23/R/24/B Dispute concerning connection charges to remote property. OFFER upheld supplier's charge of £4,636.
48. ibid.
49. Reg 6 Electricity (Connection Charges) Regulations 1990
50. s10 GA 1986
51. s8 Interpretation Act 1978
52. Sch 5 para 7(6) GA 1986
53. Sch 5 para 7(1) GA 1986. *See also* note on VAT in introduction.
54. Sch 5 para 7(5) GA 1986
55. Sch 5 para 7(5) GA 1986
56. *See also* Appendix 2.
57. Sch 5 para 7(4) GA 1986
58. Sch 5 para 7(4) GA 1986
59. s11(1)GA 1986
60. *See also* Appendix 2.
61. Sch 5 para 3(1) GA 1986
62. Sch 5 para 4(1) GA 1986
63. Sch 5 para 3(2) GA 1986
64. Sch 5 para 3(3) GA 1986
65. s10(6)(a) GA 1986
66. Sch 5 para 10 GA 1986
67. s10(6)(a) GA 1986
68. Sch 7 para 12(2) EA 1989
69. Sch 6 para 1(9) EA 1989; Sch 5 para 7(5a) GA 1986, inserted by s19 Competition and Services (Utilities) Act 1992
70. ss10(2), 46(2) and 48 GA 1986
71. s46 GA 1986
72. s10(2) GA 1986
73. *See also* Appendix 3: OFGAS Position Paper C: Liability for the payment of charges for the supply of gas.
74. s10 GA 1986
75. s3 GA 1986

76. OFGAS Annual Report 1992, p44
77. ibid.
78. ibid.
79. CS(U)A 1992
80. Reg. 2 Gas (Connection Charges) Regs 1986
81. s20 EA 1989; s11(1) GA 1986
82. s20 EA 1989; s11(3) GA 1986
83. OFFER Determination S23/C/015(B)
84. s20 EA 1989; ss 11(1) and (3) GA 1986
85. s20 EA 1989; s11(3) GA 1986
86. See case study reported in OFGAS Annual Report 1990, p40.
87. OFGAS Annual Report 1990, p19
88. s20 EA 1989
89. ss20(1) and 20(4)(a) and (b) EA 1989
90. s20 EA 1989
91. See: s18(4) EA 1989; s14(3) GA 1989
92. s20(2) EA 1989; s11(3)(a) GA 1986
93. s20 EA 1989; s11(3) GA 1986
94. OFFER Determination S23/C/015(B)
95. s20 EA 1989
96. Principle 15 PCDGD, See Appendix 2.
97. Sch 5 para 7(6) GA 1986
98. Sch 6 para 2 EA 1989
99. s23 EA 1989; s11 GA 1986 as amended by CS(U)A 1992
100. See s 24 EA 1989 and s16(1) EA 1989 - guarantors are not 'tariff customers' if they have not given notice requiring a supply. Guarantors are not entitled to a supply at another premises where they are not the owner or occupier. The supplier's power to disconnect under Sch 6 para 1(6) EA 1989 applies to tariff customers only.
101. OFFER Determination S23/C/002/B
102. s20(4) EA 1989
103. s20(4) EA 1989
104. Principle 17 PCDGD adopted under Condition 12A of the Authorisation to British Gas.

Chapter 3:   Meters and Methods of Payment

(pp25-56)

1. Overall Standards Regulations. See Appendix 6.
2. See p9 Improved Service Standards for Gas Consumers - a Consultation Document, published by OFGAS.
3. See report on Prepayment Meters by Leicester Family Services Unit.
4. Condition 19 (Electricity); Condition 12A (Gas); see Appendix 2.
5. See British Gas Code of Practice for Elderly and Disabled Customers.
6. Check your supplier's Code of Practice on Energy Efficiency.
7. See Working Group Report on MANWEB's Use of Card Meters, Merseyside and North Wales Consumers' Committee 1993.
8. s18(2)(a) EA 1989; s14(1) GA 1986
9. Sch 9 paras 1 and 2(2) SS (C&P) Regs 1987
10. See para 13 JSI; Appendix 5; Sch 9 para 6 SS (C&P) Regs
11. Sch 9 para 6 SS (C&P) Regs
12. Sch 9 para 6 SS (C&P) Regs
13. Sch 9 para 6(1) SS (C&P) Regs
14. See Joint Statement of Intent, Appendix 5.
15. See your supplier's Code of Practice for customers who need help with paying their bills.
16. Sch 9, para 6(4) SS (C&P) Regs
17. Sch 9, para 6(2) SS (C&P) Regs
18. Sch 9, paras 6(4), 7(8) and 5(5) SS (C&P) Regs
19. Sch 9, para 6(4) SS (C&P) Regs
20. See Appendix 5.
21. Case reported in OFGAS Annual Report 1990, p36.
22. para 8 Joint Statement of Intent; Appendix 5.
23. Reviews under s25(1) Social Security Administration Act 1992
24. para 8 Joint Statement of Intent; Appendix 5.
25. ibid.
26. Sch 9, para 9 SS (C&P) Regs; Reg 2 CC (DIS) Regs

27. Sch 9, para 1(b) SS (C&P) Regs
28. Sch 9, para 5(c) SS (C&P) Regs
29. Sch 9, para 5(c)(ii) SS (C&P) Regs
30. Sch 9, para 6(6), 7(8) and 5(5) SS (C&P) Regs
31. para 2, JSI; Appendix 5.
32. Sch 9, para 6 SS (C&P) Regs
33. Sch 5, para 3(2) GA 1986
34. Principle 5 PCDGD; *see* Appendix 5.
35. See OFFER's discussion of the scope of tariffs in relation to changes to the terms of conditions of supply in paras 20-21 OFFER Determination S23/C/015(B) and para 35 OFFER Determination S23/C/002(B)
36. s17 EA 1989
37. s23 EA 1989
38. s18 EA 1989
39. OFFER Determination S23/C/002/(B)
40. OFFER Determination S23/C/015/(B)
41. para 39 OFFER Determination S23/C/002/(B)
42. s20 EA 1989; see also paras 9-12 OFFER Determination S23/C/002/(B) and paras 11-14 OFFER Determination S23/C/015/(B)
43. See paras 25-35 OFFER Determination S23/C/015/(B)
44. Principle first established by OFFER Determination S23/C/002/(B) (see paras 35-37) and later elaborated on in OFFER Determination S23/C/002/(B) (see paras 22-24)
45. ss 16, 17 and 23 EA 1989; see also paras 35-37 OFFER Determination S23/C/002/(B) and paras 22-24 OFFER Determination S23/C/015/(B)
46. para 45 OFFER Determination S23/C/015/(B)
47. Para 36 OFFER Determination S23/C/015/(B)
48. See OFFER Determination S23/C/015/(B) where OFFER decided the supplier was not entitled to extra charges for a prepayment meter where this had been imposed without the supplier following the

procedure for changing the terms and conditions of supply.
49. para 35 OFFER Determination S23/C/002/(B)
50. See OFFER Determination S23/C/015/(B)
51. ibid.

Chapter 4: Responsibility for the Bill
(pp58-77)
1. EA 1989; GA 1986
2. *Jackman v Yorkshire Electricity Board* [1984] 10 December (unreported) Leeds County Court. See *Legal Action*, August 1986 for description and discussion.
3. *Husey v London Electricity Supply Corporation* [1902] 1 CH 411
4. Appendix to OFGAS Annual Report 1988
5. ss16-23 EA 1989
6. Sch 6 para 2 EA 1989
7. Sch 5 para 2 EA 1989 – applies only to tariff customers
8. s16 EA 1989
9. s64 EA 1989
10. s22(4) EA 1989
11. s18 EA 1989
12. Sch 6 para 1 EA 1989
13. Sch6 para 3 EA 1989
14. Sch 6 para 5(a) EA 1989
15. Sch 6 para 5(b) EA 1989
16. Sch 6 para 3 EA 1989
17. See 'Public utilities and liability to pay' by Nicholas Nicol, *Legal Action*, March 1993, p19.
18. See the suppliers' codes of practice for the payment of bills.
19. Sch 6 para 2 EA 1989
20. Letter to *The Adviser*, Issue No. 29, January/ February 1992
21. GA 1986
22. Sch 5 para 2 GA 1986
23. Details of two cases reported in *The Adviser*, No. 31, June 1992: *British Gas West Midlands v Behan* and a second case in Reigate County Court, information supplied by Oxted CAB.
24. ibid.
25. s10 GA 1986

26. s10(2) GA 1986
27. ss10, 46 and 48 GA 1986
28. s14 GA 1986
29. s14(5) GA 1986
30. See 'Liability for gas' by Roman Lezscysyn, *The Adviser*, No. 31, May-June 1992, p37, for a useful discussion of the question of who is a tariff customer.
31. Sch 5 para 7(2) GA 1986
32. Sch 5 para 7(4) GA 1986
33. Sch 5 para 7(4)(b) GA 1986
34. See Roman Lezscysyn, *op. cit.*
35. Letter to authors and National Association of Citizens' Advice Bureaux
36. Sch 5 para 7(2) GA 1986
37. ss10(2) and 14 GA 1986
38. s10 GA 1986
39. s10(2) GA 1986
40. Sch 6 para 2 EA 1989; Sch 5 para 7 GA 1986
41. London Electricity application form 1993.
42. Sch 6 para 6 EA 1989; Sch 5 para 4(b) GA 1986
43. s22 EA 1989
44. *See also* Sch 5 para 7(2) GA 1986
45. *See also* Sch 6 para 2 EA 1989; Sch 5 para 7(2) GA 1986
46. ibid.
47. Sch 6 para 5(a) EA 1989; Sch 5 para 7(4) GA 1986
48. OFGAS Annual Report 1990, p40
49. Sch 6 para 5(a) EA 1989; Sch 5 para 7(4) GA 1986
50. s10 GA 1986, s16(1) EA 1989
51. Sch 5 para 7(4)(b) GA 1986
52. OFGAS Annual Report 1990, p29
53. *See also* OFGAS Position Paper C: Liability for payment of charges for the supply of gas; Appendix 3.
54. EA 1989 and GA 1986 as amended by CS(U)A 1992

Chapter 5:   High Bills

(pp78-88)
1. Limitation Act 1980
2. s6 Prescription and Limitation (Scotland) Act 1973
3. Sch 6 para 1(9) EA 1989; Sch 5 para 7(5A) GA 1986

4. Sch 6 para 5(2) EA 1989; Sch 5 para 15 GA 1986
5. Sch 7 EA 1989; s17 GA 1986
6. Sch 7 para 10(2) EA 1989; Sch 5 para 4(2) GA 1986
7. Sch 7 para 7 EA 1989; s17(2) GA 1986
8. There is provision in Sch 7 para 7(3) for regulations to be made which will cover any charges for an electricity meter examiner's work and by whom they are to be paid, but no such regulations have been made.
9. Sch 7 para 8 EA 1989
10. Sch 7 para 9(5) EA 1989
11. Sch 5 para 4(4) GA 1986 – the fees to be paid to meter examiners are set out in the Gas (Meters) (Variation of Fees) Regs 1990 SI No. 686
12. Sch 5 paras 4(5) and 5(2) GA 1986
13. Sch 5 para 5(2) GA 1986
14. Sch 7 para 7(2) EA 1989
15. See OFGAS Annual Reports 1990 and 1991
16. ss12-15 Sale of Goods Act 1979
17. s12 Sale of Goods Act 1979
18. s14 Sale of Goods Act 1979
19. s75 Consumer Credit Act 1974
20. Reg 30 Electricity Supply Regs SI 1988/1057
21. Reg 8 Electricity (Standards of Performance) Regs SI 1993/1193

Chapter 6:   Arrears

(pp89-110)
1. Sch 6 para 1(6) EA 1989
2. Sch 5 para 7(6) GA 1989
3. See Appendix 2.
4. See Appendix 2.
5. See Appendix 2.
6. Welfare Rights Briefing, Electricity Debts to NORWEB, Manchester Welfare Rights Service.
7. s25 EA 198; s28 GA 1986
8. See Appendix 2.
9. Sch 6 para 2 EA 1989; Sch 5 para 7 GA 1986
10. See Chapter 3: Meters and Methods of Payment, for a discussion of the problems of self-disconnection.
11. *See also* Appendix 2.

12 para 5 PCDGD; Appendix 2.
13 para 13 PCDGD; Appendix 2.
14 para 13 and 14 PCDGD; Appendix 2.
15 para 13 PCDGD; Appendix 2.
16 para 14 PCDGD; Appendix 2.
17 Condition 19(1)(Electricity);
    Condition 12A(1)(Gas); Appendix 2.
18 s23 EA 1989
19 OFFER Determination
    S23/C/015(B). Advisers may wish to
    obtain a copy of this decision from
    the library at OFFER's Birmingham
    Headquarters.
20 Condition 19; Appendix 2.
21 Condition 19(1)(Electricity);
    Condition 12A(1)(Gas); Appendix 2.
22 Condition 19(1)(Electricity);
    Condition 12A(1)(Gas); Appendix 2.
23 Letter from OFGAS, Appendix 2.
24 Para 22 London Electricity Code of
    Practice.
25 Principle 7 PCDGD; Appendix 2.
26 See Appendix 10.
27 See Appendix 10.
28 Condition 19 (Electricity);
    Condition 12A (Gas) – see
    Appendix 2.
29 s112 County Courts Act 1984.
30 s112A County Courts Act 1984 as
    amended by s13(5) Court and Legal
    Services Act; See Appendix 1.

Chapter 7:   Disconnection
for Arrears
(pp111-121)
1 Sch 6 para 1(6) EA 1989
2 Sch 6 para 1(7) EA 1989
3 Sch 6 para 1(6) EA 1989
4 Sch 6 para 1(9) EA 1989
5 Sch 6 para 1(1) EA 1989
6 Sch 6 para 27 EA 1989
7 Sch 6 para 1(6)(a) EA 1989
8 Sch 5 para 7(5) GA 1986
9 Sch 5 para 7(5) GA 1986
10 Sch 5 para 7 GA 1986 as amended
    by CS(U)A 1992
11 Sch 6 para 2(6) EA 1989
12 Sch 5 para 4(a) GA 1986
13 Sch 6 para 1(7) EA 1989
14 Condition 19 (Electricity);
    Condition 12A (Gas)

15 Sch 6 para 1(6) EA 1989; Sch 5 para
    15 GA 1986
16 Sch 6 paras 2(1) and 2(2) EA 1989
17 Sch 6 para 2(6) EA 1989
18 Sch 5 para 7(6) GA 1986
19 Sch 5 para 7(5) GA 1986
20 Sch 6 para 6(2)(b) EA 1989; Sch 5
    para 7(6) GA 1986

Chapter 8:   Theft and
Tampering
(pp122-132)
1 The two papers are set out in
   Appendix C to OFGAS Annual
   Report 1988. Note, however, that
   its opinion on one point has been
   held to be wrong. OFGAS said that,
   where a meter has been interfered
   with or damaged, the supplier must
   reconnect as soon as the damage is
   rectified or paid for so that the
   supplier cannot also insist on
   payment for gas which it estimates
   has been stolen before reconnecting
   supply. In *R v Director-General of
   Gas Supply ex parte Smith* [1989]
   (unreported), Mr Justice Pill held
   that this was wrong and British Gas
   could insist on payment for gas it
   could prove, on the balance of
   probabilities, was stolen, before it
   reconnects.
2 cf. Sch 7 para 10(4) and 12(1)
   EA 1989
3 Sch 7 para 1 EA 1989; Sch 5 para 3
   GA 1986
4 Sch 7 para 10(1) EA 1989; Sch 5
   para 4(1) GA 1986
5 Sch 7 para 10(2) EA 1989; Sch 5
   para 4(2) GA 1986
6 Sch 6 para 4(1) EA 1989; Sch 5 para
   10(1)(a) GA 1986
7 Sch 7 para 11(1)(a) EA 1989; Sch 5
   para 10(1)(b) GA 1986
8 Sch 7 para 11(1)(b) EA 1989; Sch 5
   para 10(1)(c) GA 1986
9 Sch 7 para 11(2) EA 1989; Sch 5
   para 10(3) GA 1986
10 In the 7th edition of the *Fuel Rights
    Handbook*, the case of *R v
    Midlands Electricity Board ex parte*

Busby in *The Times*, 18 October 1987, was discussed at length. It is authority for the proposition that an electricity board can impose additional terms on a consumer when making an agreement in lieu of disconnection. Looking at the full transcript of the court judgment, the opinion of the present authors is that the case is limited to the provisions of the old legislation and is no authority for anything under the EA 1989.

11 *Edmundson v Longton Corporation* [1902] 19 TLR 15; *Martin v Marsh* [1955] CrimLR 781

12 Sch 7 para 12(1) EA 1989

13 s1 Criminal Damage Act 1971; in Scotland, the common law offence of criminal damage.

14 s1 Theft Act 1968; in Scotland, the common law offence of theft.

15 s13 (electricity) and s1 (gas) Theft Act 1968; in Scotland, the common law offence of theft

16 *R v McCreadie* [1992] CrimLR 872

17 Sch 5 para 10(2) GA 1986

18 Sch 6 para 4(2) and (3) EA 1989

19 Sch 7 para 11(3) EA 1989

20 Sch 5 para 16(1) GA 1986; Rights of Entry (Gas and Electricity Boards) Act 1954

21 *R v Director-General of Gas Supply ex parte Smith* (1989) Mr Justice Pill, unreported

22 Sch 6 paras 2, 4(2) and (3), Sch 7 para 11(3) EA 1989; Sch 5 para 10(2) GA 1986

23 *R v Director-General of Gas Supply ex parte Smith* (1989) Mr Justice Pill, unreported (see Appendix 1).

24 Sch 6 para 1(6) EA 1989; Sch 5 para 7(5) GA 1986

25 Sch 6 para 1(9) EA 1989; Sch 5 para 7(5A) GA 1986

26 ss17(2) and 29 EA 1989 and the Electricity Supply Regs 1988 SI No. 1057

27 s18(2) GA 1986 and the GS(RE) Regs

28 Reg 29(4) Electricity Supply Regs 1988 SI No. 1057

29 Reg 3 GS(RE) Regs

30 Reg 5 GS(RE) Regs

31 Reg 6 GS(RE) Regs

32 Reg 7 GS(RE) Regs

33 Sch 7 para 10(3) EA 1989; Sch 5 para 4(3) GA 1986

34 Sch 5 para 7(5) GA 1986

35 Sch 6 para 1(6) EA 1989

Chapter 9:   Rights of Entry

(pp133-135)

1 s1(1) Rights of Entry (Gas and Electricity Boards) Act 1954

2 Sch 6 para 5(1)(a) and (b) EA 1989; Sch 5 para 15(1)(a) and (b) GA 1986

3 Sch 6 para 5(1)(c) EA 1989; Sch 5 paras 4(3) and 15(1)(d) GA 1986

4 Sch 6 para 5(3) EA 1989

5 Sch 6 para 6(1) EA 1989; Sch 5 para 16(1)(a) GA 1986

6 Sch 5 para 16(1) GA 1986

7 Sch 6 para 6(2) EA 1989; Sch 5 para 16(1)(b), (c) and (d) GA 1986

8 Sch 6 para 7 EA 1989; Sch 5 para 17 GA 1986

9 Sch 6 para 7(2) EA 1989

10 s109 EA 1989; s46 GA 1986

11 Sch 6 para 5(2) EA 1989; Sch 5 para 15(2) GA 1986

12 Sch 5 para 13(4) and (5) GA 1986

13 Sch 6 paras 5(1), 6(1) and 7(1) EA 1989; Sch 5 paras 15(1), 16(1) and 17(1) GA 1986

14 Sch 6 para 8(3) EA 1989; Sch 5 para 18(3) GA 1986

15 s1(3) Rights of Entry (Gas and Electricity Boards) Act 1954

16 Sch 6 para 8(1) EA 1989; Sch 5 para 18(1) GA 1986

17 Rights of Entry (Gas and Electricity Boards) Act 1954

Chapter 10:   Fuel and Benefits

(pp137-147)

1 Reg 3 SFCWP Regs

2 SFCWP Regs as amended; para 25 Cold Weather Payments Guide

3 Reg 2(1)(a) SFCWP Regs

4 Reg 1A SFCWP Regs

5 Reg 1(2) SFCWP Regs

6 Sch 1 SFCWP Regs
7 Sch 1 para 4 HB Regs; para A4 59 GM
8 Sch 1 para 7 HB Regs
9 Sch 1 para 7 HB Regs
10 Sch 1 para 7 HB Regs
11 Sch 1 Part II para 4 HB Regs
12 Sch 1 para 5(4) HB Regs
13 Sch 1 paras 5(2) and 5(2a) HB Regs
14 ibid.
15 Sch 1 para 5(4) HB Regs
16 Sch 1 paras 5(2) and 5(2A) HB Regs
17 Reg 10(1)(e) and Reg 5 HB Regs
18 Sch 1 para 5 and Sch 6 para 9(c) HB Regs
19 para A4 S4(ii) GM
20 *Fuel Rights Handbook*, 8th Edition, p130.
21 IS: Reg 48(9) IS Regs
   FC: Reg 31(3) FC Regs
   HB: No obvious provision for the treatment as capital, but should be treated as capital.
22 IS: Reg 48(10)(c) IS Regs and Sch 9 para 39 IS Regs
   FC: Sch 2 para 34 FC Regs
   HB: Sch 4 para 34 HB Regs
23 Reg 48(10)(a) IS Regs
24 IS: Sch 9 para 15 IS Regs
   FC: Sch 2 para 13 FC Regs
   HB: Sch 4 para 13 HB Regs
25 IS: Sch 9 para 36 IS Regs
   FC: Sch 2 para 29 FC Regs
   HB: Sch 4 para 33 HB Regs
26 IS; Sch 10 para 29 IS Regs
   FC: Sch 3 para 31 FC Regs
   HB: Sch 5 para 32 HB Regs
27 Direction 25 SF Directions
28 Direction 25 SF Directions
29 Direction 26 SF Directions
30 Direction 29 SF Directions
31 Direction 8 SF Directions
32 Direction 8(b) SF Directions
33 Directions 12(n) and 12(o) SF Directions
34 Direction 14 SF Directions
35 Direction 14 SF Directions
36 Direction 23(f) SF Directions
37 para 5480 *Social Fund Guidance Manual*.

Chapter 11:   Other Sources of Help

(pp148-152)

1 s17(6) Children Act 1989
2 s2 Chronically Sick and Disabled Persons Act 1970
3 s4 Disabled Persons (Services, Consultation and Representation) Act 1986
4 s3 Disabled Persons (Services, Consultation and Representation) Act 1986
5 Part VIII Local Government and Housing Act 1989; Department of Environment Circular No. 12/90.
6 s131 Local Government and Housing Act 1989; Assistance for Minor Works to Dwellings Regulations 1990 SI No. 388; Department of Environment Circular No. 4/90.
7 s15 Social Security Act 1990; Home Energy Efficiency Grants Regs 1990 SI No. 1791.
8 *Which?* June 1993 – Home and DIY Energy Advice.

Chapter 12:   You, Your Landlord and Fuel

(pp153-175)

1 *Montagu v Browning* [1954] 2 AllER 601
2 s108 Housing Act 1985
3 s211 H(S)A 1987
4 ss13-15 Supply of Goods and Services Act 1982
5 s11 LG(MP)A 1976
6 s12(4) LG(MP)A 1976
7 *Bromley LBC v GLC* [1982] 1 AllER 129
8 Part III London County Council (General Powers) Act 1949
9 s22 London County Council (General Powers) Act 1949
10 s22(3) London County Council (General Powers) Act 1949
11 s20(3) London County Council (General Powers) Act 1949

12 *Taking Action on Cold Homes*, Tenants Resource and Information Service – see Appendices 9 and 10.
13 s18 LTA 1985
14 s26 LTA 1985
15 s27 LTA 1985
16 s19 LTA 1985
17 s20B LTA 1985
18 s19(4) LTA 1985
19 s21 LTA 1985
20 s21(6) LTA 1985
21 s38 LTA 1985 'dwelling' is defined as a building or part of a building occupied as a separate dwelling. Provided the occupants of a house in multiple occupation are tenants with exclusive occupation of at least a room, their landlord would have to provide certified accounts.
22 s22 LTA 1985
23 s29 LTA 1985
24 *Finchbourne Ltd v Rodrigues* [1976] 3 AllER 581 (CA)
25 s51 RA 1977; s34 R(S)A 1984
26 s47RA 1977; s31 R(S)A 1984
27 s47(2) RA 1977; s31(2) R(S)A 1984
28 s67 RA 1977; s46 R(S)A 1984
29 s71(1) RA 1977; s49(1) R(S)A 1984
30 s31(5) Social Security Act 1986
31 Sch 1 paras 4 and 5 HB Regs
32 *Metropolitan Properties Co Ltd v Noble* [1968] 2 AllER 313
33 s71(4) RA 1977; s49(6) R(S)A 1984
34 s77(1) RA 1977 – this refers to rent tribunals but rent assessment committees now exercise the powers of rent tribunals under s72 Housing Act 1980; s65(1) R(S)A 1984
35 s78(2) RA 1977; s66(1) R(S)A 1984
36 s80(1) RA 1977; s68 R(S)A 1984
37 s44 EA 1989
38 s37 GA 1986
39 *Landlords, Tenants & Electricity Charges* (OFFER); *Maximum Price for the Resale of Gas – A guide for landlords and tenants, industrial suppliers and their customers* (1993 edition, OFGAS).
40 Meters (Approval of Pattern or Construction and Method of Installation) Regs 1990 SI No. 791
41 s17 GA 1986

42 Sch 7 para 1 EA 1989; Sch 5 para 3(2) GA 1986
43 s97 Housing Act 1985; s57 H(S)A 1987; s81 Housing Act 1980; s101 R(S)A 1984
44 s33 LG(MP)A 1976
45 s19 Greater London Council (General Powers) Act 1972
46 s19(3)(b) Greater London Council (General Powers) Act 1972
47 Registering a charge means to attach a charge to the title of the property at the Land Registry so that the owner cannot sell the property without paying off the charge.
48 s19(8) Greater London Council (General Powers) Act 1972; s33(5) LG(MP)A 1976
49 Housing Act 1985 and H(S)A 1987
50 Sch 6 para 1(6) EA 1989
51 *McCall v Abelesz* [1976] 1 AllER 727
52 s1 Protection from Eviction Act 1977; R(S)A 1984 as amended by s38 Housing (Scotland) Act 1988
53 s27 Housing Act 1988; s36 Housing (Scotland) Act 1988
54 s18 Prosecution of Offences Act 1985
55 ss53-4 H(S)A 1987
56 Erskine's Institutes II/4/63
57 Sch 10 para 1 H(S)A 1987 as amended by Sch 8 para 9 Housing (Scotland) Act 1988
58 The Landlord's Repairing Obligations (Specified Rent) [Scotland] (No. 2) Order SI 1988 No. 2155
59 'The law of specific implement', Michael Dailly, *SCOLAG Journal*, July 1993, p102 and 'Specific Implement and Repairs', Derek O'Carroll, *SCOLAG Journal*, August 1993, p115.
60 *Ravenseft Properties Ltd v Davstone Holdings Ltd* [1979] 1 AllER 929
61 *O'Brien v Robinson* [1973] AC 912
62 s11(1)(a) LTA 1985; Sch 10 para 3(1)(a) H(S)A 1987

63 s11(1)(b) and (c) LTA 1985; Sch 10 para 3(1)(b) H(S)A 1987
64 s11(1A) LTA 1985; Sch 10 para 3(1A) H(S)A 1987
65 *Calabar Properties v Stitcher* [1984] 1 WLR 287
66 *Lee-Parker v Izzett* [1971] 1 WLR 1688; *British Anzani (Felixstowe) Ltd v International Marine Management (UK) Ltd* [1980] QB 137
67 *AC Billings & Son v Riden* [1957] 3 AllER 1
68 s4 Defective Premises Act 1972
69 s3 Defective Premises Act 1972
70 s79(1) Environmental Protection Act 1990
71 s82 Environmental Protection Act 1990
72 *Whittaker v Derby Urban Sanitary Authority* [1885] 55 LJMC 8
73 s35 Powers of Criminal Courts Act 1973
74 s18 Prosecution of Offenders Act 1985
75 Lord Justice Dillon in *Quick v Taff Ely BC* [1985] 18 HLR 66
76 *Ravenseft Properties Ltd v Davstone Holdings Ltd* [1979] 1 AllER 929
77 *Birmingham DC v Kelly* [1985] 17 HLR 572
78 ibid.
79 *Dover DC v Farrar* [1980] 2 HLR 32
80 *GLC v LB Tower Hamlets* [1983] 15 HLR 54

Chapter 13:   Remedies

(pp176-190)
1 s42B EA 1989; s33E GA 1986
2 ss42 and 42A EA 1989; ss33B and 33D GA 1986
3 s39 EA 1989 and Electricity (Standards of Performance) Regs 1993 SI 1193
4 s33A GA 1986
5 s25 EA 1989; s28 GA 1986
6 s45(4) EA 1989; s31(3) GA 1986
7 s16(1) EA 1989; s10(1) GA 1986
8 s20(3) EA 1989; s11(4) GA 1986

9 s18(1) and (2) EA 1989; s14(1) GA 1986
10 Sch 7 para 10(2) EA 1989; Sch 5 para 4(2) GA 1986
11 Electricity Licence Condition 19; British Gas Authorisation Condition 12A
12 s25 EA 1989; s28 GA 1986
13 cf. s27(3) EA 1989; s30(3) GA 1986 which state that final and provisional orders shall not be questioned in legal proceedings – this is unlikely to oust judicial review in the light of past court decisions on similar ouster clauses (see *Smith v East Elloe RDC* [1956] AC 736 and *Anisminic Ltd v FCC* [1969] 2 AC 147) and the fact that a decision not to make an order is certainly judicially reviewable (see *R v Director-General of Gas Supply ex parte Smith* (1989) unreported – see Appendix 1).
14 s25(2) EA 1989; s28(2) GA 1986
15 s25(1) EA 1989; s28(1) GA 1986
16 s45(1) EA 1989; s31(1) GA 1986
17 s25(1) and (2) EA 1989; s28(1) and (2) GA 1986
18 s25(5) EA 1989; s28(5) GA 1986
19 s25(5)(b) EA 1989; s28(5)(aa) GA 1986
20 s25(6)(b) EA 1989; s28(6)(b) GA 1986
21 s25(3) EA 1989; s28(3) GA 1986
22 s26(1) and (2) EA 1989; s29(1) and (2) GA 1986
23 s26(3) and (4) EA 1989; s29(3) and (4) GA 1986
24 s26(6) and (7) EA 1989; s29(5) and (6) GA 1986
25 *R v Director-General of Gas Supply ex parte Smith* (1989) unreported – see Appendix 1.
26 s26(5) EA 1989; s29(7) GA 1986
27 s27(1) EA 1989; s30(1) GA 1986
28 s27(4) EA 1989; s30(5) GA 1986
29 s27(5) EA 1989; s30(6) GA 1986
30 s25(5)(a) and s3 EA 1989; s28(5)(a) and s4 GA 1986
31 s25(7)(b) EA 1989; s28(7)(b) GA 1986
32 s25(8) EA 1989; s28(8) GA 1986

33 s46 EA 1989; s32 GA 1986
34 s46(4) EA 1989; s32(5) GA 1986
35 ss51 and 52 EA 1989; ss40 and 41 GA 1986
36 s33 GA 1986
37 s23 EA 1989; s14A GA 1986
38 s23(5)(b) EA 1989; s14A(7)(b) GA 1986
39 s23(1) EA 1989; s14A(1) GA 1986
40 s44A EA 1989; s15A 1986
41 s23(1)(a) EA 1989; s14A(1)(a) GA 1986
42 s23(1)(b) EA 1989; s14A(1)(b) GA 1986
43 s23(1) EA 1989; s14A(3) GA 1986
44 s23(2) EA 1989; s14A(4) GA 1986; s25 Competition and Services (Utilities) Act 1992
45 s23(3) EA 1989; s14A(5) GA 1986
46 ss23(1A) and 44A(5) EA 1989; ss14A(2) and 15A(5) GA 1986
47 s23(5)(a) EA 1989; s14A GA(7)(a) 1986
48 s23(6) EA 1989; s14A(8) GA 1986
49 s23(5)(b) EA 1989; s14A(7)(b) GA 1986
50 s25(3)(b) EA 1989; s28(3)(b) GA 1986 – it could be argued that these subsections show that the intention of Parliament was to exclude any remedies against a supplier other than those expressly allowed for in each Act. However, the provisions are not clearly drafted. In the absence of a clause which expressly prohibits court proceedings, each subsection should arguably be limited to providing that, when OFFER/OFGAS are considering their enforcement powers, the practical effect will be that a court will almost never want to duplicate matters by exercising its powers at the same time.
51 The principles are set out in *American Cyanamid v Ethicon Ltd* [1975] AC 396.
52 See note 50 above.
53 s23(5)(b) EA 1989; s14A(7)(b) GA 1986
54 s27(4) and (5) EA 1989; s30(5) and (6) GA 1986
55 cf. s27 EA 1989; s30 GA 1986 – which give suppliers a right of appeal against OFFER/OFGAS final or provisional orders.
56 Rules of the Supreme Court (of England and Wales) Order 53; Act of Sederunt (Rules of Court No.2) (Judicial Review) 1985
57 *Council of Civil Service Unions v Minister for the Civil Service* [1984] 3 AllER 935
58 *R v Panel on Takeovers and Mergers ex parte Datafin plc* [1987] QB 815
59 Rules of the Supreme Court, Order 53

Index

NATIONAL WELFARE BENEFITS HANDBOOK 1993/4 edition

In April 1993 the benefit rates and regulations change again. The new **Handbook** is therefore completely revised a updated, with all you need to know about means-tested benefits and how to claim them. There is comprehensive covera of **income support, housing benefit, family credit**, the **social fund** and **disability working allowance**, and of the maj changes affecting benefits this year, including: • the impact of the **Child Support Act** on benefits, including the bene penalty and deductions for maintenance • the new **council tax benefit** • the impact of the new **community care** arrang ments on benefits, other help for people with disabilities, and on how to appeal.

£6.95 (£2.65 for individual benefit claimants – direct from CPAG)

RIGHTS GUIDE TO NON-MEANS-TESTED BENEFITS, 1993/94 edition

Fully revised and updated, this essential, practical companion to the Handbook includes: • revised coverage of unemploymen benefit • expanded coverage of disability living allowance after a year in operation • earnings rules and disability benefit the contributions system • statutory sick pay and statutory maternity pay • pensions and benefits for widows • industri injuries and diseases • benefits administration and how to appeal. The **Rights Guide,** the handbook and the new **Chil Support** Handbook are all fully cross-referenced and indexed to law, regulations and – where relevant – Commissioners decisions.

£6.50 (£2.45 for individual benefit claimants – direct from CPAG)

CHILD SUPPORT HANDBOOK, 1st edition: 1993/94

child maintenance arrangements change fundamentally in April 1993. The National Welfare Benefits Handbook covers the impact on benefits, but **this new companion volume to the Handbook and Rights Guide provides parents and advisers with definitive, expert guidance on *all* aspects of the scheme:** the law and its implications for all claimants and all other persons affected, including • who is affected, key terms and how to apply for maintenance • the Child Support Agency, providing information and the effects on either parent of non-co-operation • a step-by-step guide to the formula for calculating maintenance • exemptions, the benefit penalty, collection and enforcement, IS deductions • shared care, second families, competing applications etc • Child Support Appeal Tribunals. Fully indexed and cross-referenced to legislation and to its companion volumes, CPAG's Child Support Handbook will become the standard guide for parents, advisers, social workers, lawyers and anyone else needing to understand the scheme.

£5.95 (£2.25 for individual benefit claimants – direct from CPAG)

All three CPAG Handbooks are available from April – place your order now as copies are sent on a first come, first served basis.

The CPAG/NACAB Benefits Poster 1993/94 (A2 size, £1.95) gives you benefit rates at a glance.

Please send me :

_____	National Welfare Benefits Handbook @ £6.95 each	£_____
_____	Rights Guide to N. M.T. Benefits @ £6.50 each	£_____
_____	Child Support Handbook @ £5.95 each	£_____
_____	Benefits Poster @ £1.95 each	£_____

PRICES INCLUDE POSTAGE AND PACKING

I enclose a cheque/PO, payable to **CPAG Ltd** for –   £_____

Name_____

Address_____

_____

_____ Postcode _____

Please return this form with your payment to CPAG Ltd, 1-5 Bath Street, London EC1V 9PY

Welfare Rights Bulletin

The Bulletin is essential reading for welfare rights advisers, providing a bi-monthly update and back-up to the CPAG Handbook and Rights Guide, and to the new Child Support Handbook. There is more detailed and comprehensive coverage of social security developments than in any other magazine.

Contents include the fullest coverage of new and significant Commissioners' decisions, as well as: Court judgements, changes in law and practice, news from welfare rights workers and how to tackle common problem areas.

ISSN 0263 2098

£15.00 for a full year's subscription (6 issues)

Sent automatically to CPAG Rights and Comprehensive members, and Bulletin subscribers.

Ethnic Minorities' Benefits Handbook, 1st edition

Paul Morris, Inderpal Rahal and Hugo Storey
edited by Janet Gurney

CHILD POVERTY ACTION GROUP

This unique *Handbook* bridges the gap between immigration and benefits advisers, giving information and practical guidance on both immigration and benefits rules for anyone entering or leaving the UK. There is a particular focus on the provisions most likely to affect ethnic minority claimants.

The major part of the *Ethnic Minorities' Benefits Handbook* consists of separate chapters on each benefit, interweaving the benefits and immigration issues throughout.

There are also key sections on the *Handbook* devoted to:

- immigration law, including immigration categories; recourse to public funds; deportation rules' the issues for visitors, students, children, adoption, cohabitees, refugees; appeals, etc

- EC law regarding both social security and immigration, with guidance on claiming benefit abroad and transporting benefits from country to country.

Fully indexed and cross-referenced to social security and immigration law, the *Ethnic Minorities' Benefits Handbook* is the only authoritative and up-to-date guide to benefits in this increasingly important area of advice work. It will be revised and updated regularly.

Advisers will find the *Ethnic Minorities' Benefits Handbook* invaluable, as will many claimants – whether they are non-EC immigrants, members of ethnic minorities in the UK, EC citizens in the UK, or UK citizens in other EC countries.

400 pages   0 946744 50 5   £8.95

**Send cheque/PO for £8.95 (incl p&p) to
CPAG Ltd (Pubs/WRB), 1-5 Bath Street, London EC1V 9PY**